M

DATE DUE

DONNIE BRASCO
UNFINISHED BUSINESS

ALSO BY JOSEPH D. PISTONE

Donnie Brasco: My Undercover Life in the Mafia
The Way of the Wiseguy
The Good Guys
Deep Cover
Snake Eyes
Mobbed Up

ALSO BY CHARLES BRANDT

I Heard You Paint Houses
The Right to Remain Silent

DONNIE BRASCO
UNFINISHED BUSINESS

SHOCKING DECLASSIFIED DETAILS FROM THE FBI'S GREATEST UNDERCOVER
OPERATION AND A BLOODY TIMELINE OF THE FALL OF THE MAFIA

BY JOSEPH D. PISTONE AND CHARLES BRANDT

RUNNING PRESS
PHILADELPHIA · LONDON

Library of Congress Control Number 2005936365

ISBN-13: 978-0-7624-2707-9
ISBN-10: 0-7624-2707-8

Cover and interior designed by Doogie Horner
Edited by Greg Jones
Typography: Bad Neighborhood, Bembo, and TradeGothic

This book may be ordered by mail from the publisher.
Please include $2.50 for postage and handling.
But try your bookstore first!

Running Press Book Publishers
2300 Chestnut Street, Suite 200
Philadelphia, Pennsylvania 19103

Visit us on the web!
www.runningpress.com

This book is dedicated to the men and women in Law Enforcement and the U.S. Armed Forces who risk their lives every day to make the world a safer place to live in.

—J.P.

As always, for Nancy.

—C.B.

Acknowledgements

I would like to thank my publisher, editor, and agents for making this book possible. Also, my co-writer Charlie Brandt (a prince of a man) for putting up with my late return calls. Thanks to all my dear friends (too numerous to name) for their belief in me. And a special thanks to my family for their support in whatever adventure I undertake.

—Joe Pistone

CONTENTS

Preface

When I give lectures or teach seminars around the world, I get a lot of questions about the state of the American Mafia—which is principally the Five Families of New York City. My answer always leads to more questions, and there is never enough time to fully explain what happened to the American Mafia and how it got that way.

I decided to write this book in an effort to do justice to these questions and to show how what we did back in the day—on the street, in the social clubs, and in the courtrooms—has led to the situation today, in which the Mafia is nothing more than a weakened, exposed shadow of its former self.

This sequel to my bestseller—*Donnie Brasco: My Undercover Life in the Mafia*—also gives me an opportunity to reveal certain details for the first time anywhere, details that I could not discuss in the original *Donnie Brasco* because, in 1988, I did not want to compromise the numerous trials that would come over the next decade and my testimony in them. In 1981, I still had much unfinished business to do after coming out from my six-year deep cover penetration of the Mafia.

At the time I wrote the first book, many of the crimes I discussed continued to pose a mystery; many of the murders were still whodunits. Over the past twenty-five years, with the toppling and falling of the Mafia dominos, trial by trial, nearly all of these mysteries have been completely solved, and I get to analyze them here.

The way I see it, the most important domino to fall was the first one, the one that set the rest in motion. It was the first of the cases to go to trial—the 1982 Bonanno family trial. Had we lost that first trial—in which we used a then-novel legal theory to apply the evidence I gathered as Donnie Brasco—there would have been no subsequent trials, and none of the good news I report in this book would have occurred. Everything was at stake in that first battle of the Mafia trials war: all we had done, all we hoped to do, and my very safety. You see, the weaker we made the Mafia as we marched on from that first victory, the more we destroyed it and its ruling Commission—which had put a price on my head—and the better my family and I felt.

As I look at the ravaged state of New York's Five Families and its Mafia Commission today, I feel more than satisfied that my unfinished business is finally finished—at least as far as the American Mafia is concerned.

Introduction
by Charles Brandt

Has America witnessed a more heroic or exciting lawman than this book's subject? Who springs to mind? Wyatt Earp? Wild Bill Hickock? Eliot Ness? Much of what many legendary lawmen got credit for doing is more myth than reality. But if one swallows their résumés as gospel, these legends still don't measure up to the prolonged heroism, tactical brilliance, and pure mental toughness of a young Italian-American FBI Special Agent from Paterson, New Jersey, named Joseph Dominick Pistone—aka Donnie Brasco, Mafia gangster.

What follows here touches on the dangers Agent Joe Pistone braved his way through and the monumental destruction his testimony caused the Mafia in trial after trial from the early '80s through today. Posing as a jewel thief to whom he gave the fictitious name "Donnie Brasco," and with no rulebook to follow and no indispensable introduction to the Mafia, Agent Pistone infiltrated the Colombo Mafia family in 1975. Six months after first contact, using his infiltration of the Colombos as his self-made introduction, he infiltrated the Bonanno Mafia family. Agent Pistone soon became a working member of the Bonanno family, abandoning his own personal life, living the daily life of a Mafia crewmember, following his capo's orders, and obeying the tangled web of medieval rules that govern the Mafia's secret subculture.

After six eventful years as Donnie Brasco, Agent Pistone was proposed by his Bonanno capo, Dominick "Sonny Black" Napolitano, for the rare honor given to very few Mafia associates—induction into the Mafia as a made man. Following the simultaneous assassination of three powerful Bonanno capos—Alphonse

"Sonny Red" Indelicato, Dominick "Big Trin" Trinchera, and Phillip "Phil Lucky" Giaccone—on May 5, 1981, Pistone's capo, Sonny Black, became the acting street boss of the Bonanno crime family. To nip a potential civil war in the bud, Sonny Black gave Donnie Brasco the contract to find and kill Sonny Red's son, capo Bruno Indelicato, who was supposed to get whacked along with the other three but missed the meeting.

Because Donnie had become such a close intimate of Sonny Black, often sleeping at Sonny's apartment, the enemies on the other side of this potential gang war might target Donnie Brasco for a bullet. Agent Pistone's FBI handler throughout the operation, retired Agent Jules Bonavolonta expressed the dilemma. "While Joe would be pretending to look for Bruno so he could whack him and leave him in the street, a bunch of other guys would be looking for Joe so they could whack *him* and leave him in the street. The only difference between Joe and the other guys was that the other guys wouldn't be faking it."

By the time Sonny Black gave Agent Pistone this murder contract in mid-1981, Pistone had spent close to six years immersed in the role of Donnie Brasco. Much to Agent Pistone's disappointment, the FBI decided to pull him from his deep cover and reveal his role to the Bonannos before he could be made—or killed. In the ensuing years, Pistone's grueling court appearances on the witness stand were an indispensable element of the biggest, longest, and most significant Mafia trials in history, including the Bonanno Family cases, the Pizza Connection Case, and the Mafia Commission Case. Other major cases—such as the Mafia Cops Case—came later and were a direct result of the chaos caused by these initial cases.

Through his testimony, Agent Pistone was revealed to America as a towering super hero. A man who commits a single act of bravery can be considered a hero; the super hero lives a day-to-day life of constant bravery. For six years, Agent Pistone committed individual acts of bravery from moment to moment. His life was one of constant courage in the face of constant risk of death or harm, including torture.

Many of the made men in the Mafia that Agent Pistone was closest to were super villains—poisonous snakes poised to snap and kill without provocation. Pistone described Tony Mirra, his first Bonanno family mentor, as, "Loud, obnoxious. The meanest man I met in the Mafia." Pistone described Benjamin "Lefty Guns" Ruggiero, his next mentor and the man with whom he had the most intimate contact, this way: "You could tell Lefty was a stone cold killer just the way he looked at you." Agent Pistone always had to be super vigilant around Lefty to keep his make-believe stories straight. "Lefty would recall conversations we had eight months earlier, and he would remember them verbatim." Pistone described his capo, Sonny Black, as follows: "When you met him you knew you had to respect him. If you didn't, he'd whack you."

After Agent Pistone's mission had moved from the mean streets to courtrooms around the country, the record of convictions became so staggering and so unique that the name he chose for his undercover role, Donnie Brasco, became a law-enforcement term in its own right. After 9/11, for instance, at least one media commentator remarked that what America needed to fight terrorism is "a 'Donnie Brasco,' someone to infiltrate Al-Queda." Former CIA Director George Tenet attempted to explain his agency's inability to predict the attacks by saying, ". . . We didn't have a Donnie Brasco." Like being an Einstein, a Casanova, or a Benedict Arnold—the latter undoubtedly being how the Napoleons who ruled the Mafia viewed Donnie Brasco—being a Donnie Brasco is now a part of our language.

During my years as a prosecutor, which ended about the time Agent Pistone first infiltrated the Mafia, I marveled at the courage of the undercover cops who brought their cases to my office. While sometimes the operation involved buying swag (stolen goods), mostly these brave men were narcs. They posed as addicts; their goal was to buy drugs and bust the dealers. To make a case that a judge wouldn't toss out on a technicality, they needed to buy one-on-one, person-to-person. And to make such a direct buy, they needed to penetrate past the justly paranoid screening tactics of drug dealers. Initially, a druggie informant had to vouch for the narc to the dealer. (An introduction was something Agent Pistone did not have the luxury of when infiltrating the Mafia.) The narc had to dress and act like a drug addict, hang around with druggies, and live the druggie life a number of hours a day for a couple of weeks per case. When the dealer was arrested, the narc was exposed and his usefulness as an undercover was over.

If a narc made a mistake, the typical result would be that the dealer would become suspicious and refuse to sell drugs to the narc. Having said that, these buy-bust operations were and still are dangerous assignments. Every once in a while, a narc somewhere in America gets shot to death when the dealer is actually interested in robbing money and not in delivering product.

In Delaware in the early '70s we never lost a man to a drug dealer's bullet, but we lost at least two to the drugs to which they daily were exposed. In order to prove himself a drug addict, a narc sometimes—at the very least—had to smoke a joint offered to him by the dealer. Just as a man might not know he has a potential gambling addiction until a casino is built near his home, so a man might not know he has a potential drug addiction until he takes his first hit. One of the narcs I knew became a heroin addict; the other became a cocaine addict. Typically these matters are swept under the carpet and, unless the drug-addicted cop commits another crime, they go unnoticed and unappreciated by the public—a public that expects its police to risk their health, indeed their very lives, to protect them. These largely unreported drug-addiction tragedies are part of the hidden costs of the shift in police tactics caused by court decisions of the '60s and '70s beginning with *Mapp v. Ohio* in 1961 (the Supreme Court decision that banned evidence gathered in violation of the Fourth Amendment protection against unreasonable search and seizure). Unable to search dealers and users in the street, confiscate their drugs, and arrest them on mere suspicion alone, narcotics squads became forced to rely on the dangerous and inefficient tactics of infiltration, buy and bust.

When I first read *Donnie Brasco: My Undercover Life in the Mafia,* I read it with this insider's knowledge and experience in mind. As if I were watching a highway pileup in slow motion, I was caught up with bated breath, hoping Agent Pistone and his family would survive the ordeal. It was and remains the best and most authentic true crime book I ever read. By the book's jacket alone I saw that Agent Pistone's infiltration was not of the genus of deadly and dangerous infiltration of a drug dealer's world, which would normally last just a matter of days. It was a distinctly more deadly and dangerous infiltration, day after day, of an organization of professional killers—an organization that punishes its own members unexpectedly with two bullets behind the ear, as the courts would say, on "mere suspicion alone." As agent Pistone said, "There were moments I thought I was going to be killed.

"If you badmouth a boss to anyone," Pistone told me, "even jokingly, and it gets back to the boss, there is a good chance your best friend in the family will be ordered to shoot you in the back of the head when you least expect it." Before he became Bonanno boss in 1992, Big Joey Massino whacked a Mafia soldier for wise-cracking that the Gambino boss—Big Paul Castellano—resembled Frank Perdue of the Perdue Chicken company, who used to appear regularly in TV commercials.

Even if you hadn't badmouthed a boss but someone thought you had and it got back to the boss—again, "on mere suspicion alone" and without being given a chance to explain—you very likely would be shot and killed by the cold-blood-ed professional beside you, whose job description includes killing people who don't show sufficient respect, whatever that means.

If you asked a question perceived to be inappropriately nosey you might be suspected of being a rat, trying to gather evidence for the government. "Mere sus-picion alone" of being a rat requires little reflection on the part of a boss in order-ing your execution. As the Teamsters official and confessed Mafia hit man Frank Sheeran expressed to me, "When in doubt, have no doubt."

And, worse for your long-neglected wife, your children, and your parents, you might simply disappear. Your real family would have the agony of waiting and worrying while you failed to return and your body failed to surface. Certainly, whatever method your close friends used to kill you, and whether they disposed of your body or left it to be discovered as a message to other soldiers in the Mafia, your murder would likely never be solved.

These unfathomable rules, even the unintentional breaking of which had deadly consequences, are rules Agent Pistone had to learn on-the-job by trial and error, all the while posing as someone who already knew the way of the wiseguy. No one before Agent Pistone had ever attempted to infiltrate the Mafia at this level to study its structure and learn its rules, to understand the mindset of the made man. Agent Pistone has since taught these secret rules to all law enforce-ment, as well as to the rest of us.

Mafia rules aside, many of the men Agent Pistone hung out with at the social club, dined with at the best restaurants, played cards with, drank with, and com-mitted crimes with, were psychopaths who might kill a newcomer like Donnie Brasco on impulse.

For those 2,100-odd days of his existence as the Bonanno crewmember

Donnie Brasco, Agent Pistone also had to navigate the murky waters of the bureaucracy of the FBI. His daily undercover performance as Donnie Brasco had a multitude of producers and directors ready to assert their authority. Luckily for him and for us, Pistone had as his chief handler Agent Jules Bonavolonta, a supervisor with a talent for his job and the willingness to play the bureaucracy while Agent Pistone played the Mafia.

Nearly every facet of the operation, from the first day to the last, was carried out in uncharted waters. In his day-to-day activities, how far could an agent go in breaking the law—like a narc taking a drug—in order to keep up appearances, gain trust, and advance up the ladder? ("To this day, I never took a drug in my life," Pistone asserted.) Under which hazardous conditions should his back be covered by agents hiding nearby, who might be spotted and get his cover blown? How often and under what circumstances should he break cover to report to his handler? After all, he couldn't take notes, everything had to be memorized and verbally reported. When should he risk instant death by wearing a cumbersome wire that might be spotted? When could he see his family? Agent Pistone literally wrote the book on how to look, think, and act like a Mafia crewmember while passing along ongoing intelligence reports from the enemy camp and making cases against made men and the Mafia itself that would stand up in court in the face of rules and procedures that often seemed to favor criminals and their frequently abusive defense attorneys.

At the termination of the long-term deep-cover operation, Agent Pistone found himself the key witness in major trials he helped produce against the Mafia. "I made Rudy Giuliani a star," he once joked with me over coffee. But there's actually a lot of truth to that. Certain homicide cops made me a star prosecutor, and those that are still living know who they are and they know I know it.

Agent Pistone did his precarious job to perfection, and without fear. He never succumbed to normal emotions of the moment; and always remained as focused as a brain surgeon. "To work deep cover long-term," Agent Pistone said, "you've got to be mentally tough. The whole secret is to be mentally tough." The mentally tough role Agent Pistone performed, creating it as he played it, became the foundation on which he helped build the cases for his courtroom crusade against the Mafia. No doubt, Joe Pistone the producer, writer, and actor made stars of many a prosecutor who directed each case's final performance.

In this sequel to *Donnie Brasco: My Undercover Life in the Mafia,* Joe Pistone will reveal, for the first time anywhere, some of the darker inside information that could not have made its way into that classic book. As a practical matter, there was a larger and more unique story to tell in that early volume. To appreciate it, and without interrupting the nail-biting drama of that story, the reader had to be educated along the way to many things that we all now seem to know about the Mafia subculture. We know these things, in great measure, because of what Agent Pistone did and wrote about. In a sense, inside information would have been too much information in that first book. Also, Agent Pistone did not want the first book to be a fertile field for cross-examination by defense attorneys in the trials that were then ongoing and upcoming. Perhaps out of a sense of self-protection, as a citizen and a witness, he omitted some things and glossed over others, such as his participation in armed hijackings, beatings, and other daily Mafia activities. He played close-to-the-vest those intense feelings such activity engendered in him as he took part in them.

Thanks to the standard set by *Donnie Brasco* and a few other books and movies that succeed (unlike *The Godfather* movies) in truly and accurately portraying the filthy business of organized crime, Joe Pistone is now ready to reveal to today's reader the dark nature of what Agent Pistone as Donnie Brasco had to do to survive each day of those dangerous days, hour-by-hour, on our behalf.

While some of the facts in *Donnie Brasco* must be recounted here to give the new revelations a proper context, Agent Pistone analyzes, for the first time, the implications and long-term results of all of the actions of his years undercover. The analysis is something that needed the passage of time and the maturity of the crops he planted for Pistone to be able to sow. A naturally modest man, Joe Pistone needed prodding to express some of this. But it is an essential part of American history that only Joe can fully analyze.

After he surfaced from his deep cover, the FBI learned that the Mafia's ruling Commission had put out an open contract for $500,000 on Agent Pistone's head. "They sent guys all over the country looking for me, but obviously they didn't find me," Pistone said. The danger was not so much that a particular hit man had been ordered to kill him for money, but that word had been put out among the cowboys, the wannabes, and the nut jobs with ambitions to be Mafia soldiers, that it would do them good somehow to kill Agent Pistone if they ever got the chance. Such a wannabe loser in search of a reputation shot Wild Bill Hickock in the back. "Getting a nut" is an expression Frank Sheeran taught me, which is one Mafia method for putting out a murder contract.

Recently, in a New York City coffee shop, when one of the stated objectives of this book was first discussed with Joe—namely, the importance of exploring details involving the dirtiest and darkest part of his undercover work—he gave a hard short laugh and said, "I've got to be careful what I tell you. It's not beyond some prosecutor to read it and decide they want to do something."

By "do something," Joe meant "prosecute" him for committing such crimes.

I didn't blame him for being concerned about this. Like a soldier in combat, he was forced by circumstances to experience and do things on our behalf he'd rather not have to explain to us. And now he was about to. I thought, what a tightrope this man has had to walk and still walks twenty-five years later. When Agent Pistone went undercover in 1975, prosecutors were not out to build reputations on the prosecuting of cops; that, too, has changed.

Joe and I ended up sipping our coffee, building a rapport, and talking about that exact phenomenon in the recent annals of law enforcement.

This conversation took place many months before the 2006 arrest of a dear friend of Joe's, Lin DeVecchio, a long-retired FBI agent whose arrest was based on alleged decisions he made during cases fifteen to twenty years ago.

While there will be a couple of chapters devoted to the dark side of his deep cover, *Donnie Brasco: Unfinished Business* lets us see through Joe's eyes how his perilous performance as Donnie Brasco ultimately caused the Mafia to unravel thread by thread over the next twenty-five years—both through their own implosion and through the U.S. Department of Justice.

When Agent Pistone was pulled and the secret undercover operation was revealed on July 28, 1981, every single wiseguy everywhere in the country was staggered. They were bewildered and stunned by what Agent Pistone had pulled off against them. Their energy was demonstrably sapped; their almighty confidence shaken to its core. Bosses who smirked at United States senators in hearings; bosses whose organizational rules were enforced by unsolvable murders;

bosses whose everyday business was carried out under chains of command with no visible links leading up to them; bosses of an organization with its own secret language, spoken, if at all, in code; bosses who over centuries perfected the art and science of making their positions as impervious to American or Italian law as Hitler's was to German law; were now shown by a single agent of the FBI to be as vulnerable to law enforcement as an ordinary low-life drug dealer. Self-destructive paranoia set in.

The more intelligent members of the five main Mafia families—Bonanno, Colombo, Gambino, Genovese, and Lucchese—became increasingly private and careful. They began distrusting everyone and started killing often on less than "mere suspicion alone." They also began allowing lesser talents to rise to more highly visible and prominent positions, which were now more vulnerable positions.

The authoritative and commanding American Mafia, organized in 1931, is today in shambles. And as this book will reveal, the super heroism of Agent Joseph Dominick Pistone is the principal reason why. More than the so-called tipping point, his brave work is the wrecking ball of demolition that made the arrest and conviction of Mafia bosses for the crimes they ordered, including murder, almost commonplace today.

Agent Pistone will recount the rewarding, exciting, and hazardous undercover work he performed in America and abroad for the FBI after the Donnie Brasco operation, as well as the training, teaching, and mentoring he has done for hundreds of other brave men and women about to go under. To wit: Agent Pistone is responsible for the FBI's undercover certification school and for establishing psychological safeguards for the deep-cover agent.

Now-retired Agent Pistone will explore the rewards that citizen Joe Pistone has reaped, besides the gratification of bringing down a significant number of Mafiosi who gave all Italian-Americans a black eye and the joy of watching the New York Mafia begin to breathe its last from the severe beating he gave it. Joe will take us inside the glamorous and well-deserved opportunities that opened up for him as a result of his undercover extravaganza as Donnie Brasco.

This tale about Joe Pistone's unfinished business will open, improbably for the young Italian-American boy from the streets of Paterson, New Jersey, in Hollywood—or more precisely, on location in 1996 in Brooklyn, as technical adviser for the making of the movie *Donnie Brasco*. Today, a grandfather in his six-ties, "over budget" are the scariest couple of words the film producer, Joe Pistone, ever has to hear.

But can the artist formerly known as Donnie Brasco ever truly let his guard down?

I wouldn't advise it. Would you?

As Joe Pistone taught the world to say: Fuggeddaboudit.

CHAPTER 1

HOLLYWOOD

IF YOU EVER GET A CHANCE to have Johnny Depp play you in a movie, go for it. Especially if you have daughters; they'll love it. And I have three beautiful, smart, and talented daughters, raised largely by their mother while I was undercover for six years and then testifying around the country for many years thereafter. My daughters loved Johnny Depp—and loved the fact that he played me in the film *Donnie Brasco*. But then everybody loves Johnny Depp. Johnny is an exceptionally thoughtful and considerate man. I'll give you an example from the filming of a scene that took place in a social club. But first, let me explain the meaning of these clubs.

Social clubs are Mafia crews' country clubs. It's where the crew hangs out. Each crew has its own private club. Most of them are storefronts. Needless to say: crewmembers only.

John Gotti, boss of the Gambinos, was infamous for planning murders and other crimes with his underboss, Sammy "the Bull" Gravano, at two social clubs— the Ravenite Social Club in Little Italy and the Bergen Hunt and Fish Club in Queens. The Gambinos didn't do much fishing, but they did stock the waters of the East River from time to time with bodies. The two friends rose together in their social clubs and fell together in their social clubs when the FBI secretly bugged the club buildings and Sammy the Bull turned rat and took down his partner, the Dapper Don.

At five-foot-ten and 300 pounds, Big Joey Massino, a powerful capo (and eventually boss) in my family, the Bonannos, planned murders, hijackings, and other illicit business in the J & S Cake Social Club in Queens. The J in the social club's name stood for Joey, and the S stood for Sal—Bonanno soldier "Good-looking" Sal Vitale—Joey's boyhood friend and brother-in-law. Both of these partners at J & S were to rise together and figure prominently in the future of the Bonanno family.

While many Mafioso end their lives as guests of the government, traditionally life in the Mafia begins for all of these people in a little social club. One of the aims of the movie *Donnie Brasco* was to give the audience the feel of the life and the rhythms inside one of these important little clubs in particular, the Motion Lounge.

The crew I was a member of for the last two years of my deep cover—from 1979 to 1981—hung out at the Motion Lounge social club in Greenpoint, Brooklyn. The Motion Lounge belonged to the capo and acting street boss of the Bonannos, Sonny Black Napolitano. His name was Dominick, like my middle name, but he was called Sonny Black because of the jet-black hair coloring he used. Nothing for nothing, but Sonny could have used help from a film's make-up department.

Getting back to Johnny, the film's art directors questioned me over and over again in order to get the interior of the Motion Lounge down perfectly for the movie. They succeeded. On the movie set of the interior of the Motion Lounge, shot in a Brooklyn armory, there is a scene where the crewmembers are simply hanging out as usual, playing cards, smoking cigarettes, having drinks, reporting to Sonny Black, and generally talking swag. One of them has the line, "I got a load of Schick razor blades." This actor kept blowing the line. The director couldn't take it any more and finally blew up at the actor. Everything was quiet for a second. The next thing you know, Johnny Depp gets up and says, "Stop picking on him. If I blow a line, are you going to yell at me?" Everybody relaxed. And knowing that Johnny had stuck up for him, the actor nailed his line on the next take.

· · ·

A number of my friends from growing up in the streets of Paterson, New Jersey, were extras in the movie, *Donnie Brasco*. A high school buddy, George

Angelica, played Big Trin, one of the three powerful Bonanno capos executed in a famous Mafia hit on May 5, 1981. The simultaneous nature of that hit is reminiscent of the famous St. Valentine's Day Massacre by Al Capone in Chicago. The three-capos hit also took place on a holiday—*Cinco de Mayo.* And what's left of the Bonanno family today is still feeling shock waves from the Fifth of May massacre of Dominick "Big Trin" Trinchera, Anthony "Sonny Red" Indelicato, and Phillip "Phil Lucky" Giaccone—all of whom were in a fatal allegiance with power-hungry Carmine Galante.

After that massacre, both my capo Sonny Black and capo Big Joey Massino moved up the ladder together. The Bonanno family boss, Rusty Rastelli, in jail at the time, gave Sonny Black the power of acting street boss, while he put Big Joey Massino in charge of the family's big moneymaker, the importation of heroin from Sicily. Technically, Sonny and Big Joey had equal power as capos, but in actual practice Sonny did the kinds of things that a boss would do on the street. For example, in the real boss's absence due to jail, Sonny had face-to-face meetings with other family bosses.

In fact, Sonny Black (along with Lefty "Guns" Ruggiero—my closest mentor in the Mafia) told me that before the hit on the three capos could be carried out, Sonny, on Rusty's behalf, met with Big Paul Castellano at his palatial home in Staten Island, known as "The White House." Big Paul was the boss of the Gambino family, as well as the boss of bosses of New York's five Mafia families—Bonanno, Colombo, Gambino, Genovese, and Lucchese. Sonny hinted that in return for cutting Big Paul in on some of the profits from the Bonanno heroin operation, Big Paul gave his blessing to the hit on the capos.

Hits bring the quickest advancement in the Mafia. Just like in corporate America, you climb the ladder by eliminating somebody. When self-appointed Bonanno boss Carmine Galante got whacked with a cigar clenched between his teeth in the backyard dining area of Joe and Mary's Restaurant in Ridgewood, Brooklyn, in 1979, both Sonny Black and Big Joey Massino instantly went from soldier to capo, and Rusty Rastelli, although still in jail, moved back in as boss.

After the May 5th murders of the three capos—remnants of Carmine Galante's faction who were suspected of plotting a coup to wrest power from jailed boss Rusty Rastelli—Sonny Black as the new acting street boss suddenly had jurisdiction over all 102 "made men" of the Bonanno family. That is, 102 men who had been formally inducted into the family in a secret, quasi-religious ceremony. Men who were now officially wiseguys and could call themselves wiseguys and goodfellas. Men who got their button, got their badge, got straightened out. Men who from the moment they were inducted suddenly had untouchable street power and a form of diplomatic immunity. One hundred and two made men in the Bonanno family to add to all the made men in the four other New York families, a force of evil with nothing to do but steal, deal, and kill.

I myself was scheduled to be "made" in December, 1981, once the big boss of the family, Rusty Rastelli, got out of jail. But for my own safety, after six years undercover, the Bureau yanked me from the operation a few months before that could happen. They thought that the three-capos massacre would lead to a Bonanno family civil war and put me in the middle—and in the most danger yet of being whacked. I thought I had my best stuff ahead of me for the later innings. Still, it was the manager's call to pull the plug on the operation. So, instead of being made, I was soon making movies.

. . .

One of my daughters, a professional actress, played the girlfriend of actor Bruno Kirby, one of the featured gangsters. One of my granddaughters played her own mother (as a child) in the movie. For security reasons, I don't like to use family names. But Anne Heche, a lovely person who was very nice to my granddaughter, played my wife; and one of my three daughters was played by the real-life daughter of that daughter.

That may sound funny and require some thought to understand, but it is nowhere near as funny as Johnny Depp's fart machine—something that required no thought to appreciate. Johnny would surprise an actor or crewman with it and the laughter wouldn't stop. People ask me if Johnny is Italian and I tell them what he said to me when I asked him: "I'm one part Cherokee and the rest mutt." Johnny had a kitchen in his trailer on location and I did a lot of cooking. What else would I cook on the set of a movie about wiseguys? Sausages, peppers, steaks, meatballs, pasta, and different sauces, of course.

Al Pacino had a personal assistant who cooked, too. We had a little friendly competition. Al Pacino was a very private man on set; no fart machines in his repertoire. But he can be hilarious at dinner when he's comfortable and gets to know you. Al was attached to the picture from the beginning. Look at me using words like "attached." I'd come a long way from my days of hanging out at the Motion Lounge. Now I found myself involved in discussions about a different kind of shooting—shooting scenes, not people.

Anyway, Al was originally going to play me. But executive producer Barry Levinson talked him out of it, correctly pointing out that Al would make a terrific Lefty Guns Ruggiero, the first made gangster and Bonanno soldier who claimed me as part of his crew. When Sonny Black became a capo in 1979 after the Galante hit, Lefty and I were folded into Sonny Black's crew—Lefty as a made man and me as a valued associate, a connected guy, not a made guy. Once Al Pacino was settled into the role of Lefty, Al then recommended Johnny Depp to play me.

At one time or another we had a lot of stars attached to the movie to play me, including Tom Cruise, Alec Baldwin, John Cusak, and Nicholas Cage. Can you imagine? Nothing for nothing, but they were all okay by me. Each one of them would have brought their own special talent and quality. Nevertheless, Johnny was a stroke of Al Pacino's genius.

All the actors were real sticklers for getting to understand and know the real people behind their character. Nearly every character was based on a real person, dead or alive. Johnny Depp spent day after day with me for over a month before any shooting began so he could get down my mannerisms and speech. Even during the shoot he would check with me before takes, which could happen at any time. The workday begins at 7 a.m. and can end at three o'clock the next morning. When Johnny wasn't actively shooting a scene, we would lift weights together and generally hang out. All the while he continued to study me and ask questions.

Another example of how Johnny looked out for the crew happened during shooting in Florida. The reason we were shooting in Florida had to do with some Mafia work I did as Donnie Brasco in order to ensnare Bonanno family members in illegal activities with a Florida Mafia family.

By way of background, in 1970 Congress passed into law the RICO section of the Organized Crime Control Act. RICO—an acronym for "Racketeer Influenced and Corrupt Organizations"—is a crucial piece of legislation written by Notre Dame Law School Professor G. Robert Blakey, a prominent consultant to the federal government and expert in wiretapping legislation from the 1960s forward. RICO was enacted specifically to take aim at Mafia bosses. In the past, the most that the government could hope to do was to convict an individual mobster it caught breaking the law. The government could not convict the chain of command and get to the bosses pulling the strings, nor could they successfully try groups of Mafia made men or bosses together. In fact, in the early sixties, Attorney General Bobby Kennedy had to have simultaneous grand juries running for each of the five New York Mafia families. But the Mafia code of *omerta*—the code of silence—kept the grand juries from getting any evidence to define the structure of the Mafia and the bosses in order to prove conspiracies were taking place. The brilliance of the RICO Act was that it made it a serious crime for anyone to be a member of a "criminal enterprise," a corrupt organization, engaged in a "pattern of racketeering." If the government could prove a person was a part of the conspiracy and could prove two crimes from a list of typical Mafia crimes like murder, drug trafficking, extortion, gambling and loan sharking, then the RICO Act could help them get a conviction.

I had the goal of gathering sufficient evidence to establish a RICO charge against the Bonanno family, as well as the other New York Mafia families by association. From my relatively low position in the Mafia I was lucky to be able to broker Bonanno family alliances with other families. These alliances would provide crucial proof of the "pattern of racketeering" by the "criminal enterprise"— the Bonannos and the other families' membership in the corrupt organization known as the Mafia, also called *La Cosa Nostra* (translated from Italian: "this thing of ours").

One of the families I brokered the Bonanno family into an alliance with was the Santo Trafficante family in Tampa, Florida. Among other crimes, the primary criminal conspiracy was that the two families became partners in illegal gambling and drug distribution at a private club called King's Court. It was in a big octagonal building on five acres near Tampa. King's Court was equipped as an illegal gambling casino with crap tables, roulette wheels and blackjack. What neither Mafia family knew was the fact that the King's Court club was set up by the FBI.

When we shot the interior of the gambling casino at King's Court, it was extremely hot in Florida. We couldn't use air conditioning because the sound equipment would pick up the hum. We had a ton of extras in the scene. The extras were playing guys and dolls gambling at King's Court. Every time the director yelled "Cut!" to shoot the scene over, he made the extras stay frozen in their positions. That way we wouldn't have to go through the effort of trying to get the extras back in the exact position they were in. Because of this policy, the extras couldn't break for food or water. Johnny Depp saw this and understood what was going on. He told an assistant director that if every extra wasn't given a bottle of water at all times he wouldn't go on with the scene.

All the actors were considerate of the crew and of each other. Michael Madsen, Anne Heche, James Russo, Bruno Kirby—they were all a pleasure to work with. Nobody had an attitude. Even though I had prepared a lot with each actor before any shooting began, they each checked with me regularly because, every morning when they showed up, they had to change their personalities and become somebody different. Now *that* was something I understood and could relate to.

Al Pacino especially checked with me on a regular basis to ask about the style of speech and mannerisms of Lefty Guns Ruggiero, the real person, as Al developed the character of Lefty. The hard work that Al put into creating his character was truly impressive. Yet even the actors in the smallest of roles checked with me. They didn't necessarily want carbon copies of the real people; part of each actor's art is to put something of his or her own into the character. For example, Al's take on Lefty was to dress Lefty down. In real life, Lefty, who was very smart in the ways and history of the Mafia, was a real sharp dresser. His winter coat was cashmere. But Al saw a way to bring to the audience another side of Lefty's character—something bordering on pathetic—by wearing a distinctively un-sharp plaid jacket with a fur collar.

While I'm talking about the jacket, I don't want to forget to commend the hard work of the costume people. I worked with them many hours to get the details down of the actual clothing the real people wore, from the wiseguys in the crew to the FBI agents who handled me.

As you may know, the movie, based on the book of the same name, was not 100% accurate. The book, of course, was 100% accurate in terms of relating what happened throughout the Donnie Brasco operation, with the exception of certain matters of a sensitive nature that were left out or couldn't be told at that time. The movie was about 85% accurate in detail, but 100% accurate in overall impression of wiseguy life and the work I did. An example of an inaccuracy in the movie is the scene in which I smack my wife. I can't imagine doing that in real life. Also, Al Pacino's character of Lefty does some things that Sonny Black actually did in real life. And the ending, when Lefty leaves his apartment en route to a sit-down meeting, the audience is led to believe that he would soon be whacked—and that never happened. However, it all falls under the jurisdiction of dramatic license.

Most importantly, I never had that sense of sentimentality toward Lefty that the movie portrayed me as having. I never felt any need to save Lefty, nor did I experience a feeling of guilt that maybe I was doing something cold-blooded by "betraying" Lefty's trust. Johnny Depp has a line in the film, "All my life I've tried to be the good guy, the guy in the white fucking hat. And for what? For nothing. I'm not becoming like them. I am them."

It may sound harsh, but throughout my six years undercover as Donnie Brasco, and to this day, quite the contrary is true. I maintained an unwavering belief in my original mission. I never experienced any doubt, uncertainty, or reservation. I did not make Lefty a Mafia gangster. Lefty chose to be a hoodlum and worked hard to become a made man in the Mafia. Lefty and his Mafia underground nation is America's enemy. I was an American FBI agent. Lefty broke the laws of my country. Every single day of his adult life, he either broke them or spent time trying to figure out how to break them. The Mafia is a criminal organization full of bad people who hurt good people for profit. Take my word for it: I saw it every day I was with them. It doesn't get any simpler than that. In the end, I was proud to bring Lefty to justice, and I'm even more proud of the devastating short- and long-term effects on the Mafia that people have credited, in part, to my work.

Was there any residual post-traumatic "Brasco" lurking in my psyche? As Lefty Guns Ruggiero said countless times a day, "Fuggeddaboudit."

• • •

In getting a book deal in the first place, and then a movie deal, I dealt with people who made wiseguys look like pillars of virtue. For the book deal, I had to interview writers who were famous for writing about the Mafia. I was searching for one who would take my words and stories and court testimony and put them into book form. With author after author, I got the feeling that it was going to be their book and not mine. Finally, I found the right man for the job, Richard Woodley, a talented writer and a terrific man. We clicked. At one point when I asked his opinion regarding something about the book, he even said to me, "Joe, this is your book, not mine." At the end of our meeting, we shook hands and made a deal. I then had a meeting with a top publishing house that had offered top dollar on the book. At that meeting, their top guy told me he didn't want me to use Richard Woodley. I explained that I had signed Woodley with a handshake, and Woodley knew that was my word.

"I'll give you $50,000 more," the publisher's top guy said, "if you don't use Woodley."

"I can't do that," I said. "I made a deal with him."

"Do you have a contract with him?"

"No, I have a handshake."

"Hell, that's nothing. That's not a contract."

"To me it is."

"It's just a handshake. You mean you are going to give up $50,000 extra on a handshake?"

"It's my word and I have to get up in the morning and look myself in the mirror and live with myself."

My agent and I walked the hell out and went with another publisher who treated Richard Woodley and me and our book with dignity. Just as a way to do business, I wondered what that first publisher thought I'd think of the original offer he had made if he could so easily come up with an extra fifty grand just like that—more than my annual salary undercover. It didn't matter; I wouldn't have to deal with him again.

The movie industry is even worse. Fly-by-night guys would make offers that could tie up the book in an option for a year with almost no money down but with the promise of an enormous payday at the end. They would wave outrageous figures around, figures that meant nothing, but were intended to tempt me into letting them own my book so they could shop it around and make the best studio deal for themselves. And these guys would never look me in the eye. At least a gangster looks you in the eye and tells you he is going to steal from you.

Another high school buddy of mine, Lou DiGiaimo, a basketball and football teammate, had become a casting director. Lou hooked us up with the excellent people who ended up making the movie, a movie we were all very proud of and which featured a dynamite Academy Award-nominated script by Paul Anastasio.

And what made the movie so satisfying, at least in my eyes, was the same thing that makes an investigation a success: attention to detail. For the sake of accuracy, we even walked the old Greenpoint neighborhood, despite the fact that the exterior scenes of the film would be shot in a less-crowded neighborhood—Brooklyn Heights near the Brooklyn Bridge.

I had spent so many hours of so many days hanging around the front room of the Motion Lounge at the corner of Graham and Withers, that it felt like home when I gave the set designers a tour of the neighborhood. I could almost picture Boobie Cerasani and Nicky Santora still in the back room manning the phones in the Motion Lounge for Sonny Black's sports betting and numbers racket. During my last months with Sonny Black's crew, I lived with Sonny in his third-floor apartment over the Motion Lounge. Now I was there as technical adviser for the film—a job, believe it or not, that required a ton of work. I was adviser to every department at all times, conversing with the director, setting up scenes. Would they say this? Would they do that? What would the reaction be to such and such?

At one point, the film personnel and I were on the street where Sonny Black kept his pet pigeons—on the roof of the Motion Lounge. Sonny loved those pigeons the way some people love their favorite dog as if it were their child. He talked to his pigeons and gave them special feed. He had ninety-five of them, and had a name for each one.

Seventeen days after he reported to the Mafia Commission that I was an FBI agent, the bosses called Sonny Black to a meeting. It was the Mafia's version of a golden parachute that a corporate officer gets when he's fired—except instead of huge wealth via stock options, Sonny would get whacked. On his way out the door, he gave his watch and house keys to Charlie, the bartender at the Motion Lounge, and said, "I'm going to a sit-down. I don't know if I'm coming back."

But he went to the meeting anyway to face his punishment. And sure enough, they killed him and chopped his hands off to show that his murder was retribution for allowing me, Agent Joe Pistone, to infiltrate the Bonanno family as Donnie Brasco. They chopped off the hands that touched me and that made the significant introductions of me to the top bosses of other Mafia families. The hit itself, on an otherwise loyal and trusted friend and partner and fellow Mafia member, was executed to set an example of what happens to anyone who causes the kind of harm to Mafia family bosses as he did—that is, introducing them to an undercover agent. In the movie, for dramatic purposes, they show Lefty stashing away his personal effects as he heads out the door to a meeting to be killed. But it was Sonny Black who did that. Lefty's planned hit was picked up on an FBI wiretap and he was arrested on a Sunday afternoon and taken off the street on his way to his death and the cutting off of his hands. He would die some years later of natural causes.

Sonny Black's body had been buried in a shoddy way—most likely on purpose so it would be found like a lost letter—with a message to Mafiosi everywhere not to ever let an agent infiltrate again. The body itself was discovered in November, three months after Sonny disappeared. A man out for a walk with his dog spotted it in a swampy section of Mariner's Harbor, Staten Island. However, the body lay on ice in the morgue and remained unidentified for several months. I learned that Sonny's body had been identified and his hands cut off during a break in my testimony in the Bonanno family trial, the first of the many Mafia trials my six years of undercover work had produced. It was a year after he had disappeared. But in my heart I knew Sonny was history a week after he disappeared—when they tore down his pigeon coops from the roof of the Motion Lounge.

By the time the film crew and I walked the streets outside the Motion Lounge in preparation of making the film, the old hijacker Big Joey Massino had become the boss of the Bonannos. We weren't on the street to do any actual filming, but rather to show the set designers what the real street looked like. They wanted absolute authenticity, just like the actors, the director, the producers, and everyone else involved in the picture. You don't realize until you get involved—at least I didn't realize until I got involved—but it takes a couple of hundred people all working together like an army to put together the film that you see. Every department has to break the script down to whatever their expertise is: pre-production, wardrobe, prop master, cameraman, photographer, and an assortment of assistants. And every single person that I worked with took their assignments to heart and wanted to make the best picture they could make.

The director was responsible for putting all these individual pieces together. If a scene was shot and it didn't feel right, he'd shoot it again. Sometimes thirty seconds of what you see on screen may have taken fourteen hours to shoot.

The gangsters in Sonny Black's crew—including me—hung out at the Motion Lounge for hours on end, day after day, scheming and plotting to steal or otherwise break the law. It was repetitive and mind numbing. The whole thing is about what can be ripped off on that particular day. Like hunters who eat what they kill, the average Mafia gangster is constantly hunting so he can eat. The social club, where they hatch many of their schemes, is also where they derive their camaraderie, their sense of belonging to a family, of being part of a crew, of being teammates. It may sound strange, but when I was with them—people with names like Boobie, Jimmy Legs, Boots, Mr. Fish, etc.—I felt that sense of belonging, too, from time to time.

The thing that bothered me most about being back on that street for the first time in fifteen years since coming out, was that I knew many of the hunters had never left. They were still here in this very neighborhood. Living here. Hanging out here. Hunting here. I also knew from FBI informants that I still had a half-million dollar Mafia contract on my head, and while I kept my face out of the media, these guys didn't have to see my picture to recognize me. I couldn't fully relax. I was a little bit on guard. I found myself glancing up at the roofs for any activity, and shooting an occasional glance behind me. I checked out anybody who passed us. You never knew about any of these guys who might still be around, what's going to click in them. Because all it takes is for something to click. Maybe somebody wants to look good in Big Joey Massino's eyes.

As we strolled and I pointed out locations to the crew—a different kind of crew than I had been used to in this Brooklyn neighborhood—shopkeepers started to come out and greet me. "Donnie, how you been?" It was as if I had never left. And they were still calling me Donnie. They were shaking my hand. They obviously didn't care who from the old crew might see them greeting me. It relaxed me. And it was a kick to still be called Donnie. Why not? That's who they knew. In a way, it was a tribute.

More and more people came out of their apartments and houses to see what was going on. "Hi, Donnie, how's it going?" They had big smiles on their faces as if I had just gotten home from the Army. "I liked your book," a couple of them said.

I suddenly felt like a celebrity in the eyes of the movie people I was with. And when a truck slowed down, and the vaguely familiar tough-looking truck driver stopped and rolled down the window and yelled, "Hey Donnie," I waved back and yelled, "Hey, how you doing?"

"You rat motherfucker, you!" he hollered, rolled up his window and drove off scowling.

CHAPTER 2
DEEP COVER DONNIE

IF ONLY MAFIA ACTIVITY were just a Hollywood invention. But of course, it's real. And I not only witnessed it in action, I lived to tell about it. Until now, I haven't exposed much detail about the daily activities I witnessed, not even in my first book, *Donnie Brasco*. At the time that book was published, there were still many trials pending involving many alleged crimes committed by many alleged members of the alleged Mafia—none of which I could discuss. Now, over twenty years later, and with over 200 proven wiseguys convicted of those crimes—including the "Last Don," Big Joey Massino, who was finally convicted in 2005—those allegations are fact and I can talk.

It was 1980. I was sitting on a beat-up unmatched hard wooden chair inside the Motion Lounge playing cards with the crew and breathing in secondhand smoke when Sonny Black walked in with Big Joey Massino. I had been under-cover for five years, and had been a part of Sonny Black's crew for about a year. From the minute I went undercover I knew that sooner or later I could come face-to-face with somebody I had locked up and it could mean death for me. A scare had already happened once before during my first six months undercover when I was with Jilly Greca's crew in the Colombo family in Brooklyn. I crossed paths with another guy named Joe I had also locked up—but he wasn't a made guy and he wasn't a very bright guy and he gave me no notice. But Big Joey Massino was far from dumb. As a soldier before he got promoted to capo, he had headed a world-class hijacking ring. It was in that setting that I first made Big

Joey's acquaintance.

Hijacking, in the sense that I'm using it here, is a term for the robbery of big tractor-trailers and their loads of consumer goods. Hijacking was a Mafia monopoly. There was no freelance hijacking permitted in New York City. A criminal couldn't just go out and decide to hijack a truck because, if he did, he'd have to deal with both the Mafia and law enforcement (mostly the FBI, but also the local police.) And guess who the would-be freelance hijacker was more afraid of? The five New York Mafia families—Bonanno, Genovese, Gambino, Colombo, and Lucchese—controlled the lucrative business of hijacking and they let nobody else in on the racket. Irish need not apply—unless Mafia-approved. The top hijacking crews in the city when I was working straight-up as an agent in hijacking in 1973 were crews belonging to the then-soldiers Big Joey Massino, Sonny Black, and John Gotti. Because they were part of the Mafia, all those crews had to deal with was the FBI. It was their job to steal a load, sell it, and keep one step ahead of us.

When Sonny Black walked in the door in 1980 with Big Joey Massino—all of three hundred pounds of capo—I had no options. I couldn't keep one step ahead of anybody. I was in a room full of gangsters with only one way out, and that was the way Big Joey came in. I was a sitting duck. Could my luck hold up twice against the Joes of the underworld who might recognize me?

Big Joey and Sonny had on new black leather jackets I recognized from a load of swag (stolen goods) we had just gotten in. But matching jackets was where any physical similarity between the two ended. Sonny was in relatively good shape. In fact, he and I used to work out together. Big Joey Massino, on the other hand, was known as "Big" Joey because of his girth. I doubted he could button his new jacket. But fat or not, he was a powerful cold-blooded killer and a made man who had made his bones—that is, committed murder, turned a human being into a pile of bones—many times over.

Like I said, in 1973, a couple of years before I went undercover, I had been working straight up as a street agent in the hijacking squad. Seven years before Big Joey walked into the Motion Lounge, I had been part of an eight-man FBI team that raided a warehouse and arrested the hijackers, including their crew leader, Big Joey Massino. I couldn't remember if I had actually put the cuffs on Big Joey or handled him during the booking and fingerprinting process at the

FBI office in New York City on East 69th Street. At any rate, when he walked into the Motion Lounge, I recognized Big Joey instantly. You couldn't miss him if you tried.

As I sat there on that hard seat gambling with my fellow crewmembers, I had one main hope stirring inside me—that Big Joey, like the other Joe, would not recognize me. The only problem is that these guys make it their business to study the faces of agents and cops. That way they can recognize them in the future. Because the possibility that he had once studied my face ate at my gut, I also had a fall-back hope. I hoped that if Big Joey did recognize me he had a clear-cut memory that I was an FBI agent, the last person on earth the Mafia should get caught killing.

The last thing on earth I wanted was for Big Joey to have a less-than-clear-cut memory, a memory that was twisted in some way harmful to me. For example, if he saw me sitting there playing cards and had a memory that he had seen me before consorting with the G (what they called the government), like a suspected rat I could have a secret and silent problem. He could secretly communicate that vague memory to Sonny Black and insist that I be whacked on the spot on mere suspicion alone. Or he could wait a day or two to communicate that thought. And Sonny could wait a day or two to act on that communication. People could sit down and talk about their own suspicions of me and I would have no idea. I would walk into the Motion Lounge in a day or two and never walk out.

When I first started hanging around the Mafia joints, sitting at the bar drinking, waiting to be included in their conversations, hoping to impress them with my knowledge of jewelry itself and the heisting and fencing of jewelry, I wore a mustache. Ordinarily a mustache was not allowed in the FBI, but since I was the first agent to go under on a long-term basis they let me wear a mustache. I thought it was a good idea to wear one in case I ran into anyone who might recognize me from before I went under. By the time I met Lefty Guns Ruggiero I had an eight-month-old mustache and had gotten used to it. But when I came under Lefty the Bonanno soldier's domain, he ordered me to shave it. The Mafia, like the FBI, wants its men clean-shaven. So there I was as clean-shaven as an FBI agent. I didn't even have a mustache to hide behind.

The only thing I had going for me besides the passage of time was that over the years I had begun to look like a wiseguy, even though I wasn't one yet in the strict sense of having been made. My face had the look. And not all wiseguys have it. There's something about the look on certain wiseguys that dominates their features. The nose and chin and other distinguishing characteristics take a back seat to that look. It's not even a menacing look. It might be that it's a quiet, supreme confidence, along with a studied secretiveness, a mouth that doesn't move much, and eyes that are always aware without staring. It's a face that says: I'm always scheming and I'm always right and you're always wrong.

Then the moment of truth arrived. Everybody in the room knew Big Joey Massino except me.

"Joey, Donnie is a friend of mine," Sonny said.

"What do you say, Joey," I said looking up from my cards and into his eyes. "Pleased to meet you."

"Donnie," is all Big Joey said.

There was no don't-I-know-you-from-somewhere look or question. Big Joey the hijacker gave no hint of awareness that he was looking at anyone he recognized from anywhere else. Big Joey and Sonny settled in at a table in the corner to huddle over whatever. They looked as deadly serious as they could look, at least to me. Looking back, I wonder if maybe they were already plotting the historic hit on the three Bonanno capos, which came about a year later.

For me, there was no sigh of relief, not even on the inside. My gut still gnawed. With my poker face I settled back into my card game. I waited a few minutes and looked at my watch.

"I've got to call my girlfriend," I said and laid my cards down. "I'll be back." I went outside as if to use the outside payphone, waited a half second, and quickly walked back in to see if I had suddenly interrupted any conversation that was going on behind my back. Everything appeared normal, which was the best I could have hoped for.

"I just remembered, she's working tonight," I said. "Deal me in."

My luck held up; Big Joey never did make me.

. . .

My participation in Mafia hijacking has always been an open sore for me, something I have hesitated to talk about until now. Any involvement in hijacking was very much unauthorized by the Bureau. Before I went under I had targeted the hijackers, and at any moment during my years under I could have found myself being targeted by the hijackers. Meanwhile, I had to prove myself to the hijackers, which I did. And the personal risks involved to me, both from the Mafia and from the law, were worth what I had to do for the sake of the mission. How else could an undercover agent possibly do it? What did the Bureau expect when they put me under and extended my operation from a six-month stint to an indefinite period as I produced results? In order to work a single day undercover as a criminal and a gangster I had to gain the trust of the criminals and the gangsters, and there is only one way to do that. You've got to do what they do. You've got to do what you've got to do.

An actual hijacking works in one of two ways: a give up or a take away. In a give up, the corrupt truck driver lets the wiseguys know that he will have a particular load available for a staged hijacking. A quiet place along the driver's normal route is predetermined for the give-up hijacking, usually in an industrial area. The driver gets out with the motor running and gives up the load. He also gives up his driver's license.

The purpose of taking a driver's license in a real take-away hijacking is to scare the driver into not ever identifying his hijackers. You know where he lives and he knows you know where he lives once you take his driver's license with his address on it. In a give up, the driver doesn't need to be scared, but the license is taken so that it looks like a real hijacking to the police or the FBI.

You'd have a pistola with you, but there'd be no reason to flash it on a give up. You'd carry a gun because you're a gangster and that's what gangsters do. You never know what's going to happen. Sometimes the driver asks to be cracked and somebody gives him a shot in the jaw to give him a bruise. Later on he'd get $500 or $1,000 depending on who he was hooked in with. For a very profitable load he might get as much as $5,000.

The take away is basically the same thing except that the driver is not in on it beforehand. There is usually inside information, maybe from the driver's company, that he will be on such and such a route. The driver might be in a diner eating breakfast, lunch, or dinner, and somebody keeps an eye on him while his rig is stolen. It's wired up in no time; just open the door and start it up. The doors are rarely locked because they'd rather that you take it when it's parked than take it from them at a red light. Unless it's a diesel, which gives the driver no option but to lock it. It's not good for the engine on a diesel to start and stop. Diesel tractors are started up for the night and not shut off. So if he's driving a diesel he's got it running while he's inside eating and his rig is locked. In the case of a diesel, he might be stopped on his way out of the diner. A jacket is opened to reveal a gun and the driver automatically hands over his keys and license. The truck drivers want no trouble, and neither do the wiseguys.

Even a take-away hijacking at a red light, a traditional armed robbery, is done very smoothly. It's done in a location with little or no car traffic, again in an industrial area. The wiseguys will watch a place such as a trucking depot or truck traffic at the waterfront docks. They especially watch for refrigerated trucks. Then they follow the truck to a red light. One guy gets up on the passenger side and flashes a pistola. Another guy gets up on the driver's side and confronts the driver. This guy on the driver's side takes the driver out of the tractor with the tractor still running, gets the driver's license, and gets back in behind the wheel. This guy on the driver's side is always the one indispensable guy who can drive a big rig. Coincidentally, I worked my way through college by driving eighteen-wheelers. The other guy gets in from the passenger side.

When the light turns green they drive away. Meanwhile, there is a car with two or three crewmembers in it right behind the tractor-trailer. The trail car follows the tractor-trailer to the drop, runs interference all the way, and keeps a lookout for cops. Everybody is careful to obey the traffic laws.

The drop is a big empty warehouse or a garage in an industrial area. If law enforcement doesn't burn the drop, it would be used again and again. The rig with its load will stay at the drop for as short a time as possible.

One lucrative load of the day was coffee, like Maxwell House in cans, ready to be put on the shelf. Shrimp, for some reason, having more to do with who the inside contacts were, was a big item then. The Mafia totally controlled the Fulton Fish Market near the Brooklyn Bridge. It was natural for a Mafia-controlled fish wholesaler to sell a load of shrimp and then tip off a hijacking crew and arrange for the load to be hijacked back so they could sell it again. Clothing was big, like men's suits, and so were over-the-counter pharmaceuticals like shaving cream, deodorant, aspirin and the like. Yes, like in the movies, even Schick razor blades were a targeted score.

A typical load that I might be involved in was worth eight hundred thousand to a million dollars at retail. The crew boss, typically a soldier, would get close to half of that when he sold it as swag. He would come along on the hijacking and be the man in charge. But nobody higher than a soldier would ever go out on a hijacking. The crewmembers, almost always mere associates, would get a few thousand for their effort.

In the Mafia, all money flows upstream. So the boss of the crew, a soldier, would usually have to float half of the money upstream to his capo and so on, all the way to the top. If a crew boss got caught lying about how much money he got for a particular load, he'd get whacked. But they did take the chance and lie on occasion to their capos if they needed money, say for their own gambling debts, or if they had some real sucker pay more than the going rate for a load of whatever.

Also, before the crew boss went out on a hijacking or did any kind of other criminal score, he had to get approval from his capo. That way the capo knew to expect an envelope with money in it. If a crew boss got caught doing a score without first telling his capo, the crew boss might be given a chance to explain, but he might not. The penalty for doing it again would certainly be death.

Lots of times the load would be sold in advance of the hijacking. There was a supermarket manager in Queens, for example, who let the crew I was with know that he would take all that the crew could deliver. In that case, the rig would be brazenly driven from the hijacking right to the supermarket where it would be left there for the manager to unload. The manager would stock the shelves with his new inventory and sell it, pocketing the money himself. The manager, or one of his men, would then "dump out" the entire rig, parking the tractor and attached trailer on a city street to be found later, again in an industrial area.

If the load weren't pre-sold, the whole rig would be driven right into the warehouse drop and then all those involved in the hijacking would take off. The load would be watched for a day or two to make sure that a snitch had not given it up. It would be unloaded as it was sold, and then the rig would be dumped out. If the whole load got sold as is, often the buyer would come with his own tractor and pick up the trailer, putting a different license plate on the back of the trailer. Our crew would then take the stolen tractor and dump it out on the street. Whoever bought the load would dump out the trailer after they emptied it at their own store. And nobody had to tell anybody how it was done or what to do. It was all strictly routine.

When I was on the lawful side of hijacking in 1973, we were losing eight loads a day to the Big Joey Massino, Sonny Black, and John Gotti crews. They tore us up. We had snitches that particular agents had cultivated. The snitch might be working off criminal charges or he might be getting thousands of dollars for his information. Or both. We had good snitches inside the crews. Still, we were lucky to recover all or parts of only half of all the loads that were stolen. And we never knew whether what we were recovering consisted of loads or parts of loads that couldn't be sold anyway—in which case we were the ones buying the swag.

If as a straight-up street agent I ever paid an informant for swag, it certainly wouldn't have been the first swag I ever bought. I grew up in a neighborhood in Paterson, New Jersey, which is basically a suburb of New York City. In any gin mill you hung out in, somebody always had swag for sale. You could get your complete wardrobe in a neighborhood bar: shoes, pants, shirts, even underwear and socks. The suit I wore my first day to the FBI was swag. I had bought it years earlier. The buying of swag stopped for me when I went into naval intelligence before the FBI, but I still had the suit and it was a nice suit.

As an undercover agent you try not to break the law, but as I said, I had to fit in and stay in character in order to stay alive. There are only so many times you can bring in gold watches and precious stones and claim you stole them. You're going to have to be a team player, leave the social club, and go out in the street with your fellow teammates. You have to cut off whatever personal feelings you have about crime and crime victims, the feelings that drew you to law enforcement in the first place. And you have to justify your actions by rationalizing that as long as you're there at a hijacking with men with guns on them, at least you're in a position to prevent violence to innocent victims.

I left Jilly Greca's Colombo crew and cultivated Bonanno family connections, in part, because the Colombos had more of a cowboy mentality. I couldn't be in a position where random violence for the sake of violence was likely to occur. The Colombos I was with tended to do a lot of house burglaries. Usually, some drug addict son of well-off parents would tell his drug dealer where the valuables were kept, how to get in, and when his parents would return from their travels. The drug dealer would then tell his drug trafficker, usually a connected or made Mafia guy. The kid would get a small cut from the score, which he would put right into his veins or up his nose. But these house burglaries were one-shot deals, usually done on Long Island, and they were fraught with danger. I got the feeling that the least valued and most expendable crewmembers did more of the house burglaries.

You do too many house burglaries and it's only a matter of time before you have to take a bust. If local cops cruised by at the wrong time and I got arrested hauling a safe out of a house, I never knew how the local district attorney would treat me. What if the local Mafia family controlled the local DA? Worse, who knew what spontaneous violence would happen if the parents walked in the door unexpectedly and surprised us? I think house burglaries should be classified as crimes of violence. A lot of murders occur during house burglaries gone wrong. I might not be able to act quickly enough to prevent a sudden killing of a homeowner. In addition to having such a thing on my conscience, I'd be guilty of felony murder. Everybody in on the burglary would be guilty of any death that occurred.

Warehouse burglaries, instead of house burglaries, would have been a big advancement for me in my gangster career.

The way that worked was fairly simple. The crew boss would get information that a warehouse had, for example, a shipment of Giorgio Armani men's suits. The crew boss would tell me to go and case the warehouse. I'd be told to clock the comings and goings of the people who worked there. I'd have to see if there was a night-time guard, and if there was one, I'd have to clock his rounds and scope out his usual activities. Does he take a meal break? Is there a second guard on duty at the same time, which is rare, or one that replaces the main guard? How often do the cops cruise by to check? I'd have to look for the best time of night to break in and steal the load of suits. Maybe a weekend is the best.

I'd also need to check out how we'd break in. Usually, if there was a door with a key, the crew would just bang open the door and break the lock. Or they'd break a window, go through it and unlock the door from the inside. Typically, they'd be looking for an entrance in back of the place or for a loading dock. Most important, they'd be looking for the alarm to see where the box that controlled it was.

When the time came there'd be about five of us. We'd have a driver of our truck. We'd have a tail car like with a hijacking. We'd have a lookout who would stay outside on foot. The truck and the driver would be parked near the loading dock. The driver and the lookout would each have a walkie-talkie to alert any of us inside if there was trouble brewing on the outside. On the inside there'd be two or three of us, and at least one would have a walkie-talkie. We'd all have flashlights.

But before we went in, they would always tell me to bypass the alarm. As a jewel thief I was expected to know how to handle an alarm. I would have to go to the box and disconnect the live wire from the box after first using alligator clips to jump the live wire so there's a continuous circuit going. The idea was to fool the live wire into thinking it was still connected, that the circuit was still going. Ironically, this is something I first learned in naval intelligence along with lock picking, both of which I learned again later in the FBI.

If there were a guard, the crew would know where he was, get the drop on him with guns drawn, and handcuff him to a pipe. The guards are not there to protect against professional thieves. They are there strictly to guard against kids—vandalism, petty thievery, whatever. They know their limitations and they act accordingly.

Adrenaline would be flowing. Warehouse burglaries were not as routine as hijackings because you have so many more things to do and you have a lot more exposure. Loading the truck would take less than fifteen minutes. We then would drive the load to a drop and it would proceed from there like a hijacking. My end would be $2,500 to $5,000, which I would turn over to my Agency handler.

Warehouse burglaries were a Sunday in Central Park compared to house burglaries. Don't get me wrong; I still hated doing them. While I foolishly bought swag as a kid, justifying it by telling myself that everyone else in the neighborhood did it, and that I didn't know for sure that it was swag, and that insurance, no doubt, covered the loss, I would never have directly stolen anything from anybody. Even as a private citizen I would have tried to stop a thief from stealing if I saw a theft occurring. And here I would be stealing some innocent person's property, in the interest of combating the Mafia in a way that had never been done before. In my heart I hoped I was doing the right thing. Years later, as you'll read later in this book, it turned out that I was.

· · ·

The Mafia gangsters I lived with were not the intelligent, almost cultured people portrayed in certain books and movies, like *The Godfather*. Such fictional portrayals have often romanticized and inflated their stature. In fact, a lot of wiseguys studied the *Godfather* movies in an effort to imitate a certain style of wiseguy. But such imitation was form over substance. The bottom line is that the wiseguys I lived with had no regard for other people; they gave no thought to the bloodshed that spread to the innocent from the sale of drugs; they certainly gave no thought to the addicts their drug distributions had created, even when their own children became addicted.

Despite Mafia propaganda, drug distributions on a large scale (and sometimes on a small scale) were a part of many Mafia family's bread and butter, practically from the start of the Mafia in America. But the Bonanno and Gambino families seemed to do more of it than the other New York families.

When I helped set up a sting operation in Florida to ensnare the Florida Mafia boss, Santo Trafficante, I had drugs practically thrown into my face.

Another undercover agent and I had set up a club called King's Court in Holiday, Florida, about forty miles northwest of Tampa. It was to be an illegal gambling casino. A gambling casino controlled by the Bonanno family, or by anyone else for that matter, could not have been operated anywhere near Tampa without the approval of old-time Tampa boss Santo Trafficante. Trafficante was known the world over for his admitted participation on behalf of the CIA in the 1961 Bay of Pigs invasion of Cuba, and in a CIA and Mafia plot to kill Fidel Castro. Trafficante was also alleged to have participated in the plot to assassinate President John F. Kennedy in Dallas in 1963. Trafficante had originally been a powerful casino owner in Havana before the Cuban revolution. After the revolution, Castro ousted him from Cuba. Trafficante ran Florida like a grandfather, and he had never been in an American jail.

To get Trafficante's approval to open the King's Court casino, Bonanno boss Rusty Rastelli, from his jail cell in Pennsylvania, had to reach out to Trafficante in Florida and vouch for Sonny Black. Sonny Black, in turn, had to vouch for me, and I had to vouch for the other undercover I had brought in. Trafficante, of course, would get half of the King's Court earnings. In short time, all details were smoothed out and the casino opened.

This was a huge pigeon feather in the cap of Sonny Black. It was an operation that, no doubt, made Rusty Rastelli very happy in his dismal jailhouse surroundings. In hindsight I can see this King's Court deal was one of the key factors that later led Rastelli to name Sonny Black acting street boss to replace Sally Fruits Farrugia. Sally Fruits had stepped down because he didn't want the headaches that went with the power, and also because his thick Sicilian accent made communicating orders to Brooklyn Americans difficult.

With the King's Court deal that I had brought to him, Sonny Black, to his great joy, was now branching out territorially. The Bonanno family territory, which had operations north of Miami on the east coast in Hallandale, Florida, was expanding into the west coast of Florida and was about to have a very powerful ally in Santo Trafficante. With a Bonanno crew of Sicilian imports (called "Zips") already established in Montreal, Canada, dealing in heroin importation under their own Sicilian capo, Nick Rizzuto, this Trafficante alliance I had brokered would further establish the Bonannos' power up and down the entire east coast. Although I never met Rusty Rastelli because he was in jail the whole time I was under, I can tell you that a boss loves the idea of expanding his territory with capable made men.

The illegal work involved in the operation required precision and thoroughness. Foremost it involved sit-downs in Florida between Sonny Black and Trafficante. Unknown to them, each sit-down was photographed and was evidence of the existence of a corrupt racketeering organization. The evidence of sit-downs was needed to bring federal RICO charges against the very structure of the two Mafia families involved. The gambling operation had to be run properly and actually function as a casino. Local law enforcement had to be paid off to protect the operation. They call a cop who will take a bribe "a meat eater." We put a crooked captain, Joseph Donahue of the Pasco County Sheriff's Office, on our pad. Donahue could afford to buy a lot of steaks with the cash we handed him.

The politics inside Sonny's crew had to be handled with a precision akin to diamond cutting. While the operation brought me closer to Sonny Black, I had to be careful not to make Lefty jealous enough to want to kill me. As a mere associate I should have been reporting to a soldier, not to a capo. In my case, that soldier was Lefty. Instead of dealing with Lefty—a soldier, a made man—Sonny had me deal directly with him. He confided in me, and not just about business but about personal matters as well. Lefty was especially miffed when Sonny gradually excluded him from much of the King's Court planning and operation.

While all this intricate work was being performed in Florida in an FBI operation code-named Coldwater, the other undercover and I began to attract a lot of drug attention. I suspected that as soon as the DEA learned that a New York Bonanno gangster named Donnie Brasco had come down to operate in Florida—a hotbed of drug distribution from South America—the DEA wisely but incorrectly assumed I was in the drug business. After all, the Bonanno family seemed to be the family with the largest stake in drug trafficking of all the families.

Soon a medical doctor began to hang around King's Court, claiming he had access to large shipments of cocaine that he could sell to me. I strung him along thinking I could work backwards through him to his suppliers. But he started making excuse after excuse. Because he never came up with anything more than promises, I became suspicious of him. Because of the strange way he acted around me, I began to think that he was a DEA snitch working off his charges, and that I was being set up by the government while I was setting up the Bonanno and Trafficante families on behalf of the government.

I certainly couldn't go to the DEA with my suspicions. For security reasons only two or three people ever knew who I really was while in an operation. I had to let the DEA and this doctor continue to think I was a Bonanno gangster. So now I had to act as a gangster would act under the circumstances.

If I was right about him I also had to beat him to the punch, keep him from bringing drugs to me and avoid getting myself arrested in his sting. Along with the other undercover, I paid a visit to this doctor's office. I asked him if he was fucking around with me. When he answered "No," I knocked something off his desk. Then I asked him that same question again. When he answered "No" again, I knocked more items to the floor. After more of that I said, "Are you an agent?" He said, "No." I knocked something else to the floor. Each time I asked and he answered, no matter what the answer, I trashed the place further. Needless to say he never called the police and I never heard from that doctor again.

I later learned that the reason the doctor had been stalling in hooking me up with the promised large shipments of cocaine was that my eyes had scared him. He thought I was a stone killer and he wanted no part of me.

There was another doctor I had a run-in with in Florida, though it wasn't related to anything I was doing down there. There was a nearby hospital from which nurses used to come to the King's Court after work to unwind, have a drink and relax a bit before going home. We would chat with them often, and one night they started talking about the head surgeon. This was the era before sexual harassment was made illegal. This head surgeon was very free with his hands. Every time he walked by a nurse he would pat her on the ass. He would make vulgar remarks and they felt they were powerless if they went to the administration because they were only nurses and he was very important to the hospital. Everybody knew the power plays he pulled and for years he simply got away with it.

One night I'd heard enough and decided to act; maybe it was because I have daughters. I asked one of the nurses to keep it to herself and to meet me in the parking lot at a time when the surgeon would be going to his car. She met me and pointed his car and him out to me. He didn't know he was being watched.

I returned the next day and waited for him by his car. When he came out I said, "Excuse me, doctor so-and-so, do you like your fingers?"

"What?" he said.

"You need those precious fingers of yours to operate, don't you?"

He didn't answer.

I said, "You lay your hands on another nurse in that hospital, you won't be operating anymore."

About a week later I asked the nurses, "How's that surgeon doing?"

"What a change!" one said. "We were just talking about him today. He hasn't touched anybody all week."

"He's real nice to us," another said.

"Somebody must have taught him a lesson," the nurse who had met me in the parking lot said.

But believe me, the next time you hear a story like that about a Mafia gangster, you can bet he's an undercover agent.

. . .

In the latter months of my deep cover I divided my time between Florida and New York. One evening after dinner in New York with Lefty, he and I decided to go to a card game in a walk-up apartment in Little Italy. As we were heading up the stairs, two young white guys were coming down. When they got a step past us they pulled out guns, put them in our backs and demanded our money. I thanked God that Lefty and I had no guns with us. I would have been afraid Lefty would pull his and start blasting away. This would put me in the position of having to blast away to defend myself from their guns and to satisfy Lefty that I was not a rat. Fortunately, we were not about to whack two drug addicts in a stairway. Yet.

Lefty said, "No problem, sport. Just give them your money, Donnie."

Obviously, the robbers had sense enough not to rob the card game, because inside they would have been whacked. They figured it would be safer to get people on their way in with their gambling money. I had about $2,500 in gambling money and Lefty had about $1,500. We turned our money over and they ran out fast.

"So much for the card game," Lefty said. "You got any money in your shoe?"

"Sorry, Left," I said.

"Me neither," he said. "You just saw two dead punks run down the stairs."

Less than two days later Lefty called me to his apartment in Knickerbocker Village on Monroe Street near Little Italy. Lefty's hobby was tropical fish and he had a few aquariums in his apartment. Lefty liked to just look at the fish and watch them swim around. A number of Bonanno wiseguys lived in Knickerbocker

Village. They had some kind of in with the management. If they got behind in rent no one bothered them. Lefty had asked me if I wanted an apartment there, but I tactfully had said no. Anyway, Lefty had gotten the names and the hangout of the two robbers. I was relieved that he moved off of wanting them dead, as all he said was, "Go solo. Teach them fucks a lesson both. Get as much of the money you can back."

The robbers hung out in an after-hours storefront on the outskirts of Little Italy. They were both Italian wiseguy-wannabes in their early twenties. They were stupid to think they could get away with it, practically in their own neighborhood, and made more stupid by the drugs they were on.

It was in the middle of the afternoon. I hoped for their sake I would find them because, if I couldn't find them, Lefty might send somebody else who would find them and kill them. Plus, let's face it: I was pissed off. First, they robbed me. Second, they put me in this position of having to cross the line into violence. What I was about to do was another one of those things that was very much unauthorized by the Bureau and that could cause me to need a criminal lawyer.

I considered the consequences of telling Lefty they weren't there as I approached. But there they were. The two morons were out in broad daylight standing in front of their hangout. There was a strong grapevine in Little Italy. At that instant I could bank on that grapevine; Lefty would hear every detail of what happened even before I could report it to him.

They were my height; about six feet tall, but at 185 I had thirty pounds on each of them. They were junky skinny. I walked up to one and, boom, I let him have an overhand right. He hit the pavement as if I'd had a roll of dimes in my right fist (no comment). The other one's eyes popped open when he recognized me.

"You stay put," I said. "I'll get to you next. Don't even think about running. You're in no shape to outrun me and it'll only go worse for you."

I looked down at the kid on the ground and realized he was out cold, and so I sprung suddenly and hauled off an overhand right on the other one and he went down. I put the roll of dimes in my pocket and went through their pockets. I got a few hundred, but they had already shot up the lion's share of the money they got from us. Getting the money back was not the point anyway. It was all about the satisfaction to know they didn't get over on you and get away with it.

What I did next I did for each kid's own good. I knew I had to throw them both a good beating or they could still get whacked. You don't put a gun into the back of a made man like Lefty Guns Ruggiero and expect to live. Lefty's son was a drug addict. His son's problems might explain why Lefty only told me to "teach them fucks a lesson both." During my time with Lefty before this incident, Lefty's son pulled a gun and robbed a connected jeweler on Jewelers Row and Lefty had to square that beef with another family that the jeweler belonged to or Lefty's son would have been whacked.

I know this much: the two junky armed robbers didn't get up on their own and walk away from that sidewalk. From the kidney blows they bled piss for weeks. And until the breaks healed they had no use of their fingers for such things as shooting a gun. The whole thing took less than three minutes.

I can't remember if I took any drugs from them. If I did I would have thrown it down the nearest sewer—another unauthorized act.

When I got to Lefty's, he said, "Is it taken care of?"

I said, "It's taken care of."

I gave Lefty the few hundred I recovered and, like a boss, bless his soul, he put it in his pocket without throwing me a dime. Not another word ever was said on the subject.

CHAPTER 3
THE DEEP END

AS AN FBI AGENT, how deep could I sink into the mud of the underworld of organized crime before I would be too far in to dig myself out? Before I would be off the deep end, out there alone? No undercover had ever been in the position I had been in for as long as I had been in it.

The principal digging tool I had to keep from becoming too deeply involved in criminal activity was what I called the "well-told fiction." I lived a life of deception all the time when I was working undercover, but sometimes I had to develop an elaborate well-thought-out fiction to get myself out of a jam or to allow the operation to continue without compromising it.

While deception had become a way of life in my deep-cover work, from my family upbringing and as a Catholic who still went to Mass when I could sneak away from the crew, and as an FBI agent who reported every few days or so to my FBI handler, distorting the truth was something that went against my grain. It went against my own deep character.

I understood that my deceptions were for a greater good, as if Nazis came to my door and I lied to save the Jews I was hiding in my cellar. To me—and to any student of ethics—that's not lying. But at some point if nearly everything you do is deceptive it can become easier for you to deceive in general. At what point would I be in so deep that I would make a decision to deceive the FBI?

When the fictions start to appear to come true after you tell them, the whole house of deception gets more than a bit eerie. The spookiest for me was when

Lefty and I were staying in a hotel in Milwaukee waiting day-after-day for word that the boss of the Milwaukee family, Frank Balistrieri, would agree to meet with us to discuss a joint operation I had promoted.

During the time we were waiting for word from Balistrieri's people, I began to miss my family more intensely than normal and I had a strong desire to dig myself out to see them. I couldn't get away from this proposed meeting with somebody as important as Balistrieri, the boss of an entire family, without an elaborate fiction. I already had a phony girlfriend who I visited in California whenever I wanted to fly home to see my wife. Now I told Lefty that my girlfriend in California had been injured in a car wreck and I had to leave him to be with her. Lefty was so mad when I said I was leaving I thought he was going to explode, or maybe blow me up.

This meeting with Balistrieri was something I had set up with the help of another undercover going by the name of Tony Conte. Our plan was to forge a partnership between the Bonannos and the Balistrieri family in the vending machine monopoly in Milwaukee. It was an expansion of a scheme the Milwaukee family had going already, one in which honest saloon keepers would be required to use only our vending machines or risk problems from the Milwaukee Mafia family. It was one of the biggest breaks of Lefty's career in what he called "the underworld field." This was 1978, a couple years before King's Court in Florida, and it was one of my biggest coups to date at the time. From the Bureau's point of view, the operation we had set up was intended to gather evidence to prove the inner workings of a criminal enterprise consisting of a racketeering alliance between the Bonanno and Balistrieri Mafia families.

While I was telling Lefty that this fictitious girlfriend of mine was in bad shape from her car wreck, he was telling me, "She ain't going to die. What are you worrying about?" Behind my back to Tony Conte, Lefty called me a jerk-off, and wanted to know what was so special about this girlfriend of mine that I never brought her to New York so people could meet her. I withstood Lefty's wrath, called my wife to pick me up at the airport and hopped a plane.

My wife was nearly killed in a car wreck en route to the airport to pick me up. The young woman driving the oncoming car that crossed into my wife's lane and hit her head-on was killed. My fiction instantly had come true. This was the most devastating time of my life. I stayed with my family during the eleven days my wife was in the hospital and for another week after that, which, no matter how you slice it, wasn't long enough. We had barbecues and lived as a family for the first time in a long time. When I was satisfied that things at home were as good as they could be under the circumstances, I returned to Milwaukee.

While we were in Milwaukee working this plan, called Operation Timber, to ensnare the Milwaukee boss in a criminal conspiracy with the Bonanno family, a Milwaukee soldier named Augie Palmisano was blown up in his car. Lefty explained to Tony Conte: "They're blowing guys up because they done something wrong."

To add to his point, Lefty said, "Tony, the responsibility I gave Donnie just now . . . if he fucks up, I'm a dead man." Lefty told us how he would be killed. "If I get sent for, I don't know what I'm getting sent for. They just say to come in. And I'd be getting killed for something I didn't even know."

When the mission in Milwaukee was pretty much accomplished, as far as evidence gathering was concerned for the Bureau, Balistrieri suddenly ended the partnership. Balistrieri refused to return anyone's phone calls. The word that came down was that Balistrieri was mad at Tony Conte for doing "something wrong," something very wrong. According to word from on high, Tony Conte had been seen flirting with Balistrieri's girlfriend. You don't ever disrespect a boss in any way and expect to live another day; you especially don't disrespect him regarding his wife or his girlfriend. As Lefty put it, "That's worse than being a rat or a pimp." On top of that, the sudden dissolving of the partnership without explanation by Balistrieri cost our Bonanno bosses a lot of money, and not just in lost profits.

"Maybe he's a snitch," Lefty said to me behind Tony Conte's back. And worse, "I'm in jeopardy over here and you brought him in." And still worse, "Conte could get whacked at any time over this."

It was now time to get Tony Conte out of the picture without Lefty and those above him dwelling for long on whether Conte was an informant or an under-cover agent or just a bad soldier in need of the ultimate punishment to square things with Balistrieri. Not to mention that, since I brought Tony Conte into our Bonanno crew and introduced him to Lefty and eventually to Lefty's capo and the family underboss for this limited undercover purpose, I had my own safety to consider. Initially we had Tony Conte fake a heart attack to buy us some time. He actually reported to an emergency room complaining of chest pains. But that was only a temporary fix to get him out of immediate harm's way.

Next, we devised an elaborate fiction to extricate Tony Conte permanently without blowing up the rest of my Donnie Brasco operation that we still had in play, or blowing us up. That was big for Conte and me, that part about staying alive. This elaborate fiction also converged eerily with reality.

The elaborate fiction was that Tony Conte had a big score coming up. We told Lefty and our capo at the time, Mike Sabella, that Tony was going to participate in a major art theft that was planned to take place in Chicago and had $250,000 coming to him as his share of the take. We chose art rather than, say, jewelry, because art thieves are in a world unto themselves. It is such a specialized field that an art heist is something Mafia mobsters would not be able to look into and check out with a few well-placed phone calls to bosses in Chicago. Why we chose Chicago, I still don't know.

I told Lefty and our capo, Mike Sabella, that Tony Conte was going to share his Chicago art heist score with us, the way a good crewmember should. All money flows upstream in the Mafia as if that's the way nature had planned money to flow. And the bosses upstream can never get enough. At least half of the $250,000 would go upstream. Such a fact instantly pushes all other thoughts into the back of wiseguys' minds, including thoughts of retribution against Conte.

We concluded this operation in Milwaukee over a year before Carmine Galante got whacked in 1979. After Galante got hit, Mike Sabella got demoted from capo to soldier and Sonny Black got upped to capo, and Lefty and I went with Sonny Black. Mike Sabella was happy to be demoted at that time because the alternative was to get whacked. At this time, however, Mike Sabella was a big wheel with a lot of power and commanded the extravagant respect these people go for. Big money is a big sign of respect. Waving this kind of big money under Mike Sabella's and Lefty's noses made them forget that they were mad at Tony Conte for doing "something wrong," and for ruining their Milwaukee plans by disrespecting Balistrieri in the girlfriend department.

Now that Tony Conte had an art-theft score to whack up, all of a sudden the word floated down from upstream that it was the inner game of petty Mafia politics—not Tony Conte's flirting with the wrong restaurant hostess—that had queered the deal with Balistrieri. The bosses upstream took Tony Conte off one hook so they could keep him on another hook, one that would put money in their pockets.

No sooner had we devised this Chicago art heist elaborate fiction and told Lefty and Mike Sabella, then out of the blue a real-life art heist worth $3,000,000 was carried out in Chicago. All the big news outlets around the world reported the heist and the enormous value of the art that was stolen. Lefty and Mike Sabella licked their chops. Another fiction of mine instantly had come true. More than spooky. Nothing for nothing, but from the time I went undercover to this very day, everything about everything just seemed to fall into place like it was all meant to happen. Art theft? Chicago? Not Boston, not Los Angeles, not Paris, France— but Chicago? And more than enough value to justify a $250,000 share to Tony Conte? The coincidence was enormous, and enormously helpful.

The rest of the fictitious plot I reported to Lefty, who reported to Mike Sabella, was that Tony Conte had to meet with his confederates to get his share of the three million. The plot twist in our fiction was that the undercover agent they believed was Tony Conte, was simply not going to return from that meeting with his accomplices.

But Lefty was one step ahead of our plot devices. Lefty gave me a firm order, saying, "I'm holding you responsible. You fly back to Chicago with him. And then you don't leave his side. You go with him to pick up the money, and then you come back in here with him and that money."

I was already responsible for Tony Conte and now I was responsible for this money. People like Augie Palmisano in Milwaukee had been killed for a lot less trouble than I had already caused and was about to cause. When I called Lefty and told him my brand new plot twist—that Tony Conte had gone to the meeting but couldn't take me with him because his pals had told him to come alone, and that Tony Conte had not returned to our hotel room—Lefty said many things. None of them was good.

I'd never experienced Lefty so mad. Among the outpouring of words from Lefty that became embedded in my mind and stuck with me were:

"There ain't a punk in the street that hangs out with a wiseguy could get away with what you two guys done. Forget about it. Youse won't last five minutes in the city of New York.

"I'm so fucking mad. I don't even want to get mad at you right now. I'm fifty-two and I'm willing to spend the rest of my life in jail over this. . . .

"I'm blowing my top here. You weren't supposed to leave his side. That's why you're there.

"You put me in fucking mean positions with these guys." These guys were Mike Sabella and the other Bonanno bosses all the way to the top. Just as Lefty held me responsible, under penalty of death, Mike Sabella held Lefty responsible, with the same penalty looming.

"Could this fucking guy be a fucking agent, Donnie?"

At that last statement, I thought, why would Lefty's mind go straight to the notion that I might have specific knowledge or insight about something like whether Tony Conte was an agent? If Conte was an agent, shouldn't I be as ignorant of it as Lefty?

And the bar-none scariest words any undercover agent can ever hear about his phony stories while he's telling them was, "Something's fishy."

When enough time had passed to make it obvious to Lefty and Mike Sabella that, whatever the truth might be, Tony Conte was not going to return to the hotel with the money, Lefty called me in Chicago.

"Get on a plane late tonight and come back to New York."

"Why late tonight?" I asked, even though it could only add to my jeopardy by questioning an order. "Why can't I come in now during the day?"

"Because that's the way it is," Lefty said flatly. "You're being sent for and you come in. You come in late at night. You get a cab at JFK and you come directly to Lynn's Bar on 71st. Don't go nowhere else. Don't be seen by anybody. Don't tell anybody you're coming. Straight from JFK to Lynn's. Be there alone at midnight."

Lynn's? A small place that would be empty at midnight. Not too many people would even be on the street at 71st and 2nd at midnight. I couldn't ask Lefty why we weren't meeting in Little Italy where we normally met, a neighborhood with 24-hour-a-day pedestrian traffic. Midnight. Alone. Straight from JFK. Don't be seen by anybody. Don't tell anybody I'm coming.

This was not the way Lefty had ever talked to me. But I knew Lefty had to do whatever he had to do for putting Mike Sabella into this bad position. And that included whacking me. As Lefty once said, "A little violence never hurt anybody."

"Something's fishy."

Something's fishy on both sides of this equation, I thought. I remembered what Lefty had said to Tony Conte and to me, "If I get sent for, I don't know what I'm getting sent for. They just say to come in. And I'd be getting killed for something I didn't even know."

I'm a lousy gambler. I never win at gambling. But I would be gambling with my life if I went to this meeting.

I never told anyone about this conversation with Lefty, or the ensuing sit-down, until now. I decided to keep the meeting a secret, go to it and take my chances. If I told my FBI handlers that Lefty had ordered me to a sit-down at midnight in an abandoned bar, they never would have let me go. They would know that if they planted backup agents for protection inside an empty Lynn's at that hour, the backup would have been spotted and made. And having backup outside Lynn's would have done me no good. Therefore, having me go to the meeting would have been unacceptable. Having me skip the meeting and return to New York on my own time would have been sure grounds for being whacked—also unacceptable. For all intents and purposes, if I told my handlers about being sent for and the sit-down that would soon follow, the Donnie Brasco operation would have been over.

I decided not to tell the FBI. I was finally in so deep that I was lying to the FBI by omission. Because of my job, I lied by omission regularly in my personal life to those I was closest to, especially my wife. There was so much about what I did that I could not tell her. But she knew it and she didn't expect me to level with her about the things I was doing or the danger I might be in. The FBI, however, expected me to tell them everything. I was finally in the mud at the deep end.

Would this lie by omission to the FBI cause the web of lies I had been telling Lefty and the rest of the wiseguys to come true instantly—like my wife's car wreck and Tony Conte's Chicago art heist? Would I become just another dead rat, a Mafia associate who had done something wrong and paid the price he knew he would pay if he ever fucked up as badly as I had? Would I be dying from the lie

I had been living? Was I lying to myself that I could handle this gamble, that it was worth the risk? On that point, I don't think so. And not just because the gamble paid off.

When I teach agents who are about to go deep, I tell them that their most important asset is their mental toughness. People don't realize the power of mental toughness. A lot of people out there don't understand how much you can accomplish just with mental toughness and focus. I saw a lot of it growing up in my Sicilian and Italian neighborhood in Paterson, New Jersey. It was prized and I had it. That doesn't mean I didn't appreciate the danger of meeting with Lefty at that time in that place, but I was focused and I refused to let go. As I look back, I know I couldn't let go. I didn't have it in me.

I knew that Lefty would go when sent for, and later, when I got to know Sonny Black, I knew that Sonny Black would go when sent for. If I didn't go when sent for, Donnie Brasco was history. If I didn't show up for the midnight meeting, the whole operation would be prematurely over and I would have had to pull myself out of it. Because if I didn't show up when sent for, I would surely be whacked. That's one of the principal grounds for a death sentence—disobedience. And especially failing to come when called. It's actually a part of the Mafia oath when an associate is made; you always come when called. Period.

Lefty knew when he spoke to me on the phone that I had to be thinking that this could be it for me. He's the one who taught me that when they send for you it could be to whack you for something that you didn't even know about. But if I showed up and everything was okay, I would go way up in Lefty's estimation as a stand-up guy who comes in when called for even when it could be the end for him.

Mental toughness includes preparing well in advance to handle whatever could be thrown at you, rehearsing it in your mind like a boxer before a fight. You roll the imaginary camera in your mind and study the film of your opponent's last fight. If you're prepared that way in advance, you don't get confused or panicky by having to make decisions on the spot.

First, I decided I'm not going into any back room. Not that that matters so much, because many hits occur the instant you walk through a door from the outside. Two times .22 with a silencer, behind the ear. I could get it walking in the joint before I even closed the door behind me. I could get it stepping out of the cab. I had to keep my eyes open from the moment the cab pulled up.

Second, I decided I'm going on instinct. If something doesn't feel right when I open the bar door, I'm closing it and turning right around. I pictured myself doing just that.

Mental toughness, at least for me, includes faith. Not a day went by as Donnie Brasco that I didn't subconsciously ask a Higher Power to look over me for the day.

The threat of death was a very real threat to me when I finally opened the front door and took that first step inside. I tried to look as relaxed and normal as possible. I could see Lefty sitting with two wiseguys I knew, but hardly. Otherwise, the place was empty of customers. Not a good sign.

The two wiseguys stood up and moved away from Lefty's table when I stepped in. My first thought was, *what are they doing here?* Did Lefty want these two to get a good look at me to be sure they recognized me if they were supposed to whack me later? Still, on pure hunch, it didn't feel like a setup, like anything would happen inside Lynn's, but you never know about hunches. And like I said, I'm a lousy gambler, unlucky at playing hunches.

Nothing for nothing, I thought as I walked to Lefty's table, I'm here. I sat to Lefty's side, not across from him. That way if he pulled out a gun, I had a chance at him. And I'd be facing the bar and the two wiseguys.

The two wiseguys sat at the end of the bar closest to the door. I saw that they were boxing me out. They were sitting between the door and me, should I have any inclination to make a broken field run out of the place.

Lefty scowled at me with complete contempt. His eyes were dead and his voice commanding. "Don't say nothing to me right now. You just sit there and take what you got coming."

If this is it, I thought, I'm not going down easy. Lefty's hands stayed on the table. The two wiseguys stayed on their bar stools. We sat in silence. I couldn't break the silence because Lefty told me to say nothing, to just sit there and take what I got coming.

"You know you fucked up," Lefty said. "But I don't know you know how bad you fucked up. Donnie, sometimes I don't know you know nothing. I know you know what happens when somebody fucks up one-tenth as much as you fucked up in this here. When you got it coming, Donnie, for doing something wrong, you got it coming. I don't give a fuck who you are."

"I'm sorry, Left, I'm really sorry. This cost me, too, Left. Some of that was my money. Plus he took my clothes, my belongings, my plane ticket. I'll make this up to you. I mean it. I'll get us all right on this. I've got some ideas for some scores."

As the apology mixed with the sound of cash, Lefty looked over at the other two wiseguys and they got up, said goodnight to us, and left. Were they there to make me understand how serious I had fucked up? Did Lefty send them away to let me know he accepted my half-assed apology? Or would they be waiting for me somewhere?

"I didn't even get a Christmas bonus due to the fact of out there and how it made me look," Lefty said.

After a lot more of this kind of tongue-lashing and poor-mouthing from Lefty, it turns out, Lefty told me, he wanted to meet me way uptown at Lynn's at that late hour because he wanted to prepare me for a meeting I was to have in the morning with Mike Sabella and he didn't want word to get back to Mike that he was doing that. Lefty's act of preparing me for my meeting with Sabella also told me that Sabella had no intention of whacking me at that meeting, as long as I followed Lefty's instructions for handling the meeting.

It looked as if my gamble had paid off. My decision not to tell my handlers that I had been sent for had not backfired on me.

Lefty's advice to me for my conduct at my meeting the next morning with Mike Sabella is advice I pass on to those undercover agents I mentor. Lefty said, "Don't offer nothing. Only answer the questions. Don't show him you're afraid. Look him steady in the eye. Don't show any fear. Don't admit you were wrong, even though we know. This Conte piece of shit was our mark and you shoulda never left him go outside by himself. You shoulda kept a better eye on him so he didn't go chasing after the hostess at the Snug Restaurant, which was Balistrieri's girlfriend. Some looker that girl, but you don't even think like that. Mike will confront you on these parts. But don't you admit none of that. How you fucked this up royally you admit to me some other time, but not to Mike. Look him in the eye. Be respectful. Like I said, Donnie, if I didn't love you how much I love you you'd be fucking dead. Mike don't love you like I do."

Lefty's advice paid off. I got off with a warning. I never again saw the two wiseguys who had been at the bar. The Donnie Brasco deep cover operation was still in business. And it's a good thing it was. Because the precise things that happened as a result of my continued undercover work ultimately, many years later, were to bring down the entire Bonanno family hierarchy.

. . .

Another potentially disastrous incident happened a few years after my gamble at Lynn's paid off. It's another matter I have never before disclosed publicly.

While there are some things I had to do that I will take to my grave and never tell a soul, this is more about something I *decided* to do rather than something I did. In the past I revealed that if there was a situation in which I had to decide between trying to save a wiseguy and risking my own life to do it, or not, I would not jump in and stop the hit on a wiseguy. But I *would* risk my life to stop a hit on a private citizen. What I didn't reveal is what I would do if I found myself in a position of having to put two behind the ear of a wiseguy or risk my own life by not doing it.

My mindset was that the wiseguy would go. I knew the FBI would not stand behind me on something like that. Well, let me call it what it is—murder in the first degree. On top of that there would also be a state charge of first-degree murder in the state in which I murdered the wiseguy, and the federal Department of Justice wouldn't have jurisdiction over the state murder. But to me, I'd rather take my chances with the judicial system than with the Mafia. I'd rather be alive fighting a murder charge.

When you get an order from your boss to kill somebody, you don't hesitate, you don't negotiate, and you certainly don't say, "No thank you, I'll just stay here and play cards."

In an undercover operation you always have to know with whom you are dealing, and I did. If you hesitate when you are given a contract, you will be killed, most likely right on the very spot of your hesitation. A wiseguy who says no to a contract is a dead wiseguy.

Even if you are out on a hit with your crew you are not above danger. If you do not do your part and pull your trigger, too, the other guns could be turned on you then or later. And you could find yourself on the same blood-soaked ground as the intended victim. If the contract happens to be yours, you'd better be the first one to pull the trigger, not the one who fires into an already dead body. That's something a snitch might do.

It goes without saying that, to begin with, you don't want to be in such a position. Even if you don't pull a trigger, but you go out on a hit, you are guilty of murder in the first degree under the theory of accomplice liability known as felony murder. The accomplice, the lookout, the wheelman, is as guilty of first-degree murder in the eyes of the law as the triggerman.

In the late spring of 1981 I was given the contract to find and kill Bruno Indelicato—a made man. He was a cokehead and the son of the murdered Bonanno capo Sonny Red Indelicato. Sonny Red was one of the three capos (along with Dominick "Big Trin" Trinchera and "Phil Lucky" Giaccone) who had been sent for to attend a meeting on May 5, 1981, and when they arrived they were whacked. This downsizing in the Bonanno family occurred a few days before I got the contract to find and kill Bruno.

Bruno, also a capo, was supposed to have attended the meeting, but failed to appear and escaped getting whacked in the massacre with his father. Now they had to find Bruno and kill him before he could retaliate against those responsible for his father's murder.

The May 5th upheaval caused Sonny Black Napolitano, who I had been with for two years by then, to be moved up a rung as acting street boss for the jailed boss Rusty Rastelli. Lefty and I were with Sonny Black's crew and that meant we were moving on up with Sonny Black. Sonny Black was now as big as you could get without being the actual boss.

As acting street boss, Sonny Black was the boss who gave me the Bruno Indelicato contract. Sonny told me to go to Miami, find Bruno Indelicato, and kill him.

"I think he went to Miami because he's got a $3,000-a-day coke habit and he's got connections with the Colombians down there," Sonny told me. "I want you to find him. When you find him, hit him. Be careful because when he's coked up, he's crazy. He's not a tough guy with his hands, but if he has a gun, you know.

. . . He might be down there with his uncle J.B. If you come across them both, just kill them both and leave them there in the street. I want the body found. He's like 140, 150 pounds. Smaller than you. Thin-faced kid. Italian-looking, dark. Always complaining about his bald head. In his late twenties. Bantamweight, petite-looking. He's a dangerous little kid. He's a wild man when he's coked up. . . . Leave him right there in the street."

Sonny gave me a .25 automatic for the job.

I saw Lefty a few minutes later and he already knew I had been given the hit. Lefty told me the Bruno hit would help me get promoted to a made member of the Mafia because it would give me a big hit under my belt. Lefty told me that Sonny had wanted me on the three capos hit, but that Big Joey Massino vetoed it. The prudent Big Joey didn't think he knew me well enough to include me in something that big. Years later Big Joey would point to this with pride.

This ordered hit on Bruno was one matter I clearly and quickly told my handlers. I called Jules the first chance I got, which was 3:30 in the morning. Now that Jules knew, both the FBI and the Mafia would be out there looking for Bruno. That made me figure that my chances of finding Bruno first were almost nonexistent. If the FBI found him they would arrest him to get him off the street so I wouldn't have to kill him. If other wiseguys stumbled on him in their ordinary course of activities they wouldn't wait for me to get there to kill him. Whatever wiseguy found him first would kill him first. If I somehow did find him first, I'd have called my handlers in the FBI to snatch him off the street. Unless other wiseguys happened to be along when I found him. Then I'd probably have to kill him or be killed with him.

Because Sonny Black sent me to Miami figuring Bruno would want to be near a supply of coke to feed his huge habit, I danced around all the usual coke haunts in Miami, getting seen everywhere. I was making sure Sonny Black would hear back in New York that I was taking my assignment seriously.

It did occur to me that Bruno Indelicato might get wind that I was the one that had the contract and try to get a shot at me first, or have one of his men who I wouldn't know or even recognize to get off first. But I kept a watchful eye and told myself that the last thing Bruno Indelicato needed to do was go out of his way to try to shoot a shooter. He needed to lay low and keep on the move. Of course, where does it say that a cokehead like Bruno always does what logic dictates?

Nevertheless, in my gut I felt that if Bruno was going to try to whack anybody it was going to be Sonny Black. Sonny Black could never really rest easy until Bruno was gone, and that's why the new acting street boss had given me the assignment in the first place.

· · ·

A side assignment Sonny gave me while I was looking for Bruno was to drop in on two made men operating for the Bonannos in Hallandale, Florida, not far from Miami. Joe Puma and Steve Maruca were two soldiers who had been under one of the three murdered capos, Phil Lucky, and owed allegiance to the three capos who were massacred. My job was to reassure Puma and Maruca that they were not going to be whacked and to tell them that they now owed their allegiance to Sonny Black.

In a strange way, this assignment was more significant under the Mafia code than the assignment to kill Bruno. Anyone—made, connected, or just some nut—could be given a contract to hit someone. But to have a sit-down of any magnitude with a made man, you had to be at least made. Here I was, a connected man only, not a made man, going to Florida to a sit-down in order to reassure two made men that they wouldn't be hit if they did the right thing. In the sit-down I would be expected to evaluate them both for the slightest attitude or sign of disloyalty or even disappointment that their friends, the three capos, had been whacked. And they would know that I, a mere associate, was sizing them up.

Puma had been so scared after the hits that he hurried to New York to pledge his allegiance to the new power. Maruca made it clear that the three capos' deaths were a part of Mafia life. "Things like this happen. You can't question," he said.

· · ·

After I was down in Florida awhile Sonny Black called me to fly back to New York. I figured or hoped that my contract to kill Bruno had expired and we would get back to whatever daily scheming presented itself to us in the Motion Lounge in Brooklyn and King's Court in Tampa. Among other things, I was hoping to hear more talk and get more evidence against those who participated in the hit on the three capos.

Which brings me to the other bad incident nobody knows a thing about. One night we were sitting around in the Motion Lounge playing cards and chatting away. Lefty, Jimmy Legs, Nicky Santora, Sonny, and I—all just doing our usual ritual when the phone rang. It was a pay phone on the wall. Sonny Black answered it and I could tell from his look and the tone of his voice when he grunted that he was getting excited.

Sonny hung up the phone and said, "Bruno's in a house in Staten Island."

Lefty got up from the card table and said, "Let's go."

Let's go, I thought. Jimmy Legs and Nicky Santora got up, too. I got up. My getting up, under the law of conspiracy to murder, was an overt act. Immediately upon committing that overt act, I was guilty of conspiracy to murder Bruno.

Lefty's maroon Caddy was parked right outside the front door of the Motion Lounge. Sonny Black, as capo, would not be going, and everybody knew that. Sonny Black gave Lefty the address and directions. Meanwhile I'm thinking, *there is no way out.* Everybody's heavy, including me. We've all been loaded up since the three capos got whacked, in case that multiple hit set off a full-scale Mafia war. I still had my .25 automatic from Miami in my pocket. The others had .38's to .45's. Lefty had a shotgun in the trunk.

If I hesitated in front of my capo, my own soldier, and my crewmates, I would not have left the Motion Lounge alive. I was on a fast-moving train. I could go to the bathroom, but there were no cell phones in those days. I positively couldn't go outside to use a pay phone at a time like this. There was no way I could contact anyone. I was alone. The statement "Let's go" from Lefty was all it took and everybody knew what to do. This wasn't the first time these guys had done something like this. It never even entered my mind to bolt and run away. They'd get in Lefty's car, catch up to me in a block and I'd be the victim of a drive-by shooting. And then they'd go kill Bruno.

As an FBI agent you're trained to question information you get. Who told you Bruno was there? How reliable is the source? How stale or fresh is the information? Was Bruno seen in the house? What's the layout of the house? All those things went through my mind, but it didn't make any difference. As a Mafia soldier you get to ask no questions. There are no questions in Mafia business. You're trained to go on the word that's given to you. There could have been something else in that call. For all I knew Sonny Black had been told there were three of Bruno's men there with Bruno Indelicato, and maybe Sonny Black chose not to tell us.

Almost from the beginning of my deep-cover penetration into the Mafia my mental toughness mindset had prepared me for this moment. The people I had been assigned to infiltrate engaged in murder the way a cabbie goes through a yellow light. I had to be mentally prepared for the near occasion of murder. I had long ago made my decision of what to do when this predictable occasion arose. If Bruno's there, he's gone. If I have to put a bullet in his head, I will, and I'll deal with the federal government and the Staten Island D.A. later. There's no doubt they would both charge me for murder. The Bureau would brand me a rogue agent and hang me out to hang. My wife, my daughters, my parents, would all be crushed right along with me, but my decision when it had been made was firmly made.

Meanwhile, we could be walking into a death trap. If not a death trap, then at least a bloody situation. We just killed Bruno's old man. He knows we're out to kill him. He's a cokehead. He's not going to come easily. There will probably be a shootout. Any of his men that are there with him to guard him will be killed, too. I could be facing multiple murder charges. Or worse yet, I got that old dreaded feeling that I would die as a gangster.

We were half out the door and on the street when the phone rang again. Sonny Black ran over and got it, said, "Hold it," and waved us back in while he took the call. We shut the door. When he hung up, Sonny Black said, "It's bad information."

"That's too bad, Sonny," I said.

In my mind, all these years I've been calling that the "miracle of the second phone call." The Higher Power I looked up to each day for protection was looking out for me.

CHAPTER 4

"YOU'RE GOING TO GET MADE"

MY INTERPRETATION OF EVENTS that I've tried to offer in this book—for example, my breakdown in the last chapter about the impact my King's Court gambling casino and the meetings with Santo Trafficante had on the rise of Sonny Black in Rusty Rastelli's eyes—is not the kind of thing I had time to think about while I was under. In those days I was too busy staying alive and trying to commit details to memory so that I would be able to verbally report the intelligence and evidence I was gathering. The past twenty years since my first book, *Donnie Brasco*, came out, have provided me more information and time to reflect. Still, at the time I was working my deep-cover operation, I knew I was having an impact and that I was about to have a dramatic impact when I surfaced. But I wanted to stay under, and to this day I think it was a mistake for the Bureau to have pulled me out before I had a chance to get made and to operate as a made man.

Could it have been my ego, my competitiveness, that caused such feelings? I gave it a lot of thought then and I've given it a lot of thought over the years, watching events unfold, and I come out the same way every time: I should have stayed under at least until I was made.

But I understand their thinking. My handler, Jules Bonavolonta, who made the final decision, was afraid for me. He did not want to lose an agent, and a close friend at that, in the middle of a Mafia war. "You're in a war here," Jules said, "a shooting war, and you're right in the middle of it. I'm not going to risk getting you whacked just to get more information."

Maybe if we hadn't been such close friends he'd have let me risk it.

And make no mistake, while a Mafia war did not ensue following the May 5th shootings of the three capos, the Sonny Black crew was anticipating a shooting war and we were all armed. The three murdered capos had their own crews who were loyal to them. This amounted to a small army that had been under them, some of whom were relatives, like Bruno. Vendetta is a word of Italian origin which seemed to be in play at this time. In contrast, following the Galante hit, no one went around armed; there was no talk of retaliation.

Over a month after the three capos hit, on June 20, 1981, there was a wedding in Staten Island involving the daughter of Sonny Black's crewmember and made man Boobie Cerasani. We all were loaded with arms at that wedding reception. I had my .25. It was a wedding, but that didn't stop it from being a gathering where wholesale vengeance could be carried out. In fact, capo Big Joey Massino was too afraid to attend. He told his good friend Sonny he thought it might be a trap and none of his crew showed up, thereby disrespecting both Boobie and Sonny. Big Joey risked certain ridicule and opted for caution. Lefty referred to Big Joey as a "jerk-off" for not coming to the wedding.

For his own purposes later on after I surfaced, Big Joey claimed he didn't attend Boobie's daughter's wedding because he didn't trust me. He knew better than to be fooled by me. But we know what he told Sonny at the time and it had nothing to do with me. Analyzing it, if he thought the wedding could be a trap, then Big Joey considered the possibility that Sonny might be behind the trap, making a clean sweep. Paranoia reigned everywhere.

The next thing I heard from Lefty about Big Joey was even more paranoiac. Lefty told me, "Sonny and Joey are feuding because Sonny's got more power. So Joey got an unlisted telephone number now. He ain't talking to anybody because of this feud with Sonny."

So the danger that Jules Bonavolonta put on one side of the balance sheet was potentially a realistic danger when he made his decision.

On the other hand, the FBI is a paramilitary organization. Anyone who joins an army voluntarily does so with the certain knowledge that death is a real and present danger. On the streets of America, every few days or so, a cop is shot and killed. Even with the advances in emergency medical care and even with the extra precautions cops have learned to take since crime escalated in the sixties—precautions such as body armor—cops get shot protecting us and they die from their wounds in the line of duty. So do FBI agents. I volunteered for that risk when I joined in the summer of 1969 and was no less ready to accept that risk in the summer of 1981.

Some supervisors at Headquarters were less concerned about my safety and more afraid I would push the envelope and whack somebody and tarnish the Bureau's image. The Mafia soldiers on the other side of this crime war, like cops, also signed up knowing that death was a risk for them.

As for the Bureau's image, Hall of Fame second baseman Joe Morgan once said something to the effect of, "Show me a batter who cares what he looks like at the plate and I'll show you a batter you can get out." Getting good wood on the ball should be a batter's only concern. The Bureau's only concern should have been public safety, to get as many murderers and heroin merchants of death and suffering off the street as quickly as possible.

Some supervisors at Headquarters had gained prominence in the Bureau under J. Edgar Hoover. It was a well-established principle under Hoover before he died in 1972 that undercover operations were forbidden because of the danger that undercover work could potentially corrupt the undercover agent. To gather intelligence on the Mafia, Hoover opted for black-bag operations instead. These were illegal bugs and wiretaps. They were illegal in the sense that whatever facts were gleaned from the taps and bugs were unusable in court. They were illegal in the further sense that to plant a bug an agent often had to secretly break and enter into private premises without a warrant. But in a broader sense the valuable intelligence that was gained could be used out in the field to thwart criminal activity and to build cases with other legally admissible evidence. Lives were actually saved by the bugging when the targets of a hit were forewarned and scooped up off the streets.

Kicking and screaming, some of these old Hooverites had to change their minds and go along with undercover operations a few years after I joined the FBI in 1969. Two years before I joined the FBI, President Lyndon Johnson's brand new Attorney General (and one of Saddam Hussein's current lawyers, Ramsey Clark)

ordered the shutting down of black-bag operations such as those under the direction of the legendary FBI Agent Bill Roemer. Roemer's various bugs and taps
were yielding great results against the Chicago Mafia during the years Bobby
Kennedy was in charge of the Justice Department. Roemer always felt that LBJ
closed down these black-bag operations because LBJ was afraid a bug had uncov-
ered evidence of corruption against one of LBJ's political allies.

One of these old Hooverite supervisors at Headquarters had gone so far in
my case as to express his belief at a meeting concerning me that I had become
corrupt and gone over to the other side. "Nobody's that good that he can go
native," this supervisor actually said to Jules Bonavolonta. All these years later that
comment still brings out the fight in me.

The ultimate devastation to the Mafia resulting from the Donnie Brasco operation—devastation that has been twenty-five years in the making—could have
taken a mere couple of years if I had been allowed to stay in just six more months.

During my last year under I was told repeatedly that I would be made. Sonny
Black told me around Christmastime in 1980 over dinner at Crisci's, a restaurant
in walking distance from the Motion Lounge. Sonny told me that if I kept my
"nose clean and didn't take a drug bust" I would be made the next time "the
books were opened up" to allow the making of new members.

The only time I was involved with drug deals was when Sonny and Lefty
were also involved, so that didn't concern me. It was just a matter of time and a
matter of the books opening up. Sonny apologized for not making me right then
at Christmas, but he had only one opening and Boobie Cerasani had been with
him longer and had earned the right to that spot on the basis of Boobie's senior-
ity. The clear implication was that I, a man who had been with Sonny Black a
mere year and a half, was on the fast track to being made on the basis of my pro-
duction and the projects for earning money that I came up with, such as the then
blossoming King's Court gambling operation in Florida.

Meanwhile, Lefty was schooling me in the way of the wiseguy for that gold-
en moment when I would be made. He even described the quasi-religious ceremony to me. He told me I had to dress up in a suit and tie. There would be three
or four capos there and a couple of other associates there to get their button. My
capo would give me the important formal introductions to the other capos. Then

we'd go in another room, one at a time. In addition to the ritual and the oaths, they would question me. Lefty told me, "If they ask you what you would do if your wife or your mother was in a hospital bed dying and you were called in for a meeting, your answer has to be that you would leave that hospital and come in for a meeting without even asking what the meeting was for or nothing. You just would come. No questions asked, no matter how close to dying your mother was or your wife."

Imagine if I had been made. It would have been the biggest humiliation the Mafia had ever suffered. And it was the one chance the FBI would ever have to pull it off. There is no chance another undercover agent will ever reach that stage again. After I surfaced, the Mafia immediately changed the rules to require that two members vouch for the prospect, and one of those members has to have known the prospect for ten to fifteen years. Especially in today's politically correct climate where public safety often takes a back seat to some principle or other, there is no way an undercover agent could do the dirty work it takes to spend ten to fifteen years inside a crew. Especially in terms of intelligence gathering, there is a world of difference between sting operations—where agents go under for a defined period for a specified purpose—and going deep.

Imagine the embarrassment for the Mafia from coast to coast and all the way to Sicily when the news got out that the exalted Bonanno crime family had made an agent. This organization depends on the sanctity of its rules and traditions to attract new members and to frighten their victims and the public. How susceptible would they have appeared? How low would their soldiers' morale have sunk? Don't forget, this ceremony of theirs, as dumb as it may sound to outsiders, means the world to them. You expose this ceremony as vulnerable and you hurt them where they live. Making an agent would have had the opposite effect on them that the morale-boosting movie, *The Godfather,* had on wiseguys like John Gotti. I say movie and not book because we're not talking about readers when we talk about these people. There was a no-questions-asked killer they actually started calling Luca Brasi after Don Corleone's loyal enforcer in *The Godfather.*

What a purge there would have been! The ruling Commission of *La Cosa Nostra* would have had every capo in the room at my ceremony whacked.

Around the time Sonny Black gave me the contract to hit Bruno Indelicato, we went up to his pigeon coops on the roof of the building above the Motion Lounge. "Donnie," Sonny said, "I'm going to put you up for membership to get made when the Old Man gets out." By his telling me that in those words, I knew that Sonny had already put me up and cleared it with the Old Man, Rusty Rastelli, who was due to get out that December, 1980. That's how they do it. Before they tell you that you are going to be made or get anything from on high, they get pre-approval. Sonny would not have put himself on the line like that without already knowing that our boss approved me, at least. I had no history with the other bosses that would stand in my way. I was approved by a boss I had never met and that would be good enough. I was approved on my resume and Sonny's say so, a capo who had developed more and more credibility in Rastelli's eyes as a result of the projects I had set up for him. I was approved by a boss with a twinkle in his little dead eyes behind bars.

As if reading my thoughts, Sonny added, "You're going to get made, Donnie. You're already up. There won't be a problem. I would have put you up last time, but I had to put Boobie up."

There was a rule that to be made you had to go out on a hit, at least as a witness. Both Sonny and Lefty were under the impression that I had killed people before, people who had cheated me on a score. Lefty explained that a hit was different. It was the killing of someone who had never done anything to you. It was the killing of someone who may or may not have deserved to die, but you had no choice. You whacked the guy because you were given the order to do so, or you got whacked yourself.

But both Sonny and Lefty made it clear that capos sometimes lied by omission on that issue to get a guy made. For example, close friends or relatives were proposed without ever having "done any work." The boss doesn't ask the capo about a particular hit the proposed Mafia associate has been on. The boss assumes the capo knows the rules and when the capo proposes someone that associate has already "made his bones." It was well known that one dummy, Joey "The Mook" D'Amico, was made because his mother, Tony Mirra's sister, paid off a capo.

Sonny Black had been trying to steer a hit my way. Like Lefty, Sonny also told me that he had wanted me to be in on the May 5th hit on the three capos, but that Big Joey Massino had vetoed it because Big Joey didn't know me. It was clear now, up on the roof with the pigeons, that whether or not I found and whacked Bruno, Sonny Black had already lied by omission to get me pre-approved by Rusty.

There it was. I was in. That was June and December was just around the corner. I swelled with pride the way one of Sonny's pigeons would puff up his chest and prance around the coop. Holy shit, I thought, how this is going to wreck the Mafia forever.

Sonny's news did take me by surprise a little in that nobody had hinted that the books were about to be opened up. Plus it looked like it was a time of war. I just thanked Sonny and assured him of my loyalty.

Wait till I tell Jules this one, I thought. During this phase I was being kept under a week at a time. I had to plead my case to stay under on a weekly basis. My ace in the hole had been an upcoming meeting in Florida at the end of July between Sonny and Santo Trafficante that I had to attend and that would put more nails in both men's coffins. I had convinced Jules that I could manage to stay alive and not get whacked until that meeting. But that ace in the hole was a deuce compared to this news. It never occurred to me that the Bureau wouldn't take advantage of this unprecedented opportunity and keep me under at least until I was made.

My man Jules and I already had had some hellacious fights over the phone about my coming out, but they got nuclear after that conversation with Sonny. Sonny's news didn't faze Jules at all. My supervisor and friend didn't budge. He believed the operation had to end.

And I wasn't alone in wanting to keep me under a while longer. We had a meeting at a motel in Washington attended by the heads of field offices from around the country who had set up stings through my personal help in the form of all-important introductions as a Bonanno gangster. They did not want their operations to fold prematurely before they had completed their missions. In some cases, money and time had been invested and there would be no arrests to show for it if I came out then.

Not to beat a dead horse, but as a made man I would have had access to discussions that were out of my league as a mere connected associate. Whenever I was introduced to a made man, the wiseguy doing the introduction would say,

"Donnie's a friend of mine." That was a signal that I wasn't made and to watch what was said in front of me.

If a made man was with us he would be introduced in a different way: "Lefty's a friend of ours." As a friend of "ours" Lefty could stay, but I would have to go to another table.

When you plant a spy you want him to have access to information. Otherwise, what's the point? As a mere connected guy I could not mingle with made men from other families unless someone like Sonny called ahead of time or unless I was formally introduced and had a made man with me. If I had been a made man I would have had the freedom to go wherever I wanted and hang out with Gambino men under John Gotti; Genovese men under Fat Tony Salerno; Colombo men in Brooklyn under Carmine Persico; and Lucchese men under Tony Ducks Corallo.

I would also have had the freedom to hang out with other crews in the Bonanno family, like eventual boss Big Joey Massino's crew at J & S Cake. In between scores, these crewmembers have almost nothing else to do but play cards and talk about crew business, gossip, brag, and bullshit. The intelligence alone that I would have harvested from such access as an equal would have been fantastic. We still don't know how much we don't know about the Mafia despite the flood of turncoats of the past decade. These turncoats play it very close to the vest. They still consider ratting a sin, and they only tell as little as they can get away with telling to get their own charges dropped.

Intelligence gathering was a huge part of what I did undercover. For example, for years the Bureau saw an influx of made Sicilians coming over and being absorbed into the Bonanno family, primarily, but also into the Gambino family. And for years no one fully understood why these Zips were coming over. The intelligence I gathered from just being talked to by Lefty revealed that these Zips were in America to facilitate the smuggling of heroin and cocaine hidden in imported cheese, pasta, or other shipments from the Sicilian Mafia. Some of the narcotics went into Montreal, where the Bonanno family had a crew of Zips under the Sicilian capo Nick Rizzuto. Most of the narcotics were smuggled into New York by the Zips who lived on Knickerbocker Ave., the same Brooklyn street where Galante was whacked at Joe and Mary's restaurant. The

Knickerbocker Ave. Zips were under their own Zip capo, Toto Catalano, a baker by trade. If I got that much from Lefty as a connected guy, as a made man I'd have heard deeper secrets, and gotten details—who, what, when, where, how—that had been off limits to me.

Nothing for nothing, but after all these years my last day as Donnie Brasco still stings a little. You keep a guy under six years, long hours day after day living with gangsters on their round-the-clock schedules, hurting his family life and depriving his family of their man around the house, their father, destroying his hobbies and his social life with friends of his own choosing, risking his life, risking going to jail himself, and when he's one rung away from totally devastating the Mafia you yank him off the ladder.

I wouldn't have just been made, which would have been plenty good enough for an enormous payoff. I would have been made by the acting street boss of the family, with all the added prestige that that would have brought under their own rules.

I spent that last day undercover in Florida at the Tahitian Court Motor Lodge. Santo Trafficante's driver drove the boss up there for that final meeting to discuss arrangements for King's Court. Under their ways of doing business I had to be present for that meeting to take place because I had introduced the other under-cover agent involved in King's Court. Introductions are another important ritual-istic part of the Mafia. They take their introductions very seriously and there are serious consequences for bringing the wrong guy around to be introduced. Even though I was needed at the meeting because I had started the ball rolling on the alliance between the families, because I wasn't made I had to excuse myself and wait outside while they talked. Other agents had placed a bug in Sonny's room, but once again the old fox Santo had the TV turned up real loud so our bug picked up nothing but daytime television.

When their meeting was over Trafficante drove back to Tampa. I drove Sonny Black to the airport for his flight to New York. On the drive Sonny was ecstatic with how the meeting with Trafficante had gone.

"Florida is going to be ours, Donnie," Sonny said to me, echoing what he'd said from the beginning. "Get going on the bingo and the dog track. Keep on top of the other guy regarding the numbers and the booking and moving shit. Florida is all about drugs. Everything's got to be big down here. With the big man involved with us, I don't want to be handing him thin envelopes. A big part of my future is going to be in Florida. I'm going to be spending a lot of time down here myself. You did a good job down here so far, Donnie. I see the future down here. Everything is really going to roll from here on out."

Sonny talked about his future, but when he got out of my car and we parted, I believed I was looking at Sonny for the last time.

While I drove to my Florida apartment I had to remind myself that if Sonny had suspected I was an informant he would have killed me in a New York minute. The next day I packed up in a miserable mood. They could always close it down if things got hot for me. Why don't they just pull some strings to let Rusty out of jail right now, claim the prison is overcrowded, so I could get made right now if they're worried about waiting until December? Close it after I get my button. Maybe there was some ego in these thoughts. I had gone under in 1975 when Ford was president. I was under for the entire Carter administration. And now as I flew first to a grand jury in Milwaukee and then on to Washington, the Gipper was in the White House. I had to leave my resentment behind me in Florida. I wasn't retiring to a farm. In a sense, my work was just beginning.

CHAPTER 5

FIRST BLOOD

AT THE LAST MEETING with my handler and the other agents involved before the end of the Donnie Brasco operation, we had to decide how we would handle my coming out. For sure we wouldn't release my real name. That part was easy. In fact, we didn't release my real name until a year later during my first day on the witness stand in my first trial.

There was a lot of scrambling for Jules and our electronics expert Jimmy Kallstrom to get court-ordered bugs and telephone wiretaps for certain Bonanno premises so that the fallout from my coming out could be monitored. Evidence from the field offices, which were handling all the other operations, had to be harvested and those operations closed down, whether productive or not.

At one time there were twenty-six wires and bugs up and running that were based on probable cause taken from intelligence reports of mine from the field. Not to mention all the physical surveillance operations that had been put in place and yielded fruit due to the intelligence I provided. Who would be where, doing what, and when. The flow of intelligence would now cease.

There were financial considerations, too. For example, Jules had an informant, a Mafia wannabe named Vinny DePenta, getting a salary of $1,000 a week in cash. Based on my intelligence about the way Toto Catalano's Zips brought heroin into the country, DePenta was put on the FBI payroll to work a pasta import scam. He tried to lure Bonanno Zips into using his import business to smuggle in heroin from Sicily. That operation had to be wound down to save the Bureau DePenta's salary. DePenta was earning more than I earned, and I had to pay taxes on my money.

Also there was the million-dollar question: Which one of the various wiseguys should we tell first? We knew that deaths were likely for all of those who were responsible for my rise in the ranks and for all those who had made introductions of me to the top bosses.

There's a line in the movie where Johnny Depp says, "If I come out alive, this guy, Lefty, ends up dead. That's the same thing as me putting the bullet in his head myself." While I never expressed that sense of regret, I certainly knew that that was the likely consequence for some of those who had vouched for me, especially Lefty. I had been ready to go to a house in Staten Island to kill Bruno Indelicato and whoever was protecting him. How much different was that from causing deaths by coming out?

Tony Mirra had been the first Bonanno to vouch for me. Mirra was the first one to bring me around Little Italy and introduce me around as an associate of his. You have to remember that Little Italy twenty-five to thirty years ago was not the tourist attraction it is today. Back then it was lined with social clubs and Mafia hangouts. Wiseguys would sit outside in front of these clubs and sip coffee and watch everybody that walked by. This was the Mafia's turf. A good look at how it was then can be gotten from the Martin Scorcese film *Mean Streets*, filmed on location in Little Italy in the early seventies. Through Mirra I was introduced to capo Mickey Zafferano, in charge of porn, and capo Fort Lee Jimmy Capasso. Either one of those two introductions could get Mirra killed when I surfaced.

I had met Mirra through my early work with Jilly Greca's crew in the Colombo family in Brooklyn. I was with Jilly's crew around 1976 or so when Jilly got made. In 1980, a year before I came out, Jilly Greca got whacked. High among the host of risk factors for getting whacked was getting indicted. A man under indictment is a man under pressure. The fear is that the man may fold under pressure. When a wiseguy rolls over he is said to have gone bad. The idea is to get rid of him before he goes bad.

If the man is only a so-so earner to begin with, his loss is no great loss. Jilly Greca's scores were never very big ones when I was with him. Jilly got indicted and Jilly got whacked. The evidence for the indictment against him was based on intelligence I had gathered and supplied to my handlers. Looking back I can see that Jilly Greca's death was the first one the Donnie Brasco operation had caused.

As I said, I wanted to get away from Jilly's crew because of its cowboy mentality. To make that happen I hung out for six months at Carmella's restaurant where Tony Mirra would come in regularly. Tony was the first Bonanno family member I hung out with and it was through Tony that I met Lefty. When I met Tony he had just gotten out of prison on an eighteen-year drug distribution sentence and he was picking up where he had left off.

Tony was loathsome and vicious as the devil. But he was a money machine for the Bonanno family. Tony and I might go to a bar, pick a fight in the bar with some citizens, break a mirror and after the commotion was over move in on the bar owner, demanding a weekly salary not to do that again, convincing him that he needed protection. The next night we might go around collecting from the slot machines Tony had installed in bars by similar strong-arm tactics. Meanwhile, Tony distributed drugs, mostly wholesale quantities. Among his clients in the discos and nightclubs we bounced around in were movie stars, politicians, and prominent lawyers.

Tony was a top soldier, but Tony was such an individualist that I didn't see that he would take me to places I wanted to go, places where I would be able to infiltrate at the next level above soldier. It didn't take me long to realize that life with Tony was not for me and that it would be wise to divide my time and cultivate Lefty.

I couldn't walk out on my new best friend Tony or he'd make me pay for the snub. I had to gauge how much time I could spend away from him. Meanwhile, my new friend Lefty was counseling me to stay completely away from Mirra because, while Mirra was a made man and entitled to respect, he could be a dangerous enemy and a more dangerous friend. Lefty said, "Don't mess with that guy. He killed more people than cancer." Mirra's weapon was a knife. If you saw him pull a knife you knew he would use it and kill with it. The only person Mirra had any kind of close relationship with was his mother, but sometimes if you asked him how she was doing he'd tell you to mind your own business. Like Anthony Perkins said to his knifing victim Janet Leigh in the movie *Psycho*, "A boy's best friend is his mother." Tony Mirra would definitely qualify as a psycho.

One night Mirra asked me to take a ride with him to Brooklyn. He didn't say a word the whole way. With a whacko like Mirra you never knew what he had in mind. I considered that maybe in his warped mind he had some secret grievance against me and he was taking me to Brooklyn to kill me. Fortunately, when we got to his destination there was a Rolls Royce waiting. The boss of the Colombo family, Carmine Persico, and his son Little Allie Boy Persico were there for some kind of meeting with Mirra. Tony introduced me to them. Looking back, that one introduction more than any other no doubt sealed Mirra's fate when I surfaced.

The problem of disassociating myself from Mirra was solved when he went back to jail on an eight-and-a-half-year sentence for another narcotics conviction, having already spent nearly half his life in jail.

With Mirra out of the picture I was free to spend every day with Lefty, who then was a soldier in capo Mike Sabella's crew. Lefty called Jilly Greca to vouch for me. Lefty said to me, "Jilly says you ain't no leech. He says you keep busy and earn good, and nobody over there had to carry you."

. . .

There's a restaurant that's still there on Mulberry Street, called CaSa Bella's. CaSa Bella's was named after its first owner and founder, Lefty's capo Mike Sabella. The only time I ever saw Carmine Galante in the flesh before he was whacked in 1979 was on the sidewalk in front of CaSa Bella's. Lefty had taken me there to help guard Galante, who was there to have a meeting with Mike Sabella and other capos.

Carmine Galante arrived with his two bodyguards, Baldo Amato and Cesare Bonventre, a couple of Zips imported from Sicily to Knickerbocker Avenue by the baker, Toto Catalano. I had met Toto, Baldo, and Cesare and some of the other Zips when I was running with Mirra and then later with Lefty. The Zips gave Galante a lot of power. The power came from the Zips' willingness to do anything for him, and the fact that other families had little contact with them so they could be fairly anonymous on a hit inside another family. Baldo Amato and Cesare Bonventre specifically covered Galante's back pretty much all the time, and under Toto Catalano they helped Galante run the heroin import business ever since he got out of jail in 1974.

After they went inside, Lefty, in a hushed tone of voice, said, "You don't know how mean this guy is, Donnie . . . a tyrant. That's just me telling you, it don't go no further. Lot of people hate him. They feel he's only out for himself. He's the only one making any money. . . . There's a lot of people out there who would like to see him get whacked. That's why we're here."

Lefty told me that when Mike Sabella had the marble done in CaSa Bella's it was imported from Sicily and heroin was smuggled in with the marble. Although Mike Sabella went back down to soldier when Galante got whacked, Sabella retained CaSa Bella's, Italian marble and all, for years.

Lefty was a 24-hour-a-day gangster. He was a degenerate gambler. He had the ability to generate money, but he never had any. Ironically, while he was doing his own gambling and losing at it, he was handling the family's bookmaking operation for the underboss Nicky Glasses Marangello. The first important introduction Lefty made for me was with Nicky Glasses. On Lefty's behalf I would often deliver gambling receipts to Nicky Glasses at his social club, Toyland. Lefty was always educating me on the ways of the Mafia and the ways of the wiseguy. He taught me how dangerous an introduction can be for the man who makes a bad one and vouches for a rat. The assumption is that if you introduce a rat or otherwise vouch for a rat, there's a good chance you yourself are a rat making introductions for the feds in order to get out from whatever trouble you might be in.

Lefty never talked to me about the hits he did, but he did tell me the best way to do a hit—two shots from a .22 in the back of the head. "The bullets rattle around in the skull," Lefty said.

I got the impression from all these guys that killing was something instilled in them when they were small. You kill a guy. He's gone. He's dead. Where are we going to eat tonight?

• • •

During the time I spent with Lefty under Mike Sabella I proposed to Lefty the idea of a vending machine business in Milwaukee. That meant that boss Carmine Galante had to arrange for capo Mike Sabella and underboss Nicky

Glasses to meet with capos in Chicago to arrange for a meeting between Milwaukee's top boss Frank Balistrieri and Lefty and me. Also on our side of the table was another undercover, Tony Conte, I had brought in on what the Bureau called Operation Timber.

Although Milwaukee was its own Mafia family, Chicago still oversaw everything out that way. So here was Lefty introducing me to his capo Mike Sabella and the underboss Nicky Marangello, and causing these two heavyweights to meet with Chicago bosses. And, to cap it all off, when everything was finally arranged, here was Lefty introducing me to the top boss of the Balistrieri family. Besides having meetings with Frank Balistrieri himself, we had meetings with his underboss Steve DeSalvo and Balistrieri's brother and both of Balistrieri's sons, who were lawyers and made men at the same time.

During one of those meetings, because the Mafia is always in search of a few good men, Balistrieri offered me the job of picking up the skim in Vegas for his family and delivering it to Kansas City. I gave Balistrieri the impression that I was considering his job offer. But it was not a job offer that would lead to prospects for my operation. In front of me Balistrieri warned Lefty, ". . . if Donnie takes this, you gotta be responsible for him. You know the consequences once I put it on record. If this guy fucks up, you're in trouble, not him. They don't look for him. They look for you."

As a side note, it was disconcerting the way Frank Balistrieri treated his brother and his sons during these meetings. They bowed down to him like the Don that he thought he was. There was no feeling of a fatherly or brotherly relationship. He barked at his brother in front of us like his brother was Fredo in *The Godfather*, and his brother took it. In the brief meeting I had witnessed with Carmine Persico and his son Allie Boy there was none of that. You could tell there was a relaxed father-son relationship that went above the relationship of a tough guy boss to a made soldier. I had seen Lefty with his troubled son and there was always that spark that a father has for his son, no matter how disappointed he might be in the son's drug use or whatever.

To make matters worse for Lefty, when Mirra went to jail, Lefty "went on record" with me. That is, Lefty put in a claim to Mike Sabella that I was now part of Lefty's crew. Putting in a claim is another of those territorial things they believe in.

I was now the property of Lefty. I belonged to him. I could now only do scores after first getting Lefty's approval and splitting the take with him. I didn't necessarily have to tell Lefty exactly what crime I was planning, just that I was going away on a score, and I had to return with money for him. Mirra might have once owned me, but as with the recording of a deed to a house, Mirra had failed to file the proper paperwork.

When Mirra got out of jail and saw how enterprising I had been while he was away, he went to the ruling Commission of the bosses of the five families and formally disputed Lefty's claim on me. Looking back, I think that of all the partnerships I brokered, the alliance in the mid-west with Balistrieri, even though it had fallen through for no known reason, was the most impressive one to a guy like Mirra. It's one thing to branch out into New Jersey or even Florida, but to expand a family's territory into the domain of Chicago was quite large.

As a result of Mirra's challenge to Lefty's long-ago claim on me, there had to be several sit-downs with the Bonanno capos to settle it. Sonny represented Lefty at these sit-downs. In the end, Lefty and Sonny won when capo Big Joey Massino, an oversized swing vote, enlisted Rusty's influence in favor of Lefty's claim. Lefty told me Big Joey had said to him, "Lefty, stick to your guns. I'll go back and tell that guy in the can."

After Lefty and Sonny won me, Mirra made another formal claim. This time he claimed that I had stolen $250,000 in a drug deal a few years back. The obvious question was why didn't he bring it up at the time. It was not like Mirra to let 250 pennies slip through his fingers without pulling his knife. Still, the punishment for stealing anything, much less $250,000, is death. We had to go through another round of sit-downs to expose it as a trumped-up charge. All the while, Lefty and Sonny, without realizing it, were exposing themselves to death as my champions.

As a side note, I had the added indignity of one of the old Hooverite supervisors in the Bureau Headquarters opening up an internal investigation on me based on Mirra's wild charge that I stole drug money. I guess I should laugh now, but a part of me can't. Here I was just trying to do the best job I could, to stay focused. I loved being an FBI agent and I was working at what I was good at—and I was good at undercover work. Yet while trying to do that job I had to handle the stresses of my own Bureau while handling the stresses of the Mafia and of my own neglected family.

. . .

After Carmine Galante got whacked in 1979 and Lefty and I were assigned to Sonny Black, it wasn't long before Lefty's new capo Sonny Black had made me his own. Lefty was kept out of things that I was put into. Lefty complained to me about that and I had to make sure Lefty's nose didn't get too far out of joint while I harvested the fruits of my close association with Sonny Black.

Sonny had charisma. Sonny was old school. He was, in their terms and mine, a stand-up guy. If I could forget what he did to earn his money, there was something very likeable about Sonny, and we clearly connected as men. Sonny was intelligent. We talked about current events, sports, life in general, not just the boring talk of Mafia life.

Sonny spent most of his time at the Motion Lounge, living a double life. His wife and kids lived a few blocks away. His son suffered from a chronic illness that needed medical care. At one point in our relationship Sonny asked me to make sure that if he ever got whacked his wife still got a thousand a week for her and his kids. Sonny said, "I want you to promise me that you'll look out for my kids if anything happens to me." That was a promise I knew I could not keep as I made it. Sonny then said, "In this life, if you get power, somebody will want to take it from you."

Sonny Black made the deadliest of all the introductions when he introduced me to Santo Trafficante in Florida and I shook Trafficante's hand. It didn't matter that I had set the whole deal in motion with Trafficante regarding the gambling operation at King's Court. I could never have met a boss as powerful as Trafficante without a direct introduction from at least a capo, if not from an acting street boss. Sonny himself could not have sat down to forge an alliance with Trafficante unless it came from Rusty in jail. In fact, a mere capo sitting down with any boss from another family, much less a boss with the stature of Santo Trafficante, was an unusual occurrence and a tribute to the rising power of Sonny as well as to the merit of the King's Court schemes I had brought to Sonny and Rusty.

When King's Court began looking like a real moneymaker for all concerned, we added the idea of running bingo games. That doesn't sound like much, but in Florida at that time bingo was huge. A charity, like a veterans' organization, would be the figurehead to make the whole thing legal. It was a license to print money. The veterans' organization would get a few hundred a night. Sonny and Santo would split the rest, and Santo never had to lift a finger. Lefty watched all this from the outside through a window. Lefty was left out of it. Rusty watched all of this from the inside through prison bars, and no doubt, salivated.

One day Lefty surprised me by telling me that when Rusty got out of jail he was going to demand to go directly under Rusty and he was going to take me with him. We were both going to report to Rusty, the top Bonanno boss, and no longer report to any capo. Lefty claimed that they had been close before Rusty went to jail, and because of things he had done for Rusty he was owed that courtesy by Rusty.

In hindsight I can see that Rusty might have allowed that to happen in some measure because of the appearance of entrepreneurial skill that my handlers and I had created. I had been demonstrating vision and talent, and I gave the appearance of bringing in big money. By reporting directly to Rusty, that money would not be split with a capo or anyone else. Rusty would get a full half with no tax coming out as the money floated upstream through the hands of others. Lefty wanted us to be viewed as a two-man starting rotation bound for the Hall of Fame, like the lefty Sandy Koufax and the righty Don Drysdale. Lefty wanted credit for my projects, credit that was then going to Sonny.

In all the years I spent undercover I never saw any soldier manipulate or fight over the ownership of any mere associate. Nor did I ever see any capo manipulate or fight over the ownership of a soldier, much less a mere associate. During this Paterson, New Jersey knock-around guy's time with the Bonannos they had me doing the old big band dance tune, "The Jersey Bounce." Like the little silver ball in a pinball machine, I had been bounced off Mirra onto Lefty; almost bounced to Balistrieri; bounced off Lefty and almost back to Mirra; bounced back to Lefty and then bounced on to Sonny; and was about to bounce back to Lefty when Rusty got out, and ultimately land directly under Rusty. All this bouncing was like the kiss of death for those who were claiming me as theirs.

The only thing that saved Rusty's hide in this was that I never got to be made and he never personally dealt with me as he was in jail the whole time. Years later during a RICO trial in which I testified against Rusty, I overheard him say to his pals in the hallway during a recess, "He woulda never met me. Even if I wasn't in the can." Yeah sure, I thought, unless I had a hundred dollar bill stuck to my forehead. Then I'd have met him.

. . .

The decision regarding which one of the likely candidates to go to first with the news that I was an agent was not to be taken lightly. The Bureau provided a psychological profiler for our meeting, one of the behavioral science guys. I gave the profiler all the details I could about the personalities of both Sonny and Lefty. The main consideration for everyone, except me, was which of the two—Sonny or Lefty—we could get to turn. Would the fear of getting whacked, coupled with the promise of lifetime protection in the Witness Security Program, work quickest on Lefty or on Sonny? Speed counted because the longer it took for the candidate to make up his mind the more likely the Mafia would kill him before he turned. The hope was that he'd turn before he even told anyone else about the FBI's visit to him.

On one issue I was in agreement with the profiler: Tony Mirra was out of the question in my mind and everyone else's mind. First he was a psycho, and second he was a psycho.

To the rest of them at the meeting, including the profiler, the man most likely to turn was Lefty.

I disagreed.

"I know these two guys," I said. "There's no shot either one of these guys will ever roll. It's not in them. Forget about it."

Nevertheless, I believed that Sonny should be told first. Sonny would have to get on the phone and self-report his monumental unprecedented fuck-up to bosses so high up that Lefty couldn't even get them on the phone. Sonny had been the capo that Lefty reported to for two years. If agents first went to Lefty all that Lefty would have done would have been to go to Sonny. Why insert an extra unnecessary step and risk a situation where the message to Sonny was watered down by Lefty's perception of it? By going directly to Sonny and explaining it all to him, there was a good chance of getting more evidence of the existence of their criminal enterprise from the tap on Sonny's phone as he made his frantic calls.

After all, I argued, prior to the hit on the three capos, Sonny himself told me that he went to Big Paul Castellano's mansion in Staten Island, the White House, to get approval for the hit. Big Paul was the boss of the Gambinos, the brother-in-law of the deceased Don Carlo Gambino. Big Paul was also reported to be the boss of bosses of the five families of New York. Sonny told me he had done a big favor for Big Paul in exchange for permission to hit the three capos. Sonny implied that the favor was to cut Big Paul in on a share of the Bonanno family heroin import trade with the Zips, and that he had cleared that with Toto Catalano and could report to Big Paul that he had the Zips lined up behind the three capos hit.

I argued that it was possible that Sonny might pick up the phone and call Big Paul after the agents visited him. Such a call could lead to evidence for probable cause to bug Big Paul. Jules ended up agreeing with me and so the decision was made to go to Sonny and let Sonny handle it from there on the phone with the bosses. We'd be on the bugs and taps listening in.

Special Agent Doug Fencl had worked on various Mafia matters for years and had known Sonny in the past. In fact Sonny had once said to me about Fencl, "He's a nice guy, a gentleman. He doesn't bullshit. He just tells me exactly what's on his mind."

Therefore, it was decided that Doug Fencl would be the leader of the team. To help convince Sonny, we posed for pictures at the motel where we had our strategy meeting. I stood with Doug and the others. They were wearing the Brooks Brothers type of clothing of an agent. I was wearing the slacks and sweater of Donnie Brasco, but I was holding my FBI credentials and smiling at the camera.

On the early morning of July 28, 1981 at 6:00 a.m., Special Agents Doug Fencl, Jerry Loar, and Jim Kinne showed up at Sonny's third floor apartment at the Motion Lounge. We chose 6:00 a.m. in case Sonny wanted to keep our visit a secret. Sonny recognized Doug and let them in. No doubt Sonny assumed they were there because of his meeting with the high profile Santo Trafficante two days earlier. Perhaps, Santo had been tailed to the Tahitian.

"Sonny," Doug Fencl said, "you know a guy named Donnie Brasco?"

"Yeah, sure," Sonny said. "Yeah, I know Donnie."

Fencl showed Sonny a group photo of me posing with the very agents that were at that moment standing with him in his apartment.

"Recognize the fourth guy, Sonny? Take a good look."

Sonny said nothing.

"Did you know Donnie Brasco is an FBI agent, Sonny?"

Sonny just glanced at the photo in disbelief without responding for a while. Then Sonny said, "I don't know the guy, but if I meet him I'll know he's an FBI agent."

Doug nodded and handed Sonny a business card. There was no need to explain. They both knew what that meant. If Sonny chose to make the call he would be protected if he came over to our side.

Doug waited for the implications to sink in, and said, "What do you suppose is going to happen, Sonny, when they find out your friend Donnie Brasco is an agent?"

Sonny said nothing.

"If there's anything I can do to help," Doug said, "you can get me at this number. You can call me any time, Sonny."

Sonny looked at Doug and said, "Doug, you know there's nothing I can do about this. It's over."

At first, the bugs and taps revealed utter and complete disbelief. Sonny told Lefty and some of the rest of the crew at a meeting at the Motion Lounge that I had been kidnapped. "Donnie's been snatched by the feds. . . . The feds came over and tried to make me believe he's an FBI agent. . . . Can you believe the balls on these guys?" Sonny went on to tell them that I had been forced to pose with the agents in photographs and was probably brainwashed by the FBI.

Obviously, looking back now, some of the things I revealed here for the first time are things that no FBI agent would be expected to have participated in: burglaries, armed robbery, hijackings, felony assault, and beatings. Sonny had to have been convinced of my authenticity by my performance in general, not to mention specific events like my willingness to walk out the door of the Motion Lounge to get into Lefty's car and to head to Staten Island to hit Bruno Indelicato.

For ten days Sonny kept the news within his own crew. He spent more than a week looking for me in New York, Florida, California, Milwaukee, and Chicago. Finally, Sonny's disbelief turned to acceptance and he made the incriminating calls we expected. Sonny called Trafficante personally, rather than go through one of Trafficante's people. That was protocol; the kind of respect Trafficante was due. But also, by calling Trafficante himself, if Trafficante chose to spare Sonny he could do so without concern that he would be setting an example of leniency within his own family. The old school Trafficante barely replied.

Sonny got word to Rusty Rastelli in Lewisburg Prison in Pennsylvania. As we had hoped, Sonny called Big Paul Castellano, boss of the Gambino family and the boss of bosses. Castellano gave the same non-response Trafficante had given.

Seventeen days later Sonny Black became the first blood drawn. On August 14, 1981 all the calls from Sonny's phone stopped. On that day Dominick Sonny Black Napolitano disappeared after handing his watch and house keys to Charlie the bartender and going to a meeting in Staten Island. Sonny had been sent for. Sonny knew why and Sonny went. Sonny had the nerve to go to that meeting.

Sonny had two rules: number one, not to rat; and number two, not to run. I told my fellow agents when he disappeared, "When you see them dismantling the pigeon coops on top of the Motion Lounge, then you know he's gone, he's dead." The next week they took down his pigeon coops. I was right about Sonny; he'd rather die than turn.

A few months after Sonny's disappearance, his girlfriend Judy called Headquarters and asked to meet with me in Washington. We took precautions and I agreed to the meeting. I assured Judy that Sonny was gone and urged her to get away from these people and make a new life for herself. Judy confided to me Sonny's deepest feelings when he learned I was an agent. "You know what he said?" Judy asked. "He told me, 'I really loved that kid.' He was really broken up when he found out that you were an agent, but he said that wouldn't change the way he felt because of the type of guy you were. You did your job and you did it right."

Others didn't feel that way at all. During the time between Sonny's disappearance and the taking down of his pigeon coops, we got word from informants that a half-million dollar open contract—open to anyone—had been put on my head, and that guys had been sent around the country with pictures of me to get the word out and to find me if they could. Commission members may come and go, but the Commission has its own sources of money, and a half a million in those days was a small matter to them.

Precautions were taken and security increased for my family and me. Here I was out of the Mafia and my family and I were in more danger than I was in when I was in the Mafia. Agents visited the bosses of each of the five New York families who had put out the contract to warn them not to even think about bothering me in any way. The bosses all feigned innocence and denied any knowledge of the contract.

Normally, the American Mafia knows better than to kill anyone in law enforcement. There is a line dividing law enforcement and the Mafia that they do not cross over. Even the Mafia understands that law enforcement officers are merely doing their jobs. But this was a unique operation. Had I crossed over the dividing line? I spent Christmas mornings with them and their families. In 1978 I was Lefty Guns Ruggiero's best man at his wedding to his wife Louise. To their way of thinking, by attending their children's baptisms and weddings and birthday parties, had I blurred the line between an agent doing his job and a member of their Mafia nation?

Because of my participation in their criminal activities—armed hijacking, warehouse burglaries, the contract on Bruno—had I become no longer an agent? Had I become one of them? Had I become their property to dispose of the way they saw fit? Because I had adopted their rules as my own, had I become subject to the punishment their world meted out for breaking their rules? Had the convincing job I'd done caused a backlash? It looked that way. The informants who told us about the contract also told us that the Mafia Commission viewed me as having crossed the line into their world, and that by doing that I made myself a murder target.

The informants, connected guys in the Mafia, believed that the Mafia was dead serious about killing me. One other consideration was the Zips under Toto Catalano. The Sicilian Mafia has no compunction about killing a law enforcement officer. At that time the Sicilian families that spawned the Zips that came over to handle the drug trade for the Bonanno family routinely killed judges, prosecutors, cops, and their wives and children in Sicily.

On his way to his scheduled execution, Lefty was arrested on a Sunday afternoon and taken off the street the same month—August, 1981— in which Sonny had disappeared and a contract had been put out on my life. I was right about Lefty. Lefty knew what was going to happen to him when he was sent for, but he was on his way there anyway when our agents, who heard it on a wire, moved in and saved his life. Lefty too would rather die than turn.

Ironically, a couple of days before FBI agents saved Lefty's life by arresting him, they heard this gem by Lefty on one of the bugs: "Any FBI agent comes to bust me, I'm gonna fucking kill him first."

Tony Mirra was finally caught up with on February 18, 1982, a little over six months after my coming-out party and exactly six months after Sonny disappeared. Mirra was found dead in a car in a parking garage near the apartment building of Bonanno family *consigliere* (adviser), Stevie Beef Cannone. Mirra had four bullets put into his head. He was in long-term parking—real long. Mirra had been set up by his uncle Al Walker Embarrato and his cousin Richard "Shellackhead" Cantarella. Mirra's nephew, Joey the Mook D'Amico—the spoiled brat whose mother, Mirra's sister, had paid off a capo to have her son get made and who's now in the Witness Protection Program—was the one who shot his Uncle Tony.

The last man to die as a result of my Donnie Brasco operation was that cop I bribed in the Pasco County sheriff's office in Florida. His job was to keep all the cops under his command off our backs while we operated our illegal gambling and drug distribution out of the King's Court club. After he was served with a federal indictment for his role in King's Court in 1983, Captain Joseph Donahue was found dead in his bathroom. Rather than face the charges, he'd killed himself.

The rest of the wiseguys who crossed paths with Donnie Brasco would soon get whacked by the U.S. Justice Department.

BEHIND THE LEGEND

THE STORY THAT AN UNDERCOVER puts together about his past life of crime is called a legend. My legend was that of Donnie Brasco, or "Don the Jeweler," a jewel thief and fence. To help establish that legend I had to attend gemology classes. I have a couple of friends who are jewelers and they added to my education. Being a jewel thief gave me a certain distinction and a bit of freedom because I could always say I had a score to make out of town. As long as I returned with money to split up and send upstream, nobody bothered me.

If I was asked something about jewelry that I didn't know, I said so. There was no point in trying to bluff. What I did know, I did know. No professional knows all there is to know about his profession. I certainly knew enough to pass as an expert in jewelry. One night when I was still with the Colombo family, a crewmember showed up at the social club with a giant diamond he had stolen in a house burglary. I took a look at it and could see it was a fake. I told him, "It's a fugazy." From that point on he held a grudge against me like it was my fault that his diamond was junk.

Another part of my legend was that I had grown up in an orphanage and had no parents or other family. That was very handy. So was being unmarried and having no children. I didn't have to produce a wife for Bonanno family cookouts. I did claim I had that very serious girlfriend in California, and that gave me protection from any attempts to fix me up as well as a reason to get out of town to visit her.

My legend had me spending a lot of time in California and Florida over the years. As a precaution, we told an informant who was mobbed up that if he ever got a call about a Donnie Brasco, he was to simply vouch for him as a stand-up guy and to claim they did scores together. One night with the Colombos, a couple of crewmembers who had just gotten out of jail and resented my status with the crew challenged me on my background. They put a gun on the table and told me to give them a name they could call to vouch for me or I wouldn't leave the social club alive. I gave them the informant's name, hoping he would remember his assignment and not screw it up. It took a while for the call to reach the informant, but when it did he did his job well. I was cleared. They put their gun away. The first thing I did was to punch the lights out of the one that was closest to me, until the others broke it up. I did it for effect, but a part of it was real for what he had put me through.

With the legend in place and rehearsed, as the new me I had to forget about my real background—an Italian-American immigrant heritage that helped shape me, that instilled a mental toughness in me, and that prepared me to serve in the way that I did all those years undercover for my country.

Both sets of grandparents were born in Italy and came over as immigrants. My mother's people were from Sicily outside of Palermo. My father's people were from Calabria across from Sicily on the Italian mainland. Both my parents grew up speaking Italian in their homes and they spoke it in our home to my brother, my sister and to me, the oldest. All of my aunts and uncles on both sides spoke Italian in the home.

My grandparents on my mother's side met in Little Italy in New York City where they had each settled after their Atlantic crossings. Shortly after they met they got married and moved to Robertsdale, Pennsylvania, a coal-mining town south of State College. I was born in their farmhouse. It was a small farm, and most of what they grew was used to feed their large family of nine children. They had pigs for meat, chickens for eggs, and horses for plowing.

My grandfather had a general store, and a saloon and beer distributorship. His son-in-law, my father, worked for him in the saloon. The farmhouse had the saloon underneath it. Across the dirt road was the general store. We used the outhouse to go to the bathroom, what Italian immigrants called the "backhouse" because it was in the back of the house.

My grandfather had a little coal mine behind the farmhouse. It was a mom and pop coal mine. The whole family worked it. It was mostly for their own use because back then everything was coal. Everybody worked hard and set an example of hard work for us kids. I used to cross the creek and walk along the railroad tracks with a coal bucket and pick coal that had fallen from the trains. I'd fill a bucket and come back for another.

We had the best spring in the town. It was the purest and coldest water I have ever had to this day. One of my uncles still has that spring. My grandfather used to let everybody in the town come to his spring for their water. This generous philosophy of life was a lesson that served me well. It helped cement who I really was and what kind of people I came from while I dealt with the gimme and grabby men of the Mafia.

We lived in that unforgettable world till I was about four, but we returned and visited it regularly while I was growing up. It was like a country vacation, and a vacation in the Old Country.

Just before I started school we moved to Paterson, New Jersey so my parents could go out on their own. They chose Paterson because, for some reason unknown to me, most of my mother's brothers and sisters had moved to Paterson. We lived in the Sandy Hill section, strictly an Italian neighborhood. My aunts and uncles who were there treated us like we were their own kids. They disciplined us when they thought we needed it.

My father ran neighborhood bars. For a while he was a part owner in one bar, but mostly he ran a bar for a good friend of his. In addition to raising three kids and taking care of the house, my mother worked from time to time for a book distributor. Who could imagine that one of her children would grow up to write books? We were poor, but nobody knew it because everybody you hung out with lived the same way. Everybody was in the same boat.

My mother was a very religious Roman Catholic. Although I was raised Roman Catholic I always went to public school. My father's family had been Catholic in Italy, but when they got here they switched to Assembly of God.

In the fifth grade we moved to Erie, Pennsylvania in the northwestern part of the state. My father had grown up there, and that is where his family settled when they came over from Calabria. We moved because my father took a job as a labor-er for his brother-in-law who owned a construction company and a toy factory.

We moved back to Paterson when I was in the eighth grade. Paterson was a great place for a young guy. The neighborhood had no crime. Nobody locked their doors. There were no drugs anywhere. Some people were bookmakers, and one time two of them disappeared. We figured it was for skimming from the Mafia. We didn't know if they were dead or on the lam.

This was Genovese family territory. Everyone knew who was involved and who wasn't. They had money and expensive cars. What you didn't see in the neighborhood was all the devious stuff that went on in their lives—the struggle for power, whacking guys for way less serious offenses than skimming.

I think I got the law enforcement bug because of the terrific cops that were a part of the community. There was a beat cop who crossed the school kids and directed traffic, all the while singing Irish songs. Of course, all the cops were Irish in those days. For some reason, I always wanted to be a cop. When I got the chance I joined the FBI. I figured if I was going to be a cop, I might as well be with the best.

I attended Paterson Eastside High School. Lou Costello of Abbott and Costello went there. So did Larry Doby, the first black baseball player in the American League. Doby starred for the Cleveland Indians and came up to the majors shortly after Jackie Robinson integrated baseball. Paterson Eastside High was integrated before the American League, and everybody got along with every-body in the late fifties, at least in my neighborhood.

I played defensive back on the football team and guard/forward on the bas-ketball team. I was a leaper and could touch the rim. I got basketball scholarships to college. The one I regret not taking was to the U.S. Naval Academy. It's an honor in my mind. But I had a girlfriend and stayed close to home. I met my future wife at a high school basketball game. I had gone to watch the game involv-ing other schools. A buddy of mine played for one of the teams. I fell in love with a cheerleader for the other team. We married while I was in college at William Paterson University, not far from my neighborhood. When I was sworn in as an FBI Special Agent on July 7, 1969—the summer of the moon landing—neither my wife nor I could have guessed where it would lead.

People often ask me how I could stand hanging out in social clubs when I was under. My answer is that that is how I spent my teenage years. All of the neighborhood guys belonged to the St. Anthony's Club. It's where you hung out. It was in the basement of the Catholic school. They had two bowling alleys for us. They had rooms with TV sets and couches, and a kitchen for our use.

The older guys in their twenties played cards. Very few from that neighborhood went to college. We learned the ropes from the older guys, and they looked out for the high school kids to make sure we didn't screw up. The worst that would happen is that guys would come around with swag. Nobody ended up going to jail. Drugs were not even thought of. Nobody had to tell us not to do them because there were none to do. This was just a minute in time before all the drugs and the drug-fueled crime took hold in the sixties.

St. Anthony's sponsored basketball and fast-pitch softball teams. There were fierce rivalries among similar clubs in North Jersey. I started shooting hoops at 8 a.m. at St. Anthony's schoolyard every Saturday morning, weather permitting, throughout my teenage years. I had odd jobs like working at a car polishing business and as a waiter. But I always found time for the great outdoors in a schoolyard in the middle of a city, with never a thought that some other teenager might be high and packing a gun. The main job that all of us kids had was to be happy.

And let me tell you how happy we were when we got our own social club. The older guys thought it was about time the young high school kids had their own place, and so they went out and got us a storefront. It had a bathroom, a couple of couches, and a black-and-white TV. Well, all TV's were black-and-white then. We still used the school basement for the bowling alley and to hang with the older guys at times, but for our own hanging out purposes, to be with people our own age—our own crew, so to speak—we had our own turf. So it was an easy, familiar, and comfortable fit later on when I started hanging out in social clubs in Brooklyn and Manhattan. I had been doing it my whole life.

As you can no doubt see, the legend I created for Donnie Brasco as a loner, an orphan, and a man without a family or ties to a community, is the exact opposite of who I am and where I'd come from. I had a family in my home and in the homes of my aunts and uncles, a family in the schoolyard, a family in the neighborhood that included a cop who sang when he crossed me at an intersection, a family of older guys, and a family of younger guys. Is it any wonder I married young and started a family of my own? Is it any wonder that so many of my neighborhood pals found their way into *Donnie Brasco* as movie extras?

Today in my sixties I'm still part of a close-knit family. I'm proud to say that my three daughters, thanks to their mother mostly, all turned out beautifully. While under, I got home two or three nights every few months and my family did not even know what I was doing when I wasn't home. During a twelve-year period, my first six in the Mafia and my first six in the courtroom, my wife and daughters were forced to uproot and move lock, stock, and barrel six times, under an assumed name. Nevertheless, my daughters are all college graduates. The oldest has a master's degree in social work and four children. Next in line is our family veterinarian, followed by our professional actress and model.

It took time and patience for all of us to rebuild after I came out. One of my daughters has yet to read my book, *Donnie Brasco*, because she doesn't want to be reminded of those years. Another of my daughters attended the first trial to hear me testify. It was very helpful for me to have her understand what I was doing when I was away from home so much. She understood and I appreciated it.

I'm blessed with grandchildren now and I see them as much as I can. While the modern age has a lot going for it, I wish that my grandkids could have the sense of public safety and freedom to roam the streets without fear, the freedom that I had my whole childhood. Nothing for nothing, but I like to think that I contributed what I could to help reduce, for a little while anyway, the flow of drugs into our country.

CHAPTER 7
UNDER OATH

IF YOU'VE NEVER PUT YOUR HAND on the Bible and testified in a courtroom you have no idea what a naked feeling that is. After I came out, I spent the next ten-plus years putting my hand on the Bible and exposing myself under oath to examination and cross-examination. My memory was tested. My integrity was impugned. I even had an arrest warrant issued for me.

It was toward the end of the 1980s. My book had been out and I was in Hollywood negotiating for the screen rights. It was the Thursday before the Fourth of July weekend. There was a trial going on in New York, and I was in L.A. I got a message from home that the prosecutor was trying to reach me. I returned his call from L.A.

"I need you on the stand first thing tomorrow morning," the prosecutor said.

"No one told me that," I said. "I'm not coming. I'm in L.A."

"What are you doing in L.A.?"

"What's the difference what I'm doing in L.A.?"

"Joe, I need you to establish the structure of *La Cosa Nostra*. I need you to explain how the family works—the boss, the capos, the soldiers, the associates. I've got no other way to establish this. You're the man."

"I'm sorry, but you've got to make it next week."

"Look, I'm out of witnesses. I have no other witness to call at that time tomorrow morning. It's the slot reserved for you, and I already told the judge I was calling you first thing."

"Well, you'll have to tell him you're not," I said and hung up.

He called me back in less than an hour. He told me the judge had issued a warrant for my arrest.

"What?" I said in disbelief.

"He said you're not running his courtroom. He wants you there at nine tomorrow morning."

"Tomorrow's the Friday before the Fourth of July weekend. You know as well as I do that the morning will start late like it always does with last-minute shit. Even if I do get on the stand, the judge will break for the day early so everybody can get a head start on the long weekend. I'll be stuck in New York all weekend and I won't even begin to testify until Tuesday."

"Look," he said. "I'm sorry about all this, but I'm only telling you what the judge told me to tell you. Meanwhile, you could get arrested."

"I don't believe this."

"I checked the flights and there's a redeye you could take tonight that would get you to court on time tomorrow, and if you do, he'll retire the warrant."

Although I had retired from the FBI by then and was on my own private citizen's time without compensation, I thought in the back of my mind that someday I might like to return to duty. If I did, an arrest for any reason, but especially for missing a court appearance, would give my one enemy in the Bureau (see Chapter 11) ammunition to keep me out . I took the redeye. I showed up in court on time. The judge and the lawyers began by arguing some legal point, and I didn't get on the stand first thing in the morning, as I knew I wouldn't. They broke for lunch and then called it an early day, and I was stuck in New York until Tuesday. But at least I wasn't in jail for contempt of court.

Tuesday morning I put my hand on the Bible and faced the jury. Before the prosecutor could ask me his first question, the judge leaned over and said, "You're the agent I issued a warrant for, aren't you?"

"Yes, sir. Sorry, I was in California."

"You wrote the book, didn't you?"

"Yes, your honor," I said.

"Ever get a movie deal?"

"As a matter of fact, I did. That's what I was doing in L.A.—negotiating a movie deal."

"Do you have a good entertainment lawyer?"

I gave him the name. I could see that the jury was all ears and fascinated by all this show business talk. I could also see that the defense attorney was none too happy about all of this.

"Excellent choice," the judge said. "He's the best in the business."

"That's what I hear," I said. "He came highly recommended by my agent. But it's all new territory for me."

"Did he explain to you about the over-the-line expenses and the under-the-line expenses?"

"Yes, he did," I said.

"Very good. I hope you get a good deal on the movie." The judge turned to the prosecutor and said, "The Government may proceed with its witness."

When the prosecutor got done with his examination, he turned to the defense attorney and said, "You may cross examine."

The defense attorney stood up, looked at the jury, and said, "The defense has no questions of this witness, your honor." At the break the defense attorney, who used to be an Assistant United States Attorney, came up to me and said, "Joe, I've got a copy of your book. Would you autograph it for me?"

That wasn't the only time that a lawyer had passed up the opportunity to cross-examine me. The first time it happened was with a defense lawyer who I had seen around the nightclubs while I was undercover. He had bought a quantity of drugs from the wiseguy I was with, and he clearly remembered the incident—and could tell I recognized him—while in court. He was obviously afraid I would somehow reveal that drug deal during cross-examination. And in that case I wasn't just testifying about the Mafia structure; I was testifying directly about his client's involvement in crimes from my personal knowledge and memory. Everybody in the room was stunned, including his client, when that lawyer said, "No questions."

• • •

In the beginning of my new career as a professional full-time witness, it was tedious and repetitive work, like it had been in the Mafia. The first thing I did after they told Sonny about me was to fly to Milwaukee to testify before a federal grand jury there. Then it was off to testify before federal grand juries in Tampa, Miami, Brooklyn, and Manhattan. I was finally out, but I was still away from my family— over and over again.

Over the years, I testified live in seventeen jury trials, sometimes as a fact witness on the particulars of the crime itself, and sometimes as a witness on the organizational structure of the Mafia and how it operates. My testimony helped convict over 200 Mafia bosses, capos, soldiers, and associates.

The thing I am most grateful for is the quality of prosecutors I had on all my cases. You can get a clunker; I never had a single one. They prepared me well and they were well-prepared, bright, aggressive, even-tempered, hardworking, and had great courtroom presence.

I worked with Rudy Giuliani when he was the United States Attorney for the Southern District of New York, which is Manhattan. He became United States Attorney just as my cases broke, replacing John Martin, who had become a federal judge. John Martin had helped guide a lot of the cases up to that point. Rudy did a great job taking over. We became good friends. Rudy was a terrific team leader and a superb manager of personnel, without micromanaging.

Louis Freeh, who went on to become a federal judge and then the Director of the FBI, tried a lot of my cases. So did lead prosecutor Barbara Jones, who went on to become a federal judge. So did Mike Chertoff, who also became a federal judge, and who is the current Director of Homeland Security. There were others too numerous to mention. The prosecutors I worked with comprised a who's who of future leaders of our country. I feel good every time I see one of these people on TV in their new fields of endeavor.

The defense attorneys tended to be the best money could buy. After some seasoning in the first couple of trials, I noticed that criminal defense attorneys like to get you in a rhythm in order to give the appearance to the jury that you're in their flow. The way to break their rhythm is by asking them to repeat their question. Also, you should never argue with a defense attorney. You're not going to win. Tell him, instead, that you don't understand the question.

After I asked one defense attorney to repeat a question twice, he asked me, in front of the jury, "What are you, a dumb lox?"

Now I started seething underneath, but I couldn't show it. I had to remain professional. I couldn't appear to be rattled, or I'd be playing into his hand. I just calmly asked him again to repeat his question, and I slowly pondered it.

You see, a defense attorney can lie in a courtroom. The government can't, but a defense attorney can, at least in New York. They'll claim to read from one of your FBI reports, what we call "302s," and say, "Isn't that right, agent?" To make sure he wasn't lying, I would say, "Let me see what you're reading from. I'll read it and see if you're right." If they don't give it to you, then you know they're lying.

Anyway, this guy who asked me if I was a dumb lox started reading from one of my 302s—blah, blah, blah. Finally, I said, "Can I see that?"

He started walking up to the witness stand, and as he got closer, I slowly leaned far back away from him so that he had to come real close to hand it to me. He reached out to give me the 302. I leaned further back, and he leaned in even closer. I grabbed his hand, and brought his ear close to my mouth. "If you ever call me a dumb lox again," I whispered, barely moving my lips, "I'll rip your heart out."

He asked for a sidebar with the prosecutor, Louis Freeh, and said to the judge, "Did you hear what he just said to me?"

The judge said, "I thought he was saying something to you, but I couldn't make it out and I'm certain the jury didn't hear it."

The defense lawyer told the judge and the prosecutor what I had said, and then he turned to the prosecutor and asked, "What are you going to do about it?"

Louis Freeh said, "I'm not going to do anything about it. But I advise you not to call him a dumb lox again. Because I know this guy, and he will rip your heart out."

· · ·

Before the trials began, there were endless days of preparation for the first batch of indictments against over fifty Mafia gangsters; of testifying at grand juries in Florida, Wisconsin, Brooklyn, and Manhattan; of reading and rereading reports and transcripts; of listening to endless tape recordings; and of interpreting the enigmatic language spoken by the wiseguys and gangsters who had been recorded.

Even for cases in which I didn't testify, I had to fly from New York to L.A. and many cities in between to meet with prosecutors and explain to them the structure of the Mafia and the mindset of the associate, the soldier, the capo, and the bosses. Remember, this was all new information back then. Except for *The Godfather* (in which the word Mafia never was uttered), our culture had no reference point at that time from which to understand the Mafia. My immersion into the Mafia gave us a perspective we'd never had, and my detailed explanation of that world helped many prosecutors understand the information they had on tape from bugs and wiretaps.

Also, there were pretrial proceedings that I had to attend for the cases in which I would be testifying. At one such proceeding in Tampa, Lefty suddenly jumped up from his seat, pointed at me, and said to the judge, "Why don't you lock him up?"

The judge's eyes popped. Lefty's own attorney backed away from him a little bit and marshals headed toward him.

Lefty started to take his seat, turned back to the judge and said, "He should be in jail! He's the gangster, not me!"

Then as the trials were scheduled I had to do the preparing all over again, this time working closely with the prosecutors that were going to present each particular case. As one case led to the next, I had to read and reread all my prior testimony. Every sentence was a potentially devastating pitfall to the prosecution's case if my memory failed me. You don't realize how boring you can be until you read your own testimony twice.

The first of the trials began almost a year to the day after I came back out to civilization. It was *United States v. Napolitano, et al.* Members of the press appropriately dubbed it the "Bonanno Family Trial." The "et al" were Lefty, some of the more prominent members of Sonny Black's crew, and capo Big Joey Massino. Napolitano was Sonny Black, of course, but he had disappeared a year earlier.

Big Joey Massino disappeared, too. Ever the cautious "jerk-off," Big Joey went on the lam around the time Tony Mirra got hit in 1982, hiding in the Pocono Mountains of Pennsylvania for over two years until he surrendered in July 1984, two years after the Bonanno family trial had ended.

Big Joey was hiding in a home owned by the parents of his good friend, an associate in his crew, Goldie Leisenheimer. The only soldier in his crew that Big Joey trusted to visit him was his brother-in-law and childhood friend—the S in the J & S Cake Social Club—Good-looking Sal Vitale. Good-looking Sal was the only one permitted to visit Big Joey in the Poconos; he went once a month to report on crew business and to get orders.

In hindsight, you have to wonder if the prudent Big Joey Massino wasn't being doubly prudent by going on the lam. It put him in a win-win position. He avoided both the trial and the Mafia.

Although Big Joey and I had minimal contact while I was with Sonny's crew, we did have contact. More importantly, Big Joey and Sonny were very close, and at times they were a working partnership. Together they orchestrated the hit on the three capos. And now Big Joey was indicted in a RICO conspiracy with Sonny, and with crewmembers of Sonny's. But why did he stay on the lam for over two years after the trial ended?

To begin with, just getting indicted for a conspiracy that involves a boss is a definite risk factor for a hit. The crewmembers would have no evidence to offer against Rusty, but Big Joey was the one who visited Rusty in jail and got approval for the work he and Sonny did. He also got the orders from Rusty for the three capos' hit.

Big Joey said a lot of things to a lot of wiseguys to distance himself from me after I came out, reminding people he didn't want me on the hit of the three capos—in fact, he vetoed Sonny's plan to have me on the hit—because he didn't trust me. He also claimed, untruthfully, that the reason he didn't attend Boobie's daughter's wedding, and the reason he got an unlisted phone number that he didn't give out, was because he didn't trust Sonny Black's rising star—yours truly. But those defenses work both ways. If he didn't trust me, then why didn't he investigate me? His failure to act and ignoring his hunch about me is a pretty big sin in a boss's eyes. And if he didn't trust me, why did he side with Sonny and Lefty in the sit-downs involving Tony Mirra's claim on me? Why did he go to Rusty in the can to influence Rusty favorably in Lefty's claim of me against Mirra?

Another black mark against him that Big Joey had to consider was that the FBI had revealed an informant in his crew who would testify in the case. In the eyes of the Commission, when it came time to dish out punishment, it was a lesser offense to have a criminal informant in your crew's midst than it was to have an undercover agent infiltrate your crew. Sonny Black's offense was such a huge offense that it had never been done before to such an extent. Still, when it comes time to mete out punishment for both greater and lesser offenses, the Mafia does not employ a wide range of punishments. The range includes two behind the ear, four in the face, a shotgun blast in the gut, an occasional car bomb—not a whole lot to choose from.

To get out from under some other charges the government had on him, the informant wore a wire and gathered RICO evidence against Big Joey. The informant was an associate named Ray Wean, a hijacker. As I said earlier, we always had paid informants in the hijacking crews who tipped us off on loads, but now Ray Wean was part of much bigger government plans.

I had a rule when I was under that I did not want to know whether there was surveillance because I didn't want the distraction of wondering where they were or who they were. I also didn't want to know who any informants might be because I might have a tendency to try to protect them, which could blow everything. I knew Ray Wean as Ray Wean the hijacker, and he knew me as Donnie Brasco the jewel thief, Sonny Black's new guy, without knowing I was an agent. During his time as an informant, he reported back to the agent handling him that there was a stone killer in Sonny Black's crew named Donnie Brasco, and that the FBI should keep a watchful eye on this Brasco. Like the doctor in Florida, Wean said Brasco had the eyes of a killer.

I often wondered after I came out whether Big Joey Massino finally woke up and recognized me from the hijacking bust years before. If any other wiseguy found out that Big Joey had actually been arrested by me in 1973 and had a clear opportunity to nip my operation in the bud—but blew it—he'd pay for that mistake with his life.

Big Joey Massino, at the end of the day, had more than one reason to hide in the Pocono Mountains. He certainly wasn't a ski bum.

. . .

So the trial went on without Big Joey Massino.

It was the Donnie Brasco operation's first trial, and for many reasons it was crucial that we get convictions. We had a RICO allegation and we had a mountain of evidence—including physical surveillance, electronic surveillance in the form of tapes made from planted bugs and telephone taps—and we had Ray Wean the informant. But lead prosecutor Barbara Jones and the second chair, Louis Freeh, repeatedly told me that the whole case depended on my credibility. I could not goof or we'd lose, as the feds too often had in the past in Mafia trials. In blunt terms, I was told that the man who lied every day for six years and lived a web of lies, now had to convince a jury that he could be believed. Innocent mistakes of memory were unacceptable.

"Joe," Barbara told me with Louis sitting beside her, "no matter how much evidence we put on, the jury has to believe you. Without your credibility, we have nothing."

Remember, while I was under I took no notes because it was too risky to keep notes on me or in my apartment. And only a few times did I wear a wire to record a conversation. I had to make mental notes. So by the time I got a chance to call my handler, there were often 500 conversations I'd had to commit to memory. Because I didn't know which conversations were more important and which one's were less important, I had to recall each one for my handler, who would then put my words into a report. Because I possessed no notes of my own made around the time of the conversations, I was fair game to be accused by defense attorneys of making things up to fit the prosecution's RICO theory.

Nothing for nothing, but if Lefty or Mr. Fish Rabito or Nicky Santora or Boobie Cerasani or Boots Tomasulo detected any exaggeration in my retelling of events and my recollection of things they had said to me, the Commission would have doubled the price on my head. I would have crossed another line in their eyes.

The reputation of the FBI as a successful fighter of organized crime was also on the line in this first trial. We weren't the first Mafia trial to go forward under the 1970 RICO law, but we were among the first few. We were in fact the first RICO trial with an FBI undercover agent as the principal witness. A year before I came out, there was a RICO trial in Philadelphia against Frank Sheeran and Lou Bottone. Sheeran was a Bufalino family hitman, a suspect in the disappearance of

Jimmy Hoffa, and a Teamsters officer. Bottone was a Philly wiseguy. The FBI had relied on wire recordings made by an informant—Bufalino associate and Sheeran's driver, Charlie Allen Palermo—to prove the RICO conspiracy and the two murders that were part of a pattern of racketeering. When the federal jury in Philadelphia returned with its verdict, the government had lost every count of each man's indictment. Charlie Allen Palermo, even with tape to back him up, had no credibility with the jury. Having an FBI undercover agent testify and lose would have been much more of a black eye and disappointment for the Bureau than that loss.

You try not to take any of this personally. But considering the sacrifices my family and I had made, a loss for me would have been a blow that would have taken a long time to heal.

More importantly, the FBI had invested a lot of time and money in Donnie Brasco. If we lost our first trial in Manhattan, it could spell disaster for the rest of our courtroom plans in Manhattan, Tampa, Milwaukee, and Brooklyn. It could also spell disaster for the whole new concept of FBI agents working deep cover.

Because of my unique role and all the legal ramifications it carried—such as whether, as a law enforcement officer, I enticed and entrapped anyone into committing a crime—we were breaking crucial new ground, and we couldn't fail. Our RICO theory, with an undercover agent as the one who gathered the most incriminating evidence, was as uncharted a stretch of water to navigate as the waters I had been in while working undercover. We were all Christopher Columbus when the trial began on July 19, 1982.

All my undercover work during my years with the Bonanno family eloquently got put into the *Reader's Digest* condensed version by Louis Freeh in his opening statement to the jury on a hot New York City day in the middle of the summer.

Louie told the jury, "The bread and butter for these defendants came from truck hijackings, armed robbery, narcotics trafficking, and gambling operations. When taken together with the acts of murder charged in this case, they constitute a pattern of racketeering—a pattern which was committed between 1974 and 1981 in New York, New Jersey, and Florida. This pattern of racketeering forms the basis for the charges in this indictment. . . . The proof will come to you in installments, one witness at a time, one piece of evidence at a time. Be assured, however, that as the trial progresses, these pieces will fall into place, and they will paint for you a clear, simple picture of a criminal enterprise known as the Bonanno family of *La Cosa Nostra*—an enterprise motivated by greed and power."

"One piece of evidence at a time," gathered up like stray pieces of coal along the railroad tracks and put into my coal bucket, was about to light a fire under the entire American Mafia.

The RICO theory of the case required proof of what they called "predicate acts of racketeering." We charged and had to prove, mostly from my memory of things that I had seen and things that had been said to me by the RICO conspirators, that the May 5, 1981 murders of the three capos was a Bonanno family crime.

The corpse of Sonny Red Indelicato was found nineteen days after the hit in an empty lot on Ruby Street on the Brooklyn-Queens border. The grave that was dug for Sonny Red's corpse was too shallow, and when rigor mortis set in, the left arm of Sonny Red, with his wristwatch still on his wrist, stiffened and shot up through the ground. Sonny Red had been wearing a self-winding Cartier watch. The watch had stopped on May 7th. An expert from Cartier testified that the watch can continue to run "after wrist action ceases" for 40 to 45 hours. This put the date of death at May 5th.

My testimony provided the backstory.

Lefty had told me that the job of disposing of Sonny Red's body had fallen to Big Joey Massino. Over a year before the trial, when boys playing in the empty lot found the body, Lefty told me that Big Joey had "screwed it up." Obviously a capo, especially a 300-pound capo, didn't go around digging graves. But Big Joey was responsible for getting the job done, and the crew he had given the job to had screwed it up, so Big Joey Massino had given a bad order.

Lefty had told me that 5' 5" roly-poly Mr. Fish Rabito's apartment in the exclusive Manhattan neighborhood of Sutton Place had been used as a base of operations for the hit. After the hit, Lefty, Sonny Black, Jimmy Legs, Boobie, Nicky Santora, and some others spent a few days there. About the time Sonny Red's watch had stopped, Lefty returned to his Knickerbocker Village apartment on a mission to get a pair of pants. His wife, Louise, had forgotten to include the pants in his suitcase when she packed for him. It was important to have a complete change of clothes in case any blood spattered on you during a hit or during the disposal and cleanup.

Lefty and I spoke on the phone during this visit to his apartment to get his pants. Lefty told me that he would be "gone a while yet . . . everything is fine . . . we're winners . . . a lot of punks ran away but . . . they came back . . . and we gave them sanctuary. . . ."

Lefty had told me that Big Trin was so big that even though he was "all cut up" in pieces, Lefty couldn't budge the body. Lefty had to get help from Boobie, Jimmy Legs, and Nicky Santora.

"I couldn't move him," Lefty had said about Big Trin. "Boobie could. Trin was all cut open and bleeding. There was little pieces lying around from the shotgun. Boobie got blood all over him trying to pick him up. I couldn't believe how strong Boobie is. He don't look it. But I was amazed. Boobie could move him. They cut him up and put him in green plastic garbage bags."

Boobie was tall and lean, pretty smart, a chess player, and to our frustration he ended up getting a fluke acquittal in this case. But despite his later Donnie Brasco operation conviction in Tampa that got him five years, and his other convictions for drug dealing and bank robbery, when the movie *Donnie Brasco* came out Boobie sued us for libel claiming the movie defamed his reputation. The judge reminded Boobie that he had no reputation to damage and threw the case out in a pretrial decision, stating, "I hold that Cerasani's reputation is so badly tarnished that . . . no reasonable jury could award him anything. . . ."

Lefty also said during that conversation that there was "one more situation . . . we gotta work out." Both Lefty and Sonny later explained to me that that "one more situation" was the hit on Bruno Indelicato. Sonny Black gave me the contract on that hit, and Lefty explained that the Bruno hit would "go on record" with the "family" and would be good in the eyes of the "bosses." Bingo, bingo, bingo— a "family" with "bosses" who ordered and sanctioned hits—evidence against the very structure of the Mafia, evidence that had eluded law enforcement throughout history before this trial.

That conspiracy to murder Bruno, like the May 5th massacre of three capos, was a predicate act of racketeering in our RICO indictment that we had to prove. Nicky Santora had solidified this predicate act in a conversation we had after I returned to New York claiming that I'd been unable to find and kill Bruno in Florida. In that conversation, Nicky said, "We'll find the kid. . . . If he comes out of it, we'll get him. . . .We got feelers out now. We'll know this week."

Thanks to one of the rare times I risked wearing a wallet transmitter, we had Sonny Black's own voice telling me, "We took care of those three guys, they're gone. . . . Bruno got away." Later Sonny Black said, "This is the first time in over ten years the Bonanno family agreed on exactly what to do."

Bingo, bingo, bingo. "The Bonanno family" is seen once again engaged in a pattern of racketeering and agreeing to commit murder.

In Florida, during the time of that very last meeting with Sonny Black and Santo Trafficante, I had a brief conversation with Nicky Santora in a coffee shop. Since it was the last day of Donnie Brasco's life, I could risk being blunt in asking nosey questions. I knew from Lefty that Nicky had been present at the May 5th hit, and I asked Nicky what the hit on the capos was like. I mentioned that Lefty had told me that after they hit Big Trin in the gut with a shotgun blast, his body was too big and heavy for Lefty to move. Nicky said, "You should have seen when they shot him; fifty pounds of his stomach went flying."

Both Lefty and Nicky had made jokes in front of me regarding a Zip who was brought in as one of the shooters in the three capos' hit. His name was Santo Giordano. During the blaze of guns, Santo Giordano had been accidentally shot by friendly fire. The shooting left Santo Giordano permanently paralyzed, and that goof-up was a source of comedy for Lefty and Nicky. Barbara, Louis, and I were confident that when I testified about Lefty and Nicky's wisecracks, the jury would be unlikely to find them as funny as Lefty and Nicky had.

Two days before I took the stand to provide all this detailed testimony, an informant in Buffalo told the FBI field office in Buffalo that the Commission had decided to hit my wife and daughters because the Commission couldn't get to me. Was this true or was it timed to rattle me before I took the stand? Either way, I took it seriously. At the time, my family was in an unknown locale under an assumed name; but no secret is impossible to find out. I thought of the Zips and how they killed the wives and children of informers in Sicily.

As soon as Jules told me the shocking news that my family was in jeopardy, I told the lead prosecutor in the Bonanno family trial, Barbara Jones, that I was going to the White House to pay a visit to Big Paul Castellano, the so-called Boss of Bosses, to inform him that "if anybody touches my wife or kids or any other member of my family, I will go after you personally. I will kill you myself." I told Barbara that I had no intention of hurting her case, but that ultimately my family came first. Barbara said that she wished I wouldn't go, but that she couldn't tell me "who to talk to and who not to talk to."

Jules assured me that he would handle it, and he sent agents to see Big Paul. If I couldn't be there to do it myself, I hoped that one of the agents would tell Big Paul what I'd said—that I would hold him personally responsible and that I would kill him if any member of my family had any problems from anybody.

Big Paul assured the agents that nothing would ever happen to my wife and children or any other member of my family. I believed him because we both knew my family had not crossed over the line into their territory. I was the only one who had done that. I believed him because Big Paul had neglected to include me in the assurance he gave to the agents who visited him. The failure to take the bull's-eye off my back boosted his credibility for me in this matter. We already knew from informants that despite the earlier visits by the agents to the heads of the five families, the contract on my life had not been lifted.

For the first time, the moment I took the witness stand and went under oath, I proudly announced my real name—Special Agent Joseph D. Pistone—to the Mafia and the media. After I testified, directly recounting the defendants' criminal incidents and the defendants' statements that supported our RICO indictment, each one of the defense attorneys took turns cross-examining me, working me over in ways that are no longer even permitted for cops who interrogate criminals. Looking back, maybe subconsciously to keep my serenity, I may have made believe I wasn't Italian.

During the cross-examination of me, one of the defense attorneys brought out a tape recording that occurred while Lefty and Tony Mirra fought over who had the rights to me. The tape included these two lines of my conversation with Lefty:

"Mirra wants to get you killed," Lefty said.

"Why don't we just kill him?" I said.

This cross-examination was designed to embarrass me and make me look bad in the jury's eyes—to make *me* look like a killer. But you have to wonder what the defense attorney was thinking. If I was serious in saying that to Lefty, then wasn't Lefty also being branded a serious killer in the eyes of the jury?

I always tried to keep my answers simple. Lefty had unwittingly given me expert advice on how to testify when, at that midnight meeting at Lynn's bar, he had prepared me for my meeting with Mike Sabella after the fiasco over Tony Conte's disappearance following the bogus art theft in Chicago. Keeping it simple, I said what should have been obvious to anyone: that my suggestion that we kill Mirra was made to enhance my credibility with Lefty. In my role as a wiseguy, that is what I would be expected to say. Their world is all about retaliation. Besides, I knew Lefty would not and could not kill Mirra, a made man, a soldier with his own capo, without getting approval for the hit at the top levels of the family, and maybe getting himself hit for even asking. Clearly, the statement— "Why don't we just kill him?"—was tactical and not practical.

A related topic on which the defense lawyers cross-examined me was Mirra's charge that I had stolen $250,000 in drug money. The timing in this cross-examination couldn't have been worse. My wife, under the circumstances, had gotten used to making important decisions without consulting me. The very day I was grilled about stealing $250,000 is the day my wife went out and bought a new car without telling me. My sole enemy in the Bureau had a field day with that coincidence. He wanted to open an investigation into the matter that would be conducted by inspectors from the Bureau's Office of Professional Responsibility, the FBI's equivalent of Internal Affairs in the NYPD. I was still on the witness stand when Jules told me about this situation. He had to nip that in the bud. I can laugh now, but there was nothing funny about it at the time.

I was on the witness stand for over two weeks in that first case, with Lefty giving me the evil eye throughout. We heard from his cellmate that, after my first day on the witness stand, Lefty said, "I'll get that motherfucker Donnie if it's the last thing I do." A bystander in the audience looked at me and pulled an imaginary trigger. We had him barred from the courthouse.

During a recess on August 12, 1982, while I was still on the witness stand, we got the news that Sonny's body had been identified. A body had been found nine months earlier in Mariner's Harbor, Staten Island, with both hands chopped off at the wrist. It was now confirmed that that body was Sonny Black's. On the one hand, I was sad for the mess Sonny had made of his life by volunteering to join the Mafia. On the other hand, I was glad for his family that they finally had proof that he was dead.

The jury returned its verdict on August 27, 1982. All the Bonanno family defendants were convicted except Boobie Cerasani, who was acquitted by a fluke. The jury had voted to acquit him on one count, and to convict him on all the rest, but they didn't understand the jury form and checked acquittal as to all counts for him. After the trial, when they realized what they had done, a couple of jurors tried to get the judge to change Boobie's verdict to guilty on all but one charge. It was too late for that, and Boobie skated, for the time being.

Out of the Bonanno family trial, Lefty got a 15-year sentence. Nicky Santoro got a 15-year sentence. Mr. Fish Rabito got a 13-year sentence. The rest got sentences of less than ten years. Sonny Black would have been convicted, but. . . . Tony Mirra would have been convicted, but. . . .

It was a joyous victory for the prosecution team, the Bureau, the Department of Justice, and all the agents and cops who did the often-tedious investigations, interviews, cultivation of informants, and physical and electronic surveillance such a case demands. A jubilee was held in a church hall across the way from the federal courthouse. I put in an appearance, but I can't explain how I felt. As gratified as I was, I just didn't feel like celebrating. Maybe the only reservation I had about what I had done to Sonny and Lefty was that I saw no reason to gloat about it. My team won the game and their team paid the price.

Also, I think it's like when you see news clips of prisoners of war getting off a plane. You see their families greeting them on the tarmac and looking far more celebratory than they do. I don't want to exaggerate, but in a funny way, I had been a prisoner of war for six years. And I still wasn't out. There were many more trials to go.

CHAPTER 8
ON THE ROAD

LIKE MOST PEOPLE, when I think of the Mafia, I think of New York City, and not just because I was with two New York families, the Colombo and the Bonanno. When Hollywood makes a movie about the Mafia, it is invariably about the Mafia families in New York City—*Goodfellas*, *Mean Streets*, *The Godfather*, and that movie with Johnny Depp and Al Pacino.

As everyone now knows, there are Mafia families throughout the country. But these families are tiny compared to the five New York City families. Places like San Francisco or St. Louis, at their peak, had maybe a dozen or so made men. The closest in size and power to a single New York family is the Chicago family, but Chicago has only one family, and Chicago itself is one-fifth the size of New York.

When the ruling Commission of the Mafia was established in 1931, it was comprised of seven bosses: the bosses of the five New York families, the Chicago boss, and the Buffalo boss. In time, the Commission pared down and evolved into just the five New York families. Off and on starting in the 1960s, it would go down to four of the five whenever the Bonanno family would get into trouble and get the boot. They were the only New York family to ever get the boot. And when that would happen, the Bonanno family would not only lose its vote, but the Bonanno boss would lose out on their share of any joint ventures the other families' bosses would have going. This isn't money that had to flow upstream; it was already upstream, and it was big money.

You have to understand that when the Commission was formed and the country was split up into about 27 families, one of the main motivating factors in doing so was self-preservation of the bosses. Sure, the Commission was intended to settle disputes like a warped United Nations—keep the bloodshed from arousing the public—and maybe it has over the years. But there's also been a lot of talk about the Commission being formed to function like a board of directors of a corporation. Yet I don't see the bosses looking out for the Mafia *per se* like a board of directors looks out for a corporation. I see the bosses looking out for themselves when they formed the Commission. With a Commission in place, unless an ambitious capo had Commission members on his side, he would be hard-pressed to kill his boss and take over because the Commission would come down on him. If the kings in Europe got together and formed a Commission of kings a few hundred years ago, there might still be a few kings in power overseas.

Unless the Commission itself sanctioned a hit on a boss, or sanctioned a takeover of a family whose boss was in jail, nobody had better try. When Philly boss Angelo "the Docile Don" Bruno was whacked in 1980, each of the Philly family capos involved was tortured and killed, some with money stuffed in their mouths to signify their greed. When Carmine Galante got out of jail and asserted himself as Bonanno boss while the official boss, Rusty Rastelli, was in jail, Carmine got whacked. None of the bosses on the Commission wanted to condone the concept that a boss could be deprived of his lucrative position just because he ended up in the can. After all, if not for the Commission, they could be next.

When I was under, in addition to the five New York families who comprised the Mafia Commission, all the old-time bosses of the families within driving distance from the city gravitated around New York and formed partnerships and alliances with the New York bosses. During my time with the Bonanno family, Philly boss Angelo Bruno and New Jersey boss Sam "the Plumber" DeCavalcante were known to be very close to the Commission bosses. Northeastern Pennsylvania boss Russell Bufalino kept a hotel suite in New York and owned a Mafia hangout in the theater district, the Vesuvio Restaurant. Bufalino would drive over two hours to New York every Thursday with Frank Sheeran. On occasion, I would be asked by Jules to drop in at the Vesuvio to try to pick up whatever intelligence I could, as Bufalino was known to be very close to the Genovese family.

When I surfaced in 1981, the eyes and ears of the Commission were fixed on the Bonanno family. The Bonanno bosses were humiliated and the family got the boot, which really meant that the boss, Rusty Rastelli, got punished because his underlings had allowed me to infiltrate and spy. The Bonannos would stay off the Commission until soon after 1991, when Big Joey Massino replaced Rusty Rastelli as boss. Big Joey got upped to boss, the proper way, when Rusty died in prison. At the time he died, Rusty Rastelli was serving a sentence based on a conviction from a trial in which I had testified, and Big Joey was still in jail as a result of the same trial.

Big Joey Massino got out of jail in November 1992 and resurrected the family's stature and reputation in the 1990s and into the next century. Big Joey, with the help of his underboss and brother-in-law, Good-looking Sal Vitale, epitomized the old school New York City Mafia gangster and ran the Bonanno family in an old-school New York City style in the decade from 1993 to 2003. Big Joey had gotten his back up off the canvas in 1993 and began winning rounds. The press routinely referred to him as "The Last Don." In that decade, the Bonanno family was the only family that did not have a single made man roll over and become a cooperating witness for the government.

I had to watch from the sidelines while all the damage I did to the Bonannos—at the Bonanno family trial, a racketeering trial involving Local 814, and the Pizza Connection Case heroin trafficking trial—seemed to get quickly repaired after Big Joey Massino got out of jail in 1992. It was frustrating to see the family doing so well in what Lefty called "the underworld field."

From the beginning, even before I came out and we began to assess what we had, Jules and I literally dreamed of a day when we would go after the heads of the five New York families in one major trial. It would be a monumental task and lots of work needed to be done by other undercover agents and cops, electronic surveillance experts, straight-up agents in the FBI, detectives in the NYPD and the New York State Organized Crime Task Force, and federal and local prosecutors. Like the team that makes a movie happen, everybody would have to work diligently in their own role for such a trial to ever take place. We had our vision, and we had the RICO law, and we were all determined.

Until that dream could come true we had plenty of other work to do to complete the unfinished business of the Donnie Brasco operation.

• • •

Despite the importance of New York City to the Mafia, there always was and still is a Mafia criminal enterprise spread north into places like New England, Buffalo, and Canada; south into Florida and New Orleans; midwest into Cleveland, Detroit, Milwaukee, Chicago, St. Louis, Kansas City, and even Youngstown, Ohio; and west into Arizona, Las Vegas, Los Angeles, and the San Francisco Bay area.

Trying to make a dent in all this, we moved on to Milwaukee with our RICO theory battle-tested and proven to be an effective weapon against the Mafia. In Milwaukee we would be using RICO to go after a family boss for the first time. Remember, we couldn't go after the Bonanno family boss, Rusty Rastelli, because he had been in jail the whole time I was under and gathering evidence. However, I had had direct contact with Frank Balistrieri, the boss of the Milwaukee family, as well as his brother, his two sons, and his underboss.

In Milwaukee, before we took the Balistrieris to trial, the prosecutor asked me to go down to the lockup and talk to Lefty to see if I could get him to turn. I think the prosecutor thought we needed more evidence against Mike Sabella, the former Bonanno capo under Carmine Galante who had first met with the Chicago made men as an entrée to Balistrieri. I had had no direct involvement with Mike Sabella on the paving of the road to Milwaukee for Lefty, the other undercover Tony Conte, and me. That was a definite hole in the case against Sabella.

"Lefty turn? I wish," I said. "There's no way Lefty will ever turn. At least not for me. Lefty hates my guts with a passion. One look at me and he'd be more inflamed. Besides, he thinks I'm the gangster, not him. Lefty's just not built that way; he'd rather die."

The prosecutor decided to try to talk to Lefty himself. He went down to the lockup and asked Lefty if he would agree to talk to me. Lefty let out a stream of expletives that made it clear that he would kill me if he could get his hands on me. Years later, Lefty got cancer in the only lung he had left. The English Ovals he smoked nonstop had caught up with him. Rather than have to take care of him in prison, the feds released him to die at home in 1993. We learned from an informant that Lefty had gone straight to Big Joey Massino, who was boss at the time and had just gotten out of jail himself, and asked Big Joey to order somebody to whack me. Agents went to Lefty and, while he denied that he had done such a thing, he wasn't very convincing. When the agents went to Big Joey, the boss only said, "Don't worry about it. Nothing's going to happen."

Our primary theory in Milwaukee was that Balistrieri was the boss of the criminal enterprise known as the Balistrieri family of the Mafia, and that he had partnered with the Bonanno family in the persons of Lefty, Mike Sabella, and Donnie Brasco to coerce saloons and restaurants to use only the partnerships' vending machines—or else. The underlying crime here was extortion. Balistrieri's underboss, Steve DiSalvo, took part in the planning of the partnership. Balistrieri's sons, John and Joseph, both lawyers, drew up the legal agreements and also played active roles in the planning of the partnership.

In front of the jury when I was on the witness stand, Balistrieri's lawyer badgered me to answer the question of where I lived. Of course, I wouldn't answer any part of that question. He went from asking me to reveal my address to asking for the city in which my family and I lived, to asking for the state, then finally to asking for the region of the country. I refused to answer each and every time he asked. Again, I wondered what this belligerent defense attorney thought the jury would be thinking. Clearly, every time I refused to answer where I lived, the jury understood why I was refusing—his client was a dangerous Mafia boss, that's why. But the lawyer went on, I guess scoring points in the eyes of his beaming, belligerent client. Maybe he was trying to send a threat to the jury implying that if I were afraid to give my address, they should be afraid to convict.

Finally, the judge took a recess and ruled that I could give the false answer of "California," because that was the state that the gangsters I dealt with thought I was from. Before we brought the jury back in, the judge was handed a slip of paper by one of the court bailiffs. It was a note from the jury asking the judge to instruct the lawyer to stop badgering the witness.

Despite a tremendous effort by the prosecutor, we lost Mike Sabella. His attorney wisely disassociated himself from the rest of the defense, and our case against Sabella, in those early days, was unique. RICO was such a new concept that things like jury instructions were still being fine-tuned. I don't think the jury understood the idea that, for us in the Bonanno family to go into another family's territory, we had to get permission, and that Mike Sabella securing this permission was a crucial part of the pattern of racketeering.

Everyone else was convicted. Milwaukee boss Frank Balistrieri got 13 years at his sentencing in 1984. After that trial, I supplied intelligence and background against him for a trial in Kansas City involving the skim from Las Vegas, based on the errand-boy job he had offered me to pick up the skim and deliver it to Kansas City. He got another 10 years in Kansas City.

My contribution in Kansas City was behind-the-scenes, but it still felt the same to make some contribution that led to bad news for the Mafia. With the huge contribution of bugs and the defection of the president of the Teamsters union, Roy Williams, as a cooperating witness, the government prosecutors in Kansas City nailed the bosses of Kansas City and Chicago, in addition to Balistrieri.

The Vegas skim had been the bosses' biggest source of money since it didn't have to flow upstream; it already was upstream. Errand boys reporting directly to the bosses for years had been walking into counting rooms in Las Vegas with empty suitcases and walking out with hundreds of thousands of dollars a month. Now it was over. They could skim in the future, but not as systematically, blatantly, or as lucratively. And not for long.

Out of the Milwaukee trial, Lefty got more time, boosting his total to 20 years. Underboss Steve DiSalvo and Balistrieri's subservient lawyer sons, John and Joseph, each got 8 years. The brothers closed their law practice and were disbarred. Years later I heard from an agent in Milwaukee that one of the sons got his license back and is again practicing in Milwaukee.

Noted crime writer and Mafia authority, Jerry Capeci, wrote in his *Complete Idiot's Guide to the Mafia, 2nd Edition*, that when Balistrieri was released prematurely from prison due to ill health, and soon after died, his daughter Benedetta sued her brother Joseph claiming that the son had grabbed the father's stash of hidden cash and refused to declare it as part of the estate and share it with her. Joseph called his sister "pathetic." Jerry Capeci also observed that after Balistrieri got released early and died, "A few members soldiered on, but for all intents and purposes, the small Milwaukee family was done."

Again, I was inwardly proud of the job the undercovers known as Tony Conte and Donnie Brasco, and our FBI handlers, had done. We permanently brought down two families: the Milwaukee Mafia family (led by Frank Balistrieri), and the Balistrieri family of Mafia members. We also exposed the Chicago family as the seat of power in that part of the country. And, for the first time ever, prosecutors applied RICO to a Mafia boss and nailed him with it. This fact alone was a huge advance in the fight against the Mafia. With this success, we were one step closer to applying RICO to all the bosses sitting on the Commission.

• • •

Next we turned to the grand jury in Florida. Because we had so much evidence in Tampa, the U.S. Attorney in Miami decided not to indict anyone for the crimes we had against them in Miami. My impression during that time frame was that the RICO law was such a novel concept that it might have influenced prosecutorial decisions.

When the indictment came down in Tampa, it triggered the bribed cop, Captain Joseph Donahue, to kill himself. It was sad. He was a small fish in a sea of sharks, but as with the rest, he volunteered to be a crook with a badge. No draft board drafted him.

Meanwhile, we had a very big fish on the line in Tampa. Santo Trafficante had been a major Mafia power his whole life. His father had run the Tampa family and, upon his death from natural causes, the title of boss went to Santo. Santo had a hand in nearly every major moment of Mafia history in the last half of the twentieth century. Santo Trafficante had been arrested at the famous Apalachin meeting in New York state in 1957 (where he was arrested with 56 other mobsters during a convention to discuss Mafia power hierarchy). He was in Cuba when Castro's revolution prevailed; Castro confiscated Trafficante's gambling and property interests and tossed him in jail. Trafficante admitted that he was an active participant in the CIA-Mafia plot to assassinate Castro, as well as in the Bay of Pigs invasion. Trafficante is still suspected of being involved in the assassination of JFK. Trafficante was arrested with a number of Mafia bosses in the Stella Restaurant in Queens in what came to be known as the Little Apalachin meeting. And, of course, Trafficante was ensnared in the Donnie Brasco operation, the first FBI deep penetration of the Mafia.

Despite this high profile, Santo Trafficante had never been jailed in the United States. We couldn't wait to bring that towering figure down.

But we would never get the chance. Almost from the outset, Trafficante realized he was done for. His health began to fail and, on St. Patrick's Day in 1987, he finally died, never to have gone to trial on the case that would have nailed him and jailed him. In the end, we took plea bargains from Boobie Cerasani, who had skated on a fluke in the Bonanno family trial, and from Trafficante's right hand man, the white-haired Benny Husick. In federal court in Tampa, Boobie got five years and Benny got three years.

• • •

Back in New York, then-capo Big Joey Massino had returned from his two-year exile in the Pocono Mountains. The U.S. Attorney's Office, under the tough and talented prosecutor Laura Brevetti, had put together a RICO case against capo Massino, boss Rusty Rastelli, and former underboss Nicky Glasses Marangello; the top officers of Local 814 of the International Brotherhood of Teamsters, the union that was supposed to be representing the moving and storage industry workers in New York; and officers of three of the big New York moving companies.

Massino, Marangello, and Rastelli were accused of being in league with the Local 814 officers in charging the moving companies an under-the-table premium for labor peace. The criminal payoff scheme guaranteed no strikes, no fire bombings, no beatings, and in some cases, the right to hire nonunion workers and fire union workers. The money for the payoffs was put together through rigged bids that inflated the cost of moving jobs and by paychecks for employees who didn't exist. The Local 814 union bosses split the payoffs they received from the moving companies with the Bonanno bosses. Because Rusty was in jail, his share was given to his brother Carmine, who just happened to be a Local 814 shop steward—that is, an officer whose job it was to represent and protect his union brothers and sisters.

The moving company officers were charged in the indictment with rigging bids. Ironically, one of the moving companies involved had moved the FBI from its offices on East 69th Street to the Federal Plaza downtown. Due to a rigged bidding process, the company was able to overcharge the FBI $5,000, which was split with the Local 814 officers and the Bonanno family officers. This was actually one of the predicate crimes charged in the applicable RICO case.

Although I had no first-hand experience with the underlying criminal acts, I had the opportunity of testifying in that trial for Laura Brevetti as an expert on the structure of the Mafia's criminal enterprise, and on the functions and responsibilities of Rastelli, Marangello, and Massino in that enterprise.

During the five-month trial, there was a lot of buzz about the planning of a movie based on the book, *Donnie Brasco*. At a recess, Big Joey asked me, "Donnie, who are you going to get to play me in the movie?"

"That's the trouble we're having, Joey," I said. "We can't find an actor fat enough to play you."

I had the occasion on October 15, 1986 of seeing Rusty Rastelli become the first New York boss to go down—with a little help from the Donnie Brasco operation. Rusty Rastelli, then 69, got twelve years added to the sentence he was already serving. In effect, it was a life sentence by degrees. My old boss would die in jail in the summer of 1991. His eventual successor, Big Joey Massino, then 44, got a ten-year sentence. No doubt he'd miss the fresh mountain air of the Poconos and maybe wish he'd stayed away a little longer. Nicky Glasses Marangello, then 74, got an eight-year sentence, again, the equivalent of a life sentence. Rusty's 65-year-old kid brother Carmine got six years.

At the end of the Local 814 trial, one of the defense lawyers for one of the other defendants came to the authorities and told us that he heard Big Joey Massino mutter under his breath that he was going to put a contract out on Laura Brevetti. Laura took a well-earned vacation.

• • •

Unfortunately, when we took Big Joey Massino to trial on the Bonanno family charges that he had lammed out on in 1982, we were dealing with a man whom I didn't really know. Although Sonny had introduced me to him at the Motion Lounge, and I had been present for conversations involving Big Joey, I had never had a one-on-one conversation with him until that discussion about who would play him in the movie. His underboss and brother-in-law, Good-looking Sal Vitale, had been added to the indictment, and before I set foot in court I had never met him, either.

The major predicate crime against the future Bonanno boss, but not his underboss, was a conspiracy to kill the three capos on May 5, 1981. This charge—conspiracy to kill—did not allege that Big Joey actually participated in the massacre itself. This distinction became important later on in the life and times of Big Joey Massino. Meanwhile, at this trial, my information had been limited to the things Lefty and Sonny told me about Big Joey's participation, and neither one was in Big Joey Massino's crew. Specifically, Sonny had told me that Big Joey vetoed my participation in the hit, and Lefty told me that Big Joey screwed up the job of burying Sonny Red's body.

In the end we didn't have enough direct evidence against Big Joey, and he was found not guilty of the major conspiracy to kill the three capos. Big Joey Massino and Good-looking Sal Vitale were found guilty of the relatively minor charges based on evidence of crimes I had nothing to do with, but on appeal, in a legal test regarding interpretation of the new RICO law, the guilty verdicts on the charges they were convicted of were tossed out as being barred by the statute of limitations. It was a bitter pill. However, the court had scheduled the Local 814 case first. The moving company union case had gone to trial before Massino's part of the Bonanno family case. So, I could take a little bit of consolation from the fact that we already had convicted Big Joey and he wasn't walking.

The man Lefty had called a "jerk-off" had been smart to go on the lam and miss the first trial. That gave his lawyers a chance to study the trial transcripts and confer with the defense lawyers in the Bonanno family trial to learn their impressions of the witness's demeanors, strengths, and weaknesses. By the time we took Massino to trial, his lawyers had seen all the government's evidence in the first trial and could prepare for it.

Watching him get paroled on the Local 814 case in 1992 and watching him take charge and rebuild the Bonanno family was one of the bad breaks of the operation. I couldn't afford to take things like that personally. I had to keep moving on, not looking back. But Big Joey Massino belonged in jail for as long as we could put him in jail. That would come later.

CHAPTER 9

THE PIZZA CONNECTION, PART 1

IN HIS BOOK, ***THE GOOD GUYS,*** Jules Bonavolonta wrote, "The press was calling it 'the Pizza Connection Case.' It was the product of a massive narcotics investigation. . . . The case had grown out of an effort that Joe Pistone and I had initiated back in 1982."

I agree with that statement. But I'd like to add that, by the time the case went to trial three years later in 1985, I believe the trial was the product of way more than "a massive narcotics investigation." Jules and I might have planted the seed based on intelligence I had gathered, but the Pizza Connection Case grew to fruition through the tireless vision of the United States Attorney for the Southern District of New York—Rudy Giuliani—and his staff, especially Assistant United States Attorneys Louis Freeh and Robert Stewart.

By the time the seeds of the Bonanno family narcotics intelligence I had gathered matured, it bloomed into one of the longest and most expensive criminal trials in American history, and the largest international heroin-smuggling case to this day.

The intelligence that I passed along as I got it, often without knowing its full significance, concerned the Zips under Toto Catalano who worked on a stretch of Knickerbocker Avenue on the Queens-Brooklyn border. The FBI Special Agent in charge of Sicilian issues, Carmine Russo, called the intelligence I provided about the Zips, "an unbelievable revelation."

Some say the Sicilians got their nickname "Zips" because they talked fast in Italian, so fast that even the Italian-American gangsters who did speak Italian couldn't keep up with them. Some say they got the nickname from a slang Sicilian word meaning peasant. Growing up in Paterson, I had heard Sicilians, including me, referred to as Zips. And since all Italians spoke fast Italian, not just the Sicilian Italians, I would go with the peasant theory. But one thing I knew, you didn't call them Zips to their face.

The Zips were fearsome, hardcore Mafia men who were made in Sicily before they ever got to New York and Knickerbocker Avenue. To understand the mind-set of a Mafia soldier, you have to understand that his head is filled with a mine-strone soup of motives to voluntarily surrender his freedom and his life to the Mafia, including but not limited to: (1) being under the umbrella of the boss's political and legal connections, (2) being protected from other rival criminals, (3) being provided opportunities to make money that might be beyond his own intel-ligence or ability to make on his own, (4) being able to instill fear in those he deals with outside the family, and (5) being provided an opportunity to advance with-in the Mafia family structure and acquire the rewards of money, prestige, and power that are yours when you are made.

The Zip in Sicily had these motives in spades. He did not live in a land of opportunity the way we know it, where Sicilians like Frank Sinatra and Joe DiMaggio could not only prosper, but could be considered the best in their cho-sen fields. In Sicily, the *padron* owned the land and made the rules, and had done so for centuries. The common man was often a peasant who was the product of peasants since time immemorial. Political corruption abounded, and the govern-ment seemed to be in league with the powerful. The Mafia held out the hope of security, protection, and money way beyond a peasant's dreams. And the peasants worked cheap.

The Zips on Knickerbocker Avenue were born and raised to be secretive, clannish, and willing to do anything for the boss. That the Zips stuck together and did not mix well with the rest of the Bonanno family was one of only a million grudges and resentments the American Mafia held toward the Zips.

My first contact with them was in my early days with the Bonanno family when I hung out with Tony Mirra. He took me to Nicky Glasses Marangello's social club, Toyland, and pointed out the Zips, including Toto Catalano, Cesare Bonventre, and Baldo Amato. He told me that Toto was one of two Zip capos. The other was Sally Fruits Farrugia. He told me that Cesare Bonventre, a young, tall, good-looking ladies-man type, was related to Carmine Galante, and that Bonventre and Baldo Amato were Galante's bodyguards. He explained that the Zips were brought into the country to wholesale heroin that Carmine Galante smuggled in from Sicily. This operation was Galante's, and nobody shared in it. Galante took all the profit and used the Zips for hits.

"They're perfect for doing work," Mirra explained, meaning murder. "Nobody knows them. They got no records. They keep to themselves. They are the meanest mothers around. They whack cops and judges. They'll whack a little kid in the playground if the boss tells them."

I never asked questions about anything that didn't pertain directly to me, but I didn't have to ask much about the Zips. The Zips were a bone of contention for the American Mafia members. The Americans hated the fact that the Zips were made in Sicily and came over here with letters of introduction and were put into the Bonanno family as made men with their own capos. Since Mafia soldiers like to complain, the information eventually found its way to my ears.

"The boss set a lot of them up in junk," Mirra told me. "They get the junk sent and distribute it to wherever the boss says."

This first bit of unbelievable intelligence that I provided about the Zips and heroin smuggling, was a "eureka" moment for the Bureau. We had seen the Zips coming in and living on Knickerbocker Avenue. We knew that some of them were smuggled in from Canada and others had come in legally, but we had no idea who was behind it or what purpose they served.

When all the information came together, it all fit. It fit what was presently going on, and it fit the Mafia history that the experts in the Bureau knew about.

The influx of Zips to New York escalated when Carmine Galante got out of jail in 1974, and that fit, too. The New York police had known Galante at least since the summer of 1943. Galante was the prime suspect that year in the murder of a journalist, Carlo Tresca. Tresca wrote articles for the Italian-American community, writings that were very critical of *Il Duce*, Benito Mussolini. We were at war with Mussolini's Italy at the time. In fact, 1943 was the year the Allied soldiers invaded Sicily and fought the Italians and the Germans for control of that island gateway to the rest of Italy. Even when I was a kid in Paterson, there was at least one New York newspaper in the Italian language, *Il Progresso*. You'd see old-timers reading it. Back in 1943 there was even more of a demand for Italian-language journalism. The story of Carlo Tresca is that his writing got under the skin of Mussolini. At the time, Vito Genovese was on the lam in Italy to avoid arrest for a murder. Mussolini asked Genovese to hit Tresca, and Genovese got Galante to shoot Tresca on the street in New York City. A car with license plates that were traced to Galante was reported leaving the scene, but the NYPD could never make a case against Galante for that hit.

The rest of the history of Carmine Galante was a history of drugs. His first conviction for heroin distribution was in 1962, for which he got twenty years. But before that, Joe "Bananas" Bonanno had sent Galante to Montreal, Canada in the early fifties. There he got involved with the French Connection heroin trafficking operation. This route of heroin came from labs in Marseilles, France, and was smuggled mostly into Montreal and New York. In the mid-fifties, the Canadian government had had enough of the American-born Galante and deported him back to the States, where he continued working the French Connection heroin traffic in New York until his 1962 drug trafficking conviction.

When the French Connection heroin route was exposed by the NYPD and a crackdown got under way, Galante was already in jail serving his heroin sentence. By the time he got out in 1974, there was a bit of a heroin drought and therefore a greater demand for heroin due to: the crackdown on the French Connection (as dramatized in the movie of the same name); President Richard Nixon's call for a War on Drugs in 1971; and the creation of the Drug Enforcement Agency (DEA) in 1973, a major expansion from the former Federal Bureau of Narcotics.

Even before he left jail, Galante saw an opportunity to fill a void using labs in Sicily. The morphine that would be turned into heroin in the Sicilian labs came from where it had always pretty much come from: Turkey. The heroin manufactured in Sicily would be put into shipments of cheese and other foods, and even into shipments of marble as Lefty pointed out to me at CaSa Bella's. This was nothing new. For a few years after World War II, until pressure from the American government stopped it, the Italians manufactured heroin for pharmaceutical purposes and—surprise, surprise—drug traffickers smuggled it into America. One smuggling technique was to place the heroin in olive oil cans that had false bottoms. The top half of the can was pure olive oil; the bottom half was pure heroin.

But what Galante added was pizza.

When I left Mirra and went "on record" with Lefty, I got an earful from Lefty about "the scumbag Zips. Galante got them in pizza parlors. He got them from New York to Chicago and every little town along the way. They got pizza parlors in places I don't even know where the fuck that is, and they got a fucking pizza parlor there. That way they can run the heroin from the pizza parlor to wherever he wants it. Then they can go launder the money in Switzerland."

Lefty told me about the special relationship between Galante and the Zips. "There's only a few people that Galante's close to. And mainly that's the Zips, like Cesare and those you see around Toyland. Those guys are always with him. He brought them over from Sicily, and he uses them for different pieces of work and for dealing all that junk. They're as mean as he is. You can't trust those bastard Zips. Nobody can. Except the Old Man. He can trust them because he brought them over here and he can control them."

Of course he could. When Galante got hit in 1979 in the backyard of Joe and Mary's Italian American Restaurant on Knickerbocker Avenue, Cesare Bonventre and Baldo Amato were supposed to be guarding him. They were not shot themselves, and they disappeared after the hit. That spelled a set-up by the very ones "he brought over here," the ones he thought he could control. Although it was a hot summer day when Galante got it, both Cesare and Baldo were wearing leather jackets, signifying a need to protect their bodies from stray pellets or flying debris.

The hit was brutal and had the mark of the Zips on it. Three men in ski masks burst into the backyard and began shooting. The famous photo of Galante crumpled on the ground with his cigar still clenched in his dead jaw, makes people forget that two innocent bystanders were also whacked. Joe Turano of Joe and Mary's was killed in front of his wife and two children, along with a friend who was there to discuss an insurance policy with Joe and Mary.

Not that Lefty and the rest cared one little bit about the innocent bystanders. "There's gonna be big changes," Lefty told me, full of excitement. That's all that mattered to him. At that point, Lefty and I went from Mike Sabella to Sonny Black. Toto Catalano went from capo to street boss of the Zips. And Cesare Bonventre, the missing bodyguard, went from soldier to capo. At 28, Cesare was the youngest capo in Bonanno family history.

Looking at Cesare Bonventre helps to understand the treachery of the Zips as a group. When Tony Mirra got out of jail, Mirra was put in Cesare's crew. Later, when Mirra contested Lefty's claim on me and accused me of stealing $250,000 in drug money, sniffing the green smell of money Cesare backed Mirra. At the sit down, Cesare went so far as to lie that he saw me at Mirra's disco, Cecil's, every night with Mirra.

"He says you were with him every night," Lefty told me during the Mafia litigation over me, full knowing that most nights I was with Lefty.

"And don't forget," Lefty added. "We're fooling around with Zips. They'll keep pecking. Greaseballs are motherfuckers. When a Zip kisses, forget about it. They hate the American people. They hate the American wiseguys."

Lefty explained that the hit on Galante had required approval from the Zips in order for Rusty Rastelli to get approval from Big Paul Castellano and the other Commission bosses. Lefty said the reason Galante "got whacked is that he wouldn't share his drug business with anybody else in the family."

Lefty added an unnecessary cautionary comment: "If they can hit a boss, nobody's immune."

On June 19, 1979, a month before Carmine Galante was whacked and two years before I came out, police in Sicily had discovered that a suitcase shipped from New York contained $497,000 wrapped in pizzeria aprons.

According to Lefty and Sonny, Cesare Bonventre had been in league with the three capos who were whacked on May 5th, 1981. The four of them had planned to hit Sonny Black. But then Cesare changed his mind. Cesare Bonventre, who was in jail on a weapons charge on the day of the hit, had switched sides, bringing his Zips with him and dooming the three capos.

The Bonanno family's biggest moneymaker was in the pizza-parlor heroin money-laundering business, and that enterprise depended entirely on the connection between the Zips and their relatives back home in the Sicilian Mafia. The boss who had the Zips was like the pirate captain who had the buried treasure. Galante's offense was that he wouldn't share any treasure with the rest of the family. So, after Galante was gone, Sonny Black promised to share some of the treasure with Big Paul Castellano, and that's how Sonny got Big Paul's approval to hit the three capos. Sonny Black could only promise to share some of the treasure with Big Paul as long as the Zips were with him. If the three capos had the Zips with them, it would have been a different story. As Rusty Rastelli's strongest capo, Sonny would have gone.

The Zips had a unique power, but they also had their limits. They knew that, to begin with, they had to be subservient to some Bonanno family boss or other. There was no way they would have been allowed to operate in America or Canada on their own. Their cunning peasant instinct informed men like capo Cesare Bonventre and his street boss Toto Catalano as to where the biggest and safest deal was for them. No doubt, Cesare and Toto understood that bosses like Big Paul and the rest of the Commission bosses would have an instinctive leaning toward the jailed boss Rusty Rastelli over the upstart coup of the three capos. Sicilians like Cesare and Toto would have needed no instruction in the self-preservation instinct of the Commission bosses when they were making decisions over matters that, at first blush, seemed to have no bearing on them.

After the three-capos hit, Sonny Black told Lefty and me that Zip capo and former street boss, Sally Fruits Farrugia, wanted to make some of the Zips capos, but Sonny told him no.

"That would be crazy," Sonny said to Lefty and me, "because those guys are looking to take over everything. That's why those three guys were killed—they went against the Zips and the Zips came over to our side. We were the ones slated to get hit, but because Sonny Red screwed the Zips, they swung over to us. There's no way we can make them captains. We'd lose all our strength."

"You're going to be in shit's creek, Sonny," Lefty said.

"Good. I been in shit's creek eighteen years."

"I advise you to be a little strong," Lefty said, "because them fucking Zips ain't gonna back up to nobody. You give them the fucking power, if you don't get hurt now, you get hurt three years from now. They'll bury you. You cannot give them the power. They don't give a fuck. They don't care who's boss. They got no respect. There's no family."

If we use the legal standard lawyers use to prove causation—the "but for" standard—there is no doubt in my mind that but for Cesare Bonventre and the Zips switching sides to go with Rusty Rastelli, the three capos would have taken control of the Bonanno family. But for Cesare Bonventre and the Zips switching sides, Carmine Galante would have finished his lunch and his cigar at Joe and Mary's, and Joe and the other murder victim would have gone on to live full lives with their families.

This is the essence of the intelligence I got on the Zips and the Bonanno family, the Sicilians and the Pizza Connection, and Carmine Galante and the three capos.

I know I've probably beaten this subject to death with a roll of dimes, and Jules would say "Amen" to that, but I want to take this last shot at putting my premature coming out in historical context at this point. Nothing for nothing, but when I was pulled, Sonny Black had just accomplished this incredible consolidation of power, bringing the Zips along with him, and I was seated at his right hand, reporting directly to him. I was also a few weeks away from Sonny being able to really confide in me the way he wanted to, and talk freely to me using explicit language. It's like we had the keys to the vault, but suddenly threw them away.

CHAPTER 18
THE PIZZA CONNECTION, PART 2

THE PIZZA CONNECTION CASE took Rudy Giuliani and his crew over three years to build. Jules and I by no means handed them even the bare bones of a case. FBI Case Agents Carmine Russo and Charlie Rooney, and other agents under supervisors Lew Schiliro and Jimmy Kossler, all worked as a team with electronics expert Jimmy Kallstrom and his bug and wiretap crew. These dedicated and incredibly hard-working men had to go out and find the evidence to use in court to prove the crimes behind the intelligence that I had provided.

One thing that my intelligence on the Zips and heroin smuggling had helped produce, was a shift in FBI policy. From the beginning, the FBI avoided narcotics investigations. Drug investigations were the turf of local police departments and of other federal agencies such as the DEA. Hoover was convinced that narcotics could be a corrupting influence on his agents. In January 1982, President Reagan reversed the Bureau's longstanding policy and announced that he had ordered the FBI to begin to take an active and leading role in the War on Drugs that Nixon had announced a little over ten years earlier.

Ten months later, in October 1982, President Reagan took the next logical step and gave a speech declaring an all-out federal effort against the Mafia. Jules, working out of Headquarters, had helped President Reagan develop the plan of attack that the president announced that day in October. No doubt the plan and the speech were encouraged by our first RICO victory in the Bonanno family trial two months prior to the speech. Part of the president's speech sounded like my undercover job description.

"Today," the president said, "the power of organized crime reaches into every segment of our society. It is estimated that the syndicate has millions of dollars in assets in legitimate businesses; it controls corrupt union locals; it runs burglary rings, fences for stolen goods, holds a virtual monopoly on the heroin trade. . . ."

. . .

Connecting a wiretap or planting a bug requires a search warrant. That's the easy part. The warrant must have a sworn affidavit attached to it setting forth the facts that constitute probable cause for the issuance of the warrant by a judge. That's the hard part.

Over the past forty years or so, the appeals courts have played with the definition of probable cause. Basically, while this is an over-simplification, an agent needs to set forth in the sworn affidavit enough facts that would allow him to arrest someone, but instead, he wants to listen in to get more evidence to support his arrest. You can't just tap a phone or install a bug merely because you have a strong suspicion of wrongdoing or you have a cop's hunch that you're dealing with bad guys who are doing bad things on the phone or in the place being bugged.

The beauty of a RICO crime is that it allowed for a new concept of "dynamic probable cause," because the crime was now the crime of being part of a criminal enterprise and not merely of committing a particular crime. Still, probable cause is never easy, and agents rely on prosecutors to steer the words in the affidavits through the tangled web of court rulings. Navigating the tangle of red tape necessary to get approval for phone wiretaps and premises bugs was never more fruitful than in the Pizza Connection Case. In this case, taps and bugs were approved and installed in pizza places throughout the northeastern part of the United States out to Chicago; in phone booths that were used by the smugglers and dealers to communicate; in import-export businesses where the goods were moved; and in other related businesses. After the electronics experts in the Bureau were finished tape-recording conversations for the Pizza Connection Case, they had enough taped conversations to play continuously for five and a half years.

The overwhelming number of these conversations was in the Sicilian dialect, which is almost a different language from Italian. The Bureau had four agents who spoke Sicilian and specialized in the Sicilian Mafia. They were under Carmine Russo, and they had to listen to every word on every tape and translate them into English. Additional interviews were conducted in Europe, and Carmine had to be present at every interview. Interrogations were conducted in Italy by the Italian investigators who were cooperating in the building of the case. Carmine had to be present for every interrogation.

When the indictment was handed down in 1984, there were 35 defendants from both sides of the Atlantic Ocean charged with smuggling $1.65 billion worth of heroin into America from 1975 to 1984. Remember, a billion dollars was a far more astonishing amount of money in those days than it is today. Using stockbrokers, they sent money back to the heroin suppliers in Sicily through banks in Switzerland. By the time the case went to trial in October 1985, the list of defendants had been pared down to 23. Then in February 1986, one died of lung cancer, and on the next day of trial, there were 22 defendants.

Cesare Bonventre had been one of the 35 indicted, but he was not among the 23 defendants to start the trial. Instead, shortly after the indictment and a year before the trial began, Cesare was whacked. Switching sides at the last minute to go with wherever you think the power lies can work in the Mafia, but only for a while. Sooner or later your pals begin to realize that you are not really a stand-up guy. They suspect that you are a one-way guy, too big for your britches, and when your character is tested by an indictment you might switch sides and turn against them. Within a week after he disappeared, Cesare's body was discovered cut up into three parts in three separate barrels at a glue factory in New Jersey.

This was a RICO indictment with a cast of defendants with Sicilian last names, some of whom had never met each other. Would the jury understand that a RICO violation is the crime of conspiracy, and that the essence of RICO is that as long as each defendant is a member of the criminal enterprise and has committed specific crimes to further that enterprise, it doesn't matter whether a particular defendant is connected to some other defendant's particular crime or even knows that the other defendant has committed a particular crime? One defendant might be engaged merely in money laundering, while another might be murdering; as long as they are both intentionally acting to further the aims of the enterprise, they're guilty of the same RICO crime.

The lead prosecutor was my old friend Louis Freeh. Along with him were the well-regarded crime fighters Robert Stewart, who was brought in from New Jersey, Andrew McCarthy, Richard Martin, and Robert Bucknam.

Because some of the defendants had two attorneys, there were 24 defense attorneys sitting with their clients at four long tables. The principal defense attorneys were Michael Kennedy, who had a national reputation, and Ivan Fisher, a New York attorney who years earlier had been retained by writer Norman Mailer to secure the release of convicted rapist and jailhouse writer Jack Abbott, a Mailer literary protégé. Much to Fisher and Mailer's discredit, a few months after they sprung Abbott, he flew off the handle in a Greenwich Village restaurant and knifed another patron to death.

Michael Kennedy represented the 62-year-old kingpin of the Sicilian faction, Gaetano Badalamenti. Ivan Fisher represented the 44-year-old kingpin of the American Zips, Toto Catalano. These two defendants were the principal focus of the prosecution's case.

The judge was Pierre Leval, a former United States Attorney in the days before RICO. Early in the trial, Judge Leval made a ruling that would permit at least part of my testimony to be heard by the jury. He ruled, "I have been persuaded by the government's argument that the existence of the Mafia—and its structure and its rules—is integrally a part of the conspiracy charged, concerning trafficking in heroin and cocaine." The other major part of my testimony dealt with the hit on Carmine Galante, but the judge's ruling on that would come later, just before I took the witness stand.

There was an isolation booth for translators, and the Sicilians who did not speak English wore headphones and heard the witnesses through simultaneous translation, like at the U.N.

Jury selection began on September 30, 1985. There were twelve jurors selected, and twelve alternate jurors selected to take the place of any jurors who dropped out along the way. They were informed that their names were not going to be released to either side in the trial, nor to the media. They were not told the true reason for their anonymity, but this was to be an anonymous jury for their own safety and to prevent bribery attempts, or worse. Judge Leval told the jurors that the trial would take six months of their lives. He was wrong by nearly a full year. During the trial, despite the anonymity of the jury, one of the jurors had to be excused because her daughter had received a threatening phone call.

I once remarked in an interview that the trial itself was a circus. What I meant was that the defense attorneys made it a circus by their explosive arguments during recesses. They had their own conference room, but even with the door shut you could stand in the hallway and hear them screaming at each other. They argued over tactics and over who was betraying whom. It was dog-eat-dog. One lawyer's defense of his client often undermined another lawyer's.

During the long ordeal of the trial, it became obvious that a rift had developed between the Knickerbocker Avenue Zips headed by Toto Catalano, and the Sicilian faction headed by Gaetano Badalamenti.

With three months of trial left to go, one of the Knickerbocker Avenue Zip defendants, Tommy Mazzara, was found wrapped in two plastic garbage bags in the gutter in Greenpoint, Brooklyn, two miles from Knickerbocker Avenue. There were two bullets in his head and his body had been mutilated as if with a meat cleaver.

A week after that, bullets struck Gaetano Badalamenti's nephew, the defendant Pietro Alfano, and an innocent bystander on a street in Greenwich Village. Alfano was the owner of a pizza parlor in Oregon, Illinois, a tiny town of about 3,800 lying 100 miles west of Chicago. At the time he was arrested on the indictment in April 1984, agents found an arsenal of weapons including submachine guns in his house and garage. Nevertheless, Alfano was out on bail during the trial. On the night he got shot, Alfano was shopping with his wife on the Avenue of the Americas near West Ninth Street. Alfano had just left the Italian gourmet delicatessen, Balducci's, carrying a bag of Italian bread, cheeses, and salami. Two men approached him from behind. One stuck a .38 caliber gun in the small of Alfano's back and fired three quick rounds. Bang, bang, bang. One bullet struck his spine. It permanently paralyzed him from the waist down. Another bullet passed through his body and lodged in the thigh of a passerby, a transit worker named Ronald Price.

The Bureau had had Alfano under physical surveillance for the first few days following Tommy Mazzara's murder. In the course of following Alfano they noticed a Cadillac that also seemed to be following Alfano. They jotted down the license number. Later, when Alfano was shot, they worked backward from the license-plate number and solved the hit in no time. Three Brooklyn wannabes had been paid $40,000 to hit Alfano—$10,000 each and $10,000 for expenses.

Six days after Alfano's shooting, the FBI arrested multimillionaire supermarket tycoon Patsy Conte, Sr. for the murder-for-hire of Alfano. Conte owned twelve Conte's Supermarkets and was a director on the board of the Key Food chain of seventy-eight supermarkets sprinkled through the five boroughs of New York. Conte, a known heroin trafficker, was an ally of Toto Catalano. Conte refused to answer any questions. Unfortunately, down the road, the charges against Conte had to be dropped when the informants' memories took a nosedive.

• • •

The trial itself began on October 24, 1985 and took seventeen months to reach a verdict. When it was over, it had generated 41,000 transcript pages of testimony from over 275 witnesses. Each prosecution witness was vigorously cross-examined, and each defense attorney had the right to participate in the cross-examination. The 24 jurors had to pay attention and sit like prisoners through every second of it.

Both the devil and the angel were in the details, and the jury was expected to remember it all. And they were expected to be able to deliberate and consider the evidence as to whether it applied or did not apply to each defendant as if there were 22 separate trials.

The principal witnesses were turncoats and me.

Tomasso Buscetta of Sicily, a lifelong friend of Gaetano Badalamenti, was the highest-ranking Sicilian Mafioso ever to turn. Almost a year and a half before the jury began deliberating, Buscetta was the first witness called by the prosecution. His testimony was "criminal enterprise" testimony. Buscetta told the jury that in 1957 he was present at a high-level meeting in Palermo, Sicily. He testified that among those present at the meeting were the defendant Gaetano Badalamenti, who was at that time the boss of the Sicilian Mafia; Lucky Luciano, the drug trafficker and American Mafioso who created the Commission in 1931 and who had been deported to Italy after the war; Bonanno underboss Carmine Galante; and his boss, Joe Bananas Bonanno. Buscetta testified that in 1959, at the suggestion of Joe Bananas, the Sicilian Mafia set up their own Commission patterned after the American Mafia Commission. Buscetta testified that a Mafioso in Sicily, Saca Catalano, told him that his cousin Toto Catalano was a capo in the Bonanno family in America under Joe Bananas. Buscetta said that he had turned on the Mafia out of concern for his family's safety. He did not tell the jury that rivals in the Sicilian Mafia had killed several members of his family, including two of his sons.

Buscetta was in the Witness Protection Program, one of the powerful new law and order tools that were created in 1970 at the time of the passage of the RICO statute. Buscetta was amazed at how he could be protected in this program in America, still the land of opportunity. Basically, the Program is used as an incentive to get convicted wiseguys to turn and testify against other criminals. For their cooperation they get reduced sentences and then are placed with their families in a community far away where they have to make a new life for themselves as ordinary citizens. The Program—administered by federal U.S. Marshals who keep these guys in check—has been an invaluable tool in getting the goods on countless criminals in order to put them away.

Salvatore Contorno, a former member of the Sicilian Mafia, was the next witness. Contorno testified that he had been arrested in Italy on narcotics charges and began cooperating to lessen his punishment.

As far as I could ever tell, the only family that made a serious effort to outlaw narcotics trafficking was the Chicago outfit. Their fear was that narcotics arrests, carrying severe penalties, would create rats and jeopardize their lucrative gambling, labor, and extortion rackets, and their share of the Las Vegas skim. At the other extreme, the Bonanno family and John Gotti's crew in the Gambino family practically specialized in narcotics. The rest of the bosses did the occasional narcotics deal or looked the other way when narcotics money flowed upstream, pretending not to know where the money came from.

Badalamenti and Catalano were able to operate pizza parlors as fronts for heroin smuggling in Chicago's territory, in part I believe, because the Chicago outfit did not traffic in narcotics. Salvatore Contorno, as he put his hand on the Bible, was a poster boy for the Chicago outfit's ban against narcotics.

Contorno testified that in February 1980 he attended a meeting in a house in a lemon grove in Bagheria, Sicily. Toto Catalano and Tommy Mazzara (the defendant later found in the gutter in Greenpoint) were also in attendance. The purpose of the meeting was to test the purity of a shipment of heroin bound for America.

Cuts and dots had been put on the bags containing the heroin. Contorno explained, "The envelopes had markings in order to avoid arguments. . . . They were particular markings so that the merchandise could not be confused. . . . The goods that we had seen in Bagheria had been lost, had been seized in Milan. . . . The police had seized it in Milan."

Contorno testified that a cousin of one of the defendants had offered him an opportunity to invest in the defendant's heroin smuggling operation. "He had pizza parlors here in America as a front, and there would be no problem in shipping the goods to America because he was a man of honor, as we were."

Did Contorno invest? "No," he explained. "I had no money."

Of course not, he was a soldier.

• • •

On December 17, 1985, in the second month of the trial, Judge Pierre Leval summoned the jury into his courtroom and addressed remarks to them, saying, "Some of you may be aware that yesterday in New York City, a defendant in another trial in this courthouse was killed on the streets of the city. There has been so much publicity; it will come to your attention, if it hasn't already. So now let me repeat something I have said to you many times before: Do not allow yourselves to be exposed to any publicity. There are certain to be many articles. Do not read or watch TV. Second, the events of yesterday have absolutely nothing to do with the case before you. There is no conceivable connection. Anyone have a problem with that? All right. Let's proceed."

On the evening before, at 5:15 p.m., the boss of bosses, 69-year-old Big Paul

Castellano, and his right-hand man Tommy Bilotti had been whacked getting out of their Lincoln in front of Sparks Steakhouse on 46th Street in Manhattan.

At the time, Big Paul was a defendant in a Gambino family RICO trial involving a stolen-car ring. I didn't testify in that case, but my intelligence helped establish probable cause for the bug in Big Paul's White House. If our jury knew what was going on in that courtroom they would have demanded a transfer. The star witness in that trial was Vic Arena, "the gay hit man." In exchange for his cooperation, Vic wanted his gay jailhouse lover to be put in the cell next to his, and he wanted Rudy Giuliani's office to treat him to a face-lift.

• • •

Nothing for nothing, but things in our courtroom were about to get at least a little more colorful with the next witness. Luigi Ronsisvalle, 47 years old, came to Knickerbocker Avenue in 1966 at the age of 26 armed with a letter of recommendation to the Bonanno family from the Sicilian Mafia in his native Catania, and possessing a fourth-grade education.

Luigi confessed to 13 murders the way you or I might confess to having eaten the last slice of cake in the refrigerator. His first slice of cake was at 18 in Sicily. His last slice was the 1979 pay-for-hire shooting of a restaurant chef who had allegedly raped a Brooklyn father's 14-year-old daughter. The girl's father had gone to the Mafia instead of the criminal justice system seeking the death penalty to avenge his child. Luigi walked into the restaurant and asked to see the chef. The chef said, "That's me," and Luigi blew him away on the spot.

Luigi explained his hits to the jury in English with a heavy Italian accent. "That was a job. It had nothing to do with destroying people. . . . If you give me $30,000 to kill a person, *you* kill him, not me."

Pressed further about the 13 hits, Luigi explained further: "I'm-a no kill. I'm-a the messenger. The bullet kill. I'm-a just-a the messenger."

I got to know Luigi during preparation for the trial. For some reason, he liked me a lot. He was nearly six feet, round and balding with glasses. He was a character and could make people laugh, but there was a dangerous edge to him. Everybody was afraid of him. We had a blue suit made for him to testify in, and the tailor was scared to death of him. "Where's the red handkerchief?" Luigi wanted to know, pointing to the pocket on the suit jacket. He was a hell of a cook, too. He came in one day with a delicious birthday cake he had made for Louis Freeh's birthday.

One morning the cross-examination droned on and on. Finally, close to one o'clock, Luigi turned to Judge Pierre Leval and asked, "How about lunch, your honor?" The jury exploded with laughter.

Luigi educated the jury on the art of transporting heroin through airports. He was always the last one to board the plane. He carried a garment bag to cover the bulge created by the two kilos of heroin taped to his body. About fifteen times he had been paid $5,000 a trip to drive 80-pound shipments from the Bonanno family in Brooklyn to the Gambino family in Manhattan. About fifteen times he availed himself of the Amtrak system to deliver 40-pound loads to pizza parlors in Chicago, again for the standard fee of $5,000.

Luigi recalled for the jury that in 1978 he and another Zip had driven 220 pounds of heroin from Miami Beach to Knickerbocker Avenue in the trunk of a red Porsche. Actually, Luigi the killer's role was to guard the heroin with his pistola and shotgun. They were met on Knickerbocker Avenue by Toto Catalano, who went into the Café del Viale and walked out with another Zip who immediately took possession of the red Porsche and its load of heroin, and drove it away.

Regarding the Zip who had driven the red Porsche from Miami Beach, Luigi testified that, before the trip, in a conversation in a café with Toto Catalano in attendance, "He say, 'Luigi, you know the pipe from Canada with the oil. Well we got the same thing, from Sicily, with *heroina*.'"

Luigi explained to the jury his motivation for initially turning himself in and cooperating in 1979, long before there was even a remote thought of a Pizza Connection Case happening some day.

Luigi had been hired by the crooked Italian financier Michelle Sindona to frighten a Wall Street figure into not testifying against Sindona. In true Sicilian Mafia fashion, Sindona had also offered Luigi $100,000 to whack the United States Attorney running the case against Sindona, John Kenney. Before he could whack anybody, Luigi got arrested for an attempted purse-snatching robbery. Luigi contacted Sindona's right-hand man for $30,000 to help him with the robbery charge, and when Sindona refused, Luigi decided to fix him. Anger, resentment, and revenge became more important to Luigi than anything else. Luigi turned himself in and implicated himself in the 1979 murder of the suspected child rapist, even though nobody suspected Luigi. For the murder, he was sentenced to five to 15 years. But it was all worth it because Luigi got an opportunity to turn state's evidence against Sindona and expose his efforts to intimidate the Wall Street witness and conspire to murder the prosecutor.

Two months after Luigi testified to all of this in the Pizza Connection Case in Manhattan, somebody poisoned Michelle Sindona in his jail cell in Italy. Someone higher than Sindona obviously suspected that Sindona might be sensing that his goose was truly cooked and he needed silencing before he could follow the lead of Luigi.

. . .

Then came my turn. But first the judge had to rule on whether I could testify about the predicate crime of the murder of Carmine Galante in 1979 in this heroin-smuggling RICO case. In his opening statement months earlier, Assistant United States Attorney Robert Stewart had described the murder to the jury and detailed the involvement of Baldo Amato and Toto Catalano in the hit.

Before recessing for the day, Judge Pierre Leval ruled that it would be prejudicial to allow me to mention the hit on the three capos, or anything pertaining to the importation of Zips to pizza parlors for the purpose of trafficking in heroin.

Overnight, Judge Leval considered the legal challenge to that part of my testimony concerning the Galante hit, and ruled that I could not mention that, either. The judge's reasoning was that the Galante hit was not in any way in furtherance of the heroin smuggling conspiracy, but was Mafia politics and the result of an internal Bonanno family power struggle. Obviously, Louis Freeh and Robert Stewart and the rest of the prosecutors disagreed, or they would not have included the Galante hit as a predicate crime in the narcotics conspiracy charge. I certainly disagreed, but I had no say.

If I'd had a chance to address Judge Leval, I would have told him that, at least in one important way, the motive to whack Galante was clearly in furtherance of the narcotics conspiracy. The Commission considered Galante an illegitimate boss who was greedy and wasn't sharing his narcotics-conspiracy treasure. For the Zips to continue their profitable heroin partnership with the Sicilians back home in the old country, they needed to side with the legitimate boss approved by the Commission, and that was Rusty Rastelli. And the time-honored golden parachute for a boss about to be forcibly retired is a shotgun blast or two. The time-honored method of showing your loyalty to the legitimate boss sanctioned by the Commission is to whack the illegitimate boss yourself. In this case, the deceased heroin-smuggling Zip Cesare Bonventre and his childhood playmate Baldo Amato took active parts in the murders at Joe and Mary's. Toto Catalano, as street boss of the Zips, equally participated in the murder of Galante because it was good for business. In fact, it was essential for the continued success of his heroin business.

At any rate, all I could do was take the stand and do the best I could on the issues I was being called to testify on, namely, the criminal enterprise, the structure of the Mafia, and details of the Bonanno family.

"The Commission," I told the jury, "was the governing body of the Mafia."

And, "Paul Castellano was one of the most powerful men on the Commission in New York City."

Judge Pierre Leval permitted me to testify—without mentioning the Galante hit or the three-capos hit—that there was "friction and tension in the Bonanno family" and that Sonny Black met with Paul Castellano in 1980 after first forming a new alliance with the Zip faction of the Bonanno family, led by Toto Catalano. It was this new alliance that resolved the friction.

The prosecutor showed me a surveillance photo of Tony Mirra and Toto Catalano kissing each other, and asked me, "Agent Pistone, were you ever kissed . . . in this manner?"

"The whole assignment—till 1981," I said, and the jury laughed.

The jury also seemed to be amused when I explained that the entire Mafia shut down for Mother's Day every year. No one was allowed to work on that day.

I later read that Badalamenti's lawyer, Michael Kennedy, said in the hallway that I was one of the bravest men he had ever heard of. He also said about me, "He's pissed off because ninety percent of his testimony was cut out." Kennedy called out to a newspaperman, "I've got your next headline—'Pierre pissed on Pistone.'"

On cross-examination, one of the other defense attorneys started to ask me a question and prefaced it by exaggeratedly referring to "this dangerous task" of infiltrating the Mafia. I jumped in and said, "Yes, it was *very* dangerous," and he steered away from trying to minimize the danger. Then he tried to make Lefty look like an idiot and an exaggerator by asking me, "Do you recall him ever telling you that he had a personal friend whose name was Supreme Court Justice William O. Douglas?"

"I don't know if [Lefty] Ruggiero said that or not," I said. "But someone mentioned it one night. There was a group of us in a night club."

Nothing for nothing, but this was 1986. This was fourteen years after *The Godfather* had won the Academy Award for best picture. Somebody on that jury must have remembered how the Corleone family owned Congressmen and had a United States Senator from Nevada in their pocket. If any of the jurors remembered Justice William O. Douglas, they would have remembered that he had a reputation for always siding with the criminal in every Supreme Court case. He was controversial, and he got headlines for creating more and more rights for criminals in the 1960s. In the last years of his life as a Justice, in the 1970s, he married a 23-year-old girl when he was 65. When that marriage quickly went on the rocks, he married a 22-year-old waitress when he was 68. Then he lied about having served in World War One so he could be buried in Arlington National Cemetery, which was supposed to be reserved for war veterans. He had been in an informal student corps in college, but even that was after the war was already over. Douglas had never served a day in the Army.

The squawking coming from the defense attorney's conference room escalated after that brilliant so-called cross-examination.

On a piece of paper used in connection with the transfer of $1.54 million in cash from "some pizzerias in New York and New Jersey" to Swiss bank accounts, the FBI lifted a latent fingerprint that belonged to the right thumb of Toto Catalano. This evidence came in near the six-month mark, and there was still nearly a year to go.

Wiretaps of long-distance calls were played of Badalamenti and one of the New York Zips. They spoke in an easily penetrated code. They referred to "pure cotton," meaning pure heroin from Sicily; "ten percent acrylic," meaning 90 percent pure heroin; "shirts," meaning cocaine from South America; and "22 parcels," meaning 22 kilograms. Duh.

After the government rested its case at the one-year mark, Badalamenti's lawyer moved for a mistrial on the grounds that the jury had become "irreparably benumbed."

Failing with that attempt, he called Badalamenti to the stand. Looking like a kindly old uncle, Badalamenti denied dealing drugs and assured the jury that he was a man of honor and dignity whose only interest was to help the downtrodden masses. He said he was the baby among nine children, raised on a family dairy farm. He had a fourth-grade education and had fought in the Italian Army before deserting in 1943 when the Americans invaded Sicily. He came to America illegally after the war and worked in his brother's grocery store in Michigan until he was deported. He claimed that his only crime was to smuggle tobacco into Sicily.

On cross-examination he defied the judge and the jury and refused to answer a single question regarding the Mafia or his membership in the Mafia. Judge Pierre Leval threatened Badalamenti with contempt of court, but he remained silent. He was taking a shot. If the jury bought his man-of-dignity nonsense, he might win the case. If he lost the case, another six months for contempt of court would be meaningless.

Badalamenti believed he was in a win-win situation when he testified and stonewalled on cross-examination. But when the jury came back on March 2, 1987 after a mere six days of deliberation, Badalamenti had lost-lost.

Of all the defendants that were left, the only one to get a complete acquittal was Badalamenti's son, Vito, a minor figure. But Vito stayed in jail pending his deportation. Two other equally minor defendants had copped pleas during the trial.

Badalamenti and Catalano got 45 years each. Under the terms of his extradition agreement, Badalamenti would serve no more than 30. Ringleaders a notch below kingpin got either 30, 25, 20, or 15 years each. Alfano, in his wheelchair, got 15 years. Lesser Zips got sentences between one and 12 years. The Zip that got one year did less time than the jury.

Judge Leval applied the federal restitution law in a unique way. The judge ruled that the kingpins were responsible for injuring countless drug addicts during the years of the narcotics conspiracy, from 1975 to 1984. Following this logic, he ordered restitution in the millions to be paid to a fund for the rehabilitation of drug addicts. A total of $3.3 million in restitution was to be paid by eight of the bigger and more prosperous players in the Pizza Connection Case. Toto Catalano alone was ordered to pay a million in restitution, on top of a $1.5 million fine.

. . .

The sentencings were in June 1987. Twenty-one months had passed since jury selection began in September 1985.

Rudy Giuliani said, "No one case can result in a massive destruction of the Mafia. However, the momentum is building."

On September 28, 1987, two days shy of the two-year anniversary of the start of jury selection, a long article appeared in the *New York Times* that cast doubt on whether Toto Catalano would ever be required to pay his restitution and his fine, and whether he would remain imprisoned in Leavenworth.

Times reporter Ralph Blumenthal wrote that Toto Catalano's lawyer, Ivan Fisher, had contacted him and asked him to attend a meeting in a Holiday Inn near Cincinnati, Ohio with Luigi Ronsisvalle. Luigi had dropped out of the Witness Protection Program and wanted to talk to Ivan Fisher, and Ivan Fisher wanted an unimpeachable witness at any such meeting. Blumenthal attended and tape-recorded the entire meeting. A few days later, on September 22nd, a second meeting was held in the motel.

Luigi recanted his trial testimony that implicated Toto Catalano in the receiving of 220 pounds of heroin in the trunk of a red Porsche on Knickerbocker Avenue. Luigi recanted his testimony that Catalano was present for the conversation about the pipeline "from Sicily, with *heroina*."

Luigi, as if singing an aria, said to Toto Catalano's lawyer, "Mr. Fisher, I want you, please, from the bottom of my heart, I want you to accept my apology for what I done to Toto Catalano. I swear to God, I feel so bad, I feel like crying."

Luigi continued, "I got three daughters. God is my witness. If I lie to you now, may my daughters drop dead with the worst things God can give to human beings. I'm swearing to you on my three daughters."

As for Catalano, Luigi said, "Somehow I put him in the middle, I don't know how. I'm trying to give it to you straight, but he's not there. I don't know what happened. Somehow the guy pops out on the corner."

Luigi explained how it happened. "It sound like they washing my brain. They not telling me this is what you got to say, but the way they were talking, it sounds like that is what they would like."

"And while they were talking I put two and two together," Luigi added. "I live like a dog because I can't take what I did in this court—a liar." Luigi said he was so upset by the lies he told that he had to drink a bottle of scotch every night to get to sleep.

When Ivan Fisher announced he would seek a new trial based on Luigi's changed testimony, Rudy Giuliani, who had supervised the trial, said his office would oppose the motion. Rudy said, "There was an overwhelming amount of testimony against him."

Louis Freeh said, "Had Ronsisvalle not testified, it would have made absolutely no difference. There were numerous other witnesses who convicted him." In the law, this is called "harmless error"—it wouldn't have mattered. It may not be the strongest position to take, but it was the only position available under the circumstances. The prosecutors, however, had to worry that they were already saddled with the harmless error from all the prosecution talk about Catalano's involvement in the Galante hit in the two months before Judge Pierre Leval had ruled the Galante hit out of the case. You can only pile on so much harmless error before you get a reversal.

Blumenthal was objective and candid in his article, reporting that he had no way of knowing if any conversations had taken place between Luigi and Fisher prior to the first meeting he attended. Blumenthal also reported the many references Luigi made to wanting Ivan Fisher to supply him money.

Luigi rubbed his fingertips together and said, "You still not talking about them goddamn things."

To pay for the motel room and expenses for Luigi to visit his daughters, Ivan Fisher gave Luigi $2,620. "Okay," Luigi said. "This is not buying me. Like I told you, I have to see my daughters." And then, squeezing the last nickel, Luigi said, "You no think Mr. Toto Catalano after say thank you, send me a few dollars someplace, buy a pack of cigarettes?"

Luigi switched subjects to another demand. "You got to guarantee for my life.

. . . Because once we are having some kind of business, your client don't want me to drop dead now."

"I no gonna have no six months life. I tell you that."

When Ivan Fisher asked Luigi why he was willing to expose himself to a perjury indictment, Luigi said, "How I got to speak? In Chinese? In Japanese? What kind-a language? You understand a man who can't swallow some things? You forget one point: in 1979 I give up myself because I can't take no more of that goddamn life."

Five days later, on October 3, 1987, Ralph Blumenthal wrote another article in the *New York Times* under the headline: WITNESS IN MOB "PIZZA" TRIAL SAYS HE LIED IN RECANTING.

Ah, life with Luigi. In court, when pleading guilty to his feeble attempt at obstructing justice, Luigi explained, "About three weeks ago some people approached me saying where my family are, my daughters are, the names, the town. In my own language, in Sicilian. And they ask me after 30, 35 minutes of speaking to me, to call a Mr. Ivan Fisher and tell him I was wrong in two points of my witness, and I said okay because I know my kids, now they are under shotgun or whatever. . . . I know at the moment I was doing something wrong, but I have pressure because my family was in danger. People were watching."

On October 15, 1989, four years after the first day of the trial, the federal appeals court in Manhattan upheld the heroin smuggling RICO verdicts, with the exception of one count regarding one of the Zips. This reduced his sentence from twenty-five years to twenty years. The conviction of the Zip who had received a one-year sentence was completely overturned, but he had long ago served his full sentence. Sadly, the appellate judges knocked out the $3.3 million in restitution Judge Pierre Leval had ordered to be paid by eight defendants to a fund for the treatment of drug addicts. While it was a great idea that the public liked, it was an idea that could never be used again based on this precedent.

At the same time the Pizza Connection Case was in trial, the fearless Italian anti-Mafia crusader Giovanni Falcone was conducting the "Maxi Trial" of Mafiosi in Palermo, Sicily, from 1986 to 1987. Falcone and Rudy Giuliani praised and encouraged each other. Falcone's efforts led to the conviction of 338 Mafiosi, including the Sicilian Boss of Bosses, Salvatore Riina. Tragically, Riina went into hiding and from his underground quarters plotted revenge. Five years later, on May 23, 1992, Falcone, his wife, and three police bodyguards were blown up and killed by a powerful bomb hidden under a bridge over which their car was traveling.

Two months after that, in July 1992, a bomb in Palermo killed Falcone's protégé and replacement, the new chief anti-Mafia prosecutor in Italy, the brave Paolo Borsellino, along with five others. Borsellino had just driven up to his mother's house when the explosives were ignited. Borsellino was literally blown to bits and his body was never found.

In a very short period of time, many more were added to the list of "the honest dead" in Italy and Sicily, including the two chief investigators who handled the Italian end of the Pizza Connection Case investigation, Cesare Terranova and Boris Giuliano.

Twenty years after his arrest and extradition in the Pizza Connection Case, Gaetano Badalamenti, who had spent most of his 30-year sentence in the worst of the Federal prisons—the underground tomblike pen in Marion, Illinois—died on May 3, 2004 at the age of 80 in an American prison hospital.

Over the years, Luigi called me from time to time. He was a severe alcoholic and very depressed. I was a sounding board. They had him in the Witness Protection Program in someplace like South Carolina. He was out of his element. Every so often during one of these calls he would ask for a "loan of $500." I was doing well with the book and the movie, so I'd send him some of "them goddamn things." Alcohol is a depressant, and as his disease progressed Luigi got more depressed. A few years ago, Luigi committed suicide.

CHAPTER 11
SOUTHERN DISCOMFORT

IN THE EARLY EIGHTIES the work itself was spectacular. I loved being an FBI agent and I loved doing the particular work I was doing in the FBI. We had set lofty goals for ourselves and we were pursuing those goals as a team. But at least one important person I had to deal with in the Bureau's hierarchy was not cheering us on.

We had so many things going on at once that it was often hard to keep track. During the time that members of Rudy Giuliani's crew were working with the FBI and the Italian government on putting together the Pizza Connection Case, another part of Rudy's office was working with supervisory special agent Lin DeVecchio of the FBI, case agent Pat Marshall, the NYPD, and the New York State Organized Crime Task Force to put together the dream case—the Mafia Commission Case—that Jules and I had nurtured a couple of years before I came out in 1981. The goal behind the Mafia Commission Case was to indict and convict the bosses of all five New York City families in one trial and send them away to die in prison.

Over the years there has been some discussion about whose idea it was and when it was hatched. I know that Jules and I talked about it early on, and he and Jimmy Kossler talked about it with the man they called their *consigliere*, the author of the RICO statute, Bob Blakey. Blakey's law was invented for the sole purpose of destroying the Mafia. The 1970 passage by Congress of the Witness Protection Program and RICO created a one-two combination punch. The Witness

Protection Program was designed to trap as many rats as possible and then use them, like Luigi, with all their baggage, in RICO prosecutions. If Witness Protection was the setup, RICO was the knockout punch.

I like to think that the Mafia Commission Case was such a logical strategy that many minds could have "originated" the idea. In fact, Big Paul Castellano came up with the idea on his own in 1983. Big Paul was picked up on a bug in the White House, two years before the indictment, predicting that all the bosses soon would be charged "in one tremendous conspiracy."

Whoever thought of it first, it was Rudy Giuliani who understood the strategy instantly and got the necessary approvals from FBI Headquarters to mobilize manpower and make it a reality.

The strategy to convict all the bosses and send them away forever was intended to have far-reaching consequences, more consequences even than adding to the momentum that was starting to swing our way, as Rudy had publicly stated. The strategy was to kill the snake by cutting off its head. The strategy was intended to, in time, kill off the entire Mafia.

From my experience with how these people think, I came to believe that the primary purpose of the organized crime syndicate's Commission that Lucky Luciano and his pals created in 1931 was to insulate and perpetuate the bosses at the top. Without a Commission to protect themselves, bosses would be forever walking around with little bull's-eyes pinned to the backs of their heads. On their backs like "Kick Me" signs would be "Shoot Me and Take Over" signs. Who would want to assume such a vulnerable position?

It was our strategy to pin targets back on the bosses, not on the backs of their heads for two shots behind the ear, but rather on their faces for the taking of mug shots. Get the bosses. Without bosses there would be no leadership, and without leadership there would be no organization to organized crime.

It was our strategy to send a message downstream. As Lefty said after the Commission sanctioned the hit on Galante, "If they can hit a boss, nobody's immune." Get the bosses, and destroy the illusion of an umbrella of protection for everyone under the bosses.

It was our strategy to create a vacuum at the top. While not rocket scientists, the bosses still were usually the brainiest and the most cunning. Get the bosses and start the brain drain.

While the various pieces that would become the Commission Case were being assembled, the prosecutors and people in the Bureau like Jules and Lin DeVecchio, who was in charge of the investigation, kept me in the loop. The Commission Case began as five separate FBI RICO investigations against each one of the five families. It was called Operation Genus, and I was consulted from time to time to provide intelligence that went into the affidavits of probable cause for wiretaps and bugs, like the one on Big Paul's White House.

When I came out and I wasn't traveling to consult or testify, I did most of my work in a city in the South which will remain confidential.

Because New York was the Grand Central Station of the Mafia, it was decided early on in the Donnie Brasco operation that my family should not live in New York City or in the New York Metropolitan Area, which includes New Jersey, Long Island, Upstate New York, and Connecticut.

About a year and a half after I had gone under, the Bureau gave my wife and me two choices for my family's safe relocation: San Diego or this city in the South. They would move my family, under an assumed name, to either city. They would assign me to the field office in that city, but they would keep me in an apartment in New York City out of which I would continue to do my work as Donnie Brasco in New York, Tampa, Miami, Chicago, Milwaukee, L.A., or wherever events took me. Because the southern city was closer to New York, we chose it. With less travel time my wife and kids could more easily visit our families in New Jersey. And I could come home more frequently, or so we thought.

It looked good on paper, but once I notified the Bureau of our decision and they moved us to a house about 40 miles outside of the city in the South, I was stuck with the decision. What I hadn't figured on was the aggravation the decision would bring my way for the almost ten years I was assigned to that city's FBI field office under the supervisor of that office and the rules by which the FBI operates.

In my book *Donnie Brasco* I was kinder to the Bureau regarding my decision to resign than Jules Bonavolonta was in his book, *The Good Guys*. I wrote that I resigned from the FBI in 1986 to write my book. Jules said I resigned because of the aggravation I was getting from the head of the southern city's field office the whole time I was undercover and the whole time I was testifying. I did resign and write the book. However, using that same legal phrase for causation—the "but for" standard—I have to admit that but for my problems in the field office in the South, my service in the FBI would not have been interrupted by my resignation in 1986, five years shy of qualifying for a pension.

Jules, bless him, didn't pull any punches in his book, so since it's in print anyway I don't mind giving the rest of the story. My southern discomfort made the job I did harder on a daily basis.

Sometimes it takes dramatic events to change established policy in the FBI. Until 1933, Hoover's FBI agents were not allowed to carry guns at all times. That year unarmed agents were gunned down and killed while escorting a prisoner in Kansas City. After that we were trusted with guns.

The SAC (Special Agent in Charge) of the southern field office to which I was assigned did not like undercover operations or undercover agents. He did not like the change in policy that undercover operations represented. I don't know if he was an old-school Hooverite or if he just had his own old-school opinions. But I do know the guy never worked the streets. His only experience with undercover was what he saw on TV: spending money, driving flashy cars, wearing leather jackets, and all the other stereotypical fluff television offered. He believed all undercover agents were slackers because they didn't come in to the office; they didn't sign in and sign out. Of course, he didn't consider that coming into an FBI office, besides being a waste of time, could get you two behind the ear. Many a Mafia soldier was whacked after someone reported seeing them go into or out of an FBI office without telling their boss first.

Not to mention that undercovers, when you think about it, are actually "signed in" 24 hours a day at times. We often work round-the-clock for weeks on end without overtime pay. When my day did end at six in the morning, I didn't go home. I went to my New York apartment or Sonny's apartment, and I was still working. If I got home to my real home three nights in five months, it was a good five months.

What made the SAC's bias more intense was the fact that when an agent is transferred to a field office, the agent goes on that office's books for statistical purposes, like going "on record" with a Mafia crew. And like a Mafia crewmember, the agent is expected to be an "earner," to carry his own weight statistically. But when I arrived, I wasn't producing any stats for the SAC's office. I counted as an agent, but I was not producing any arrests or convictions. In effect, I was watering down and weakening the SAC's statistics when the inspectors came by to evaluate his office.

Hoover had set up a system of periodic inspections that was like a bank audit. Stats were kept on the amount of time an agent spent per criminal case. I wasn't keeping any of that time because I was not working on a specific case. I certainly was not working on any cases out of my own field office since there was no connection between the Bonanno family and that city.

In 1981, when they finally swept everybody up after Donnie Brasco came out, the field office in the South didn't get a single conviction. The SAC got no credit on his office's books for anything I did. And all the time he carried me while I was under, he knew that's exactly what would happen when I came out. In comparison to other field offices, he'd come up empty in the field-office-stats department.

Meanwhile, the Bureau had made no allowance for this supervisor because a long-term undercover operation like this had never been done before. Jules tried to get me on Headquarters' roles, but there was no provision for me to be listed at Headquarters—not even on paper—because I wasn't a supervisor. So I had to stay on that field office's rolls.

While I was working undercover, despite his rumblings and some petty moves, my southern SAC had no efficient way to exercise any real control over me. I was in New York or wherever, but not in my own field office in the South. However, once I became a witness and consultant on cases, and had a chance to be home in my own field office's territory near my family, the S.O.B. SAC vigorously campaigned to assert his dominion and control over me—even though I was actually working for various prosecutors and field offices around the country at the same time.

To facilitate my trial preparation and their trial preparation, the prosecutors and Jules installed another phone line in our home. They wanted me available at all times to answer questions of prosecutors and other FBI agents. They installed state-of-the-art electronic equipment for me to review the hours and hours of seemingly endless tapes of bugs and wiretaps, almost all of which I had never heard before. In a sense, while I was strategizing and preparing for my own testimony by reading mounds and mounds of material and listening to tapes, I was a glorified translator of Mafia code talk for the Bureau.

I was on the phone all the time with prosecutors and FBI field offices. I was basically working out of my house if I wasn't traveling. And I wasn't dealing with just one federal district and the personalities of those in that district; I was dealing with many districts at once—Milwaukee, two districts in New York, and two districts in Florida. Plus I was on the phone with districts in Los Angeles, Detroit, Chicago, and elsewhere. Everyone wanted to better understand the cases they had by understanding the structure and rules of the Mafia and the ways of the wiseguys they were prosecuting. In many cases, I knew important details about defendants from snippets of conversations I had picked up in the course of six years. Despite the lawyer jokes, prosecutors are honest and dedicated, but they are not all alike. Some got it quickly, some needed handholding, and some needed convincing, especially about RICO. I also spent a lot of time at the United States Marine Corps training camp at Quantico, Virginia, the site of the FBI's training academy, giving lectures on the Mafia and on undercover work.

Meanwhile, my SAC was constantly bitching to the Bureau about me. I don't know why, because if I said I was home, I was always home. Still, he would often call my house to make sure I was there. One time, my wife told him off. He would ask my buddies in the field office whether I was actually working when I was at home. As if I would jeopardize the tough undercover work I did by slacking in my trial preparation or by failing to continue striving toward the goals and the unfinished business of the Donnie Brasco operation.

His direct bitching to the Bureau at Headquarters went on for years and years, both while I was undercover and during the strategizing and the legal and educational phases of the operation.

Unfortunately for me, there was little I or Jules or his supervisor Sean McWeeney, the head of Organized Crime for the Bureau, could do about it. A Special Agent in Charge is like a general in the military. There are four-star generals at Headquarters, and the SAC of a field office is like a one-star general. But they are all generals, and a general will not go against another general, right or wrong. As Lefty had explained to me about a made man, "When you're not a wiseguy, the wiseguy is always right and you're always wrong. It don't matter what. Don't forget that, Donnie. Because no other wiseguy is going to side with you against another wiseguy."

Finally, after the bitching went on for years, the SAC convinced the Bureau that I should come into the field office every day. He gave me an office right near his so he could watch me. I had my phone, my electronic equipment, and my paperwork sent to the office. I had to drive 40 miles each way so he could watch me work.

But still he wasn't satisfied. One day I went to lunch and when I came back a buddy of mine greeted me.

"The boss was looking for you," my buddy said. "I told him you went out to lunch. He said to me, 'Why did Pistone go out to lunch if there's a contract on his head?' I told him because it was lunch time, I guess."

One time I had to go to New York to meet with Barbara Jones and Louis Freeh, and then south to Quantico, Virginia to give a lecture. In the back of the lecture room I spotted a supervisor from my home field office who, I assumed, was getting his in-service training. After my talk I said to him, "Nice of you to come, I really appreciate it."

"Joe," the supervisor said, "I've got to be honest with you. The boss told me to come here to make sure you were here."

I played varsity sports. My wife was a cheerleader. Cheerleading really can work; the old home-court advantage from a crowd on your side. The reverse is also true. Naysayers can drain your morale. I vowed I would not let this guy get to me.

He was the one who tried to make waves when I was accused of stealing $250,000 by a defense attorney in the Bonanno family trial. I don't know how he found out, but he started asking my friend Jimmy about the new car my wife had bought. "You got a problem with Joe, ask him," Jimmy said. When he tried to get an investigation out of Headquarters, Jules stepped in and stopped him.

Can you imagine the trouble for all my cases—past, present, and future—if the FBI had launched an investigation of my integrity? And I'm not just talking about the headache he was causing me; this wrongheaded supervisor with a grudge could have ruined all our work by undermining my trustworthiness as a witness. I was not going to let anything stand in the way of our getting the Commission.

During a holiday break in a New York court case, I was back in my office in the South going over testimony and preparing on the phone with Barbara Jones when an agent walked in.

"We got a wiretap at Huntsville Prison," he said. "You're on Saturday."

That meant that I had been scheduled to sit in a van with headphones on listening in on a wiretap regarding an investigation into alleged corruption at a large Texas prison.

"Who gave you the authority to put me on a wiretap?" I asked.

"Joe, it's not me," the agent said. "He put you on."

The agent didn't have to tell me who "he" was.

"I ain't going on the schedule," I said.

I headed straight for his office. He was there behind his desk. I didn't sit down.

"You put me on the schedule at Huntsville?" I said.

"That's right. You're on and you're going."

"I'm not going."

"What do you mean you're not going?"

"I'm not going. I'm in the middle of a major case and you know it."

"You're being insubordinate."

"I'm using my head, which you're not."

He picked up the phone. "I'm going to have you fired," he said.

"Go ahead," I said. "Like the Bureau's going to fire me in the middle of all this."

"I want you fired. I'll have your job. You undercovers aren't really agents."

"I'm a better agent than you are, ever were, or ever will be. It's bad enough when you question my integrity. Don't you ever question my ability as an agent. I'll throw you out this window."

He saw my eyes and put the phone down and didn't say anything.

"I'm not going on the wiretap," I said and walked out of his office and back to mine.

The phone rings. It's Jules.

"Joe, come to New York," Jules said, and that's all he said, but I knew why. I was being sent for. Like in the Mafia, when they send for you, you don't question. You just go.

Meanwhile, I'm still in trial. On the plane I had to read transcripts I could have been reading at home. Just when I got a break and got a chance to be with my family in the South, here I was flying back to New York. In New York I sat down with Barbara Jones, Louis Freeh, and Jules.

"I'm fucking quitting right now," I said. "If the Bureau can't keep this guy from breaking my balls I'm quitting."

"Let's talk to Rudy," Barbara said.

We went into Rudy's office and we filled him in. Rudy picked up the phone and called FBI Director William Webster, the only man to ever head both the FBI and the CIA.

Rudy ran the entire story by Webster and I was assured that I would be left alone from now on to do the work that I had been assigned to do by the Department of Justice itself. I was really in no position to quit, anyway, because I did not have 20 years in to qualify for a pension.

Things did cool down a bit after that, but he couldn't help himself. The nit-picking never went away entirely, and over time it gradually increased again.

I tried to stay focused on the glass being way more than half full. We got an indictment on the Mafia Commission Case. We had a trial date and we were working with a missionary zeal.

I was getting offers on the book and I knew there was plenty more work ahead for me. My testimony was coming up in the Commission Case and I viewed it as the most significant moment of my career. I wanted to be fresh as a daisy for it. I knew I needed a break. I especially needed a break from the petty aggravation in my field office. I didn't want to be in any kind of grumpy mood on the stand. I decided to take a little time off and go on leave.

I filled out a CBR, which means "Can Be Reached." You have to leave a phone number at which you can be reached while you're away. Even on leave you have to be reachable. This was before we all got cell phones. And the rules required that you had to be reachable at the specific number you wrote down on the CBR. You can't leave a number of somebody else who can then reach out for you. It has to be a direct connection to you. If you leave a number where you can be reached, it had better be a number where you will be reached if you are called.

You guessed it. I got a call. He had a supervisor call just to check up on me to make sure I followed regulations and left a number that I could be reached at. When I answered the phone, the supervisor was embarrassed because he had no reason to call me.

I said, very simply, "I fucking quit."

. . .

I'm the only person I know who quit the FBI on the telephone.

Many people I respected and cared about tried to talk me out of it: Jules; Jimmy Kallstrom, head of the New York office; Lin DeVecchio, in charge of the Mafia Commission Case; Sean McWeeney, head of the Bureau's Organized Crime section; prosecutors Barbara Jones, Louis Freeh, and Rudy Giuliani; and many others. I listened to them and weighed what they said to me. But I'd had it, and there was no turning back. The FBI was already too inflexible to accommodate the job I did and was still doing, and it would only get worse for me in the Bureau when I got a book deal. That kind of personal glory coming my way would create petty jealousies that would only add fuel to the fire.

I told them I would continue to testify with no pay from the Bureau. And I did, from 1986 until I returned to the Bureau in 1992 and was put back on the payroll. That was around the time Big Joey Massino got out of jail.

They did pay for my hotel and my airfare, like they would for anybody else. And I continued to be available to prosecutors and field offices for consultation, at no charge to the Bureau. But when I testified in the Mafia Commission Case, I was Mr. Joseph D. Pistone, not Agent Pistone.

And as much as I missed being an agent, the same hand from above that guided every step of the Donnie Brasco operation was still in charge. Things continued to be spectacular in my life. I could continue to fight the Mafia and do whatever Rudy and Jules and the crew needed me to do, but not on a leash extending from my SAC in the South to wherever I was.

And I could fight the Mafia by making everything I knew about the Mafia available to the public. A book about my experiences deep inside the Mafia would also educate prosecutors and law enforcement in the same way I had been educating them one-on-one, but much more efficiently.

When I look back, I see that what the SAC in that nameless southern city did was a gift. I never got a bad break. When I look at what they did to Lin DeVecchio years later—accusing him of feeding information to his informant in the Mafia so his informant could use that information to whack rivals and snitches—I'll never have a reason to complain. That could have been me.

Joseph "Joe Bananas" Bonanno, the original boss and namesake of the Bonanno Mafia family.

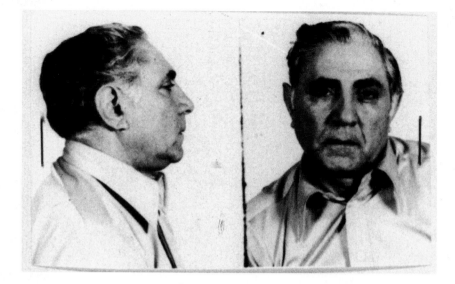

Phillip "Rusty" Rastelli, Bonanno boss while I was under.

Me (left) and my Bonanno capo Sonny Black (right) lounging poolside in Florida.

npa boss Santo Trafficante (left) and Sonny Black meeting in Florida.

nanno capo Big Joey Massino outside yland.

Frank Balistrieri, head of the Milwaukee crime family and Bonanno family collaborator.

Bonanno boss Carmine Galante lying dead with a cigar clenched between his teeth in the back-yard of Joe & Mary's Restaurant in Brooklyn.

Bonanno captain Dominick "Big Trin" Trinchera.

Bonanno captain Philip "Phil Lucky" Giaccone.

l-r: Nicky Santora (with hand in pocket), Boots Tomasula, and Sonny Black (far right) outside the Motion Lounge.

l-r: Joey "The Mook" D'Amico, Cesare Bonventre, Tony Mirra, and Toto Catalano.

l–r: Bonanno underboss Nicky Marangello (left) and Bonanno consigliere Steve "Beef" Cannone.

Bonanno capo Bruno Indelicato.

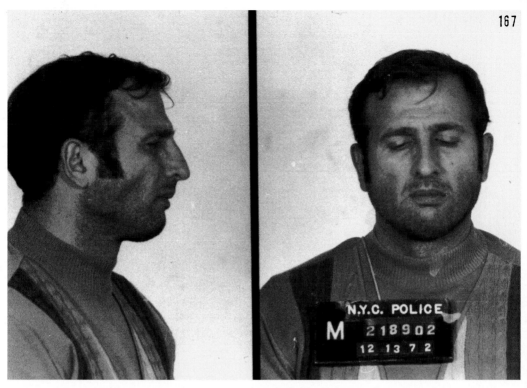

Bonanno soldier, and the target of my one and only Mafia contract, Sonny Red Indelicato.

l–r: Bonanno soldiers "Good Looking" Sal Vitale (left) and Anthony "Mr. Fish" Rabito outside Toyland.

l–r: FBI agents Jerry Loar, James Kinne, and Doug Fencl emerge from Sonny Black's apartment after informing him that "Donnie Brasco" was an FBI agent.

Rudy Giuliani (left), lead prosecutor in many of the crucial Mafia trials, with FBI Director William Webster.

Luigi Ronsisvalle (seated), lifetime criminal and star witness in the Pizza Connection Case.

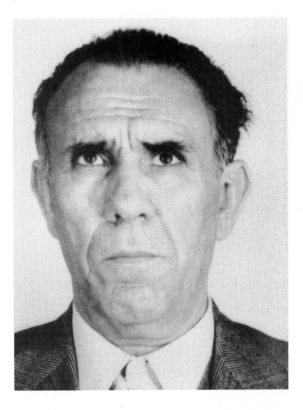

Gaetano Badalamenti, the Sicilian "Zip" boss convicted in the Pizza Connection Case.

Genovese boss "Fat" Tony Salerno.

Genovese boss (succeeding Salerno) Vincent "The Chin" Gigante.

Gambino boss, and boss of bosses of the Mafia Commission, Paul Castellano.

Gambino boss Paul Castellano's second-in-command, Thomas Billoti, lies dead in the street outside Sparks Steak House in Manhattan. Castellano's fresh corpse lay on the other side of the car.

Gambino boss (after Castellano) John "The Dapper Don" Gotti.

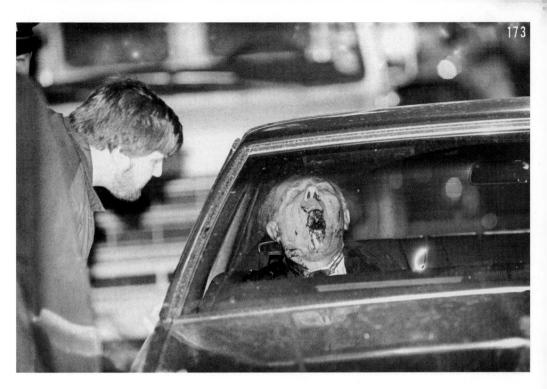

Longtime Philly family boss, Angelo Bruno, sits dead in his car as a Philadelphia policeman looks on.

Lucchese family boss Tony "Ducks" Corallo.

Lucchese underboss Salvatore "Tom Mix" Santoro.

Lucchese underboss (after Santoro) Anthony "Gaspipe" Casso.

The "Mafia Cops", l–r: Steve Caracappa and Louis Eppolito.

Colombo family soldier "Crazy Joey" Gallo.

Colombo boss Carmine "The Snake" Persico.

Ralph Scopo, Colombo soldier and president of the New York District Council of Cement and Concrete Workers.

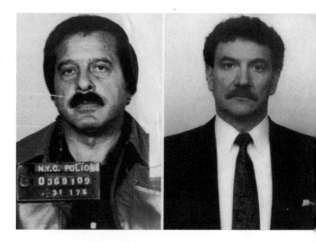

"Little Allie Boy" Persico, Colombo soldier and son of Carmine.

Colombo capo Greg Scarpa Sr. (left) and FBI agent Lin DeVecchio.

CHAPTER 12
THE MAFIA COMMISSION CASE

"IF IT WASN'T FOR ME, there wouldn't be no Mafia left."

That was the gruff voice of Genovese family boss Fat Tony Salerno. With a cigar stuck in the corner of his mouth, Fat Tony was talking to another Tony, the Lucchese family boss, Tony Ducks Corallo. They were singing sweet music to the FBI, but they didn't know it. Thanks to another law drafted by Bob Blakey that allowed bug and wiretap evidence in trial (as long as the affidavit for the warrant contained sufficient facts), Jimmy Kallstrom's wizards had bugged Fat Tony Salerno's Palma Boys Social Club on East 115th Street in the Italian section of East Harlem.

"I made all the guys," Genovese boss Fat Tony Salerno explained.

"You pick them," Lucchese boss Tony Ducks Corallo responded, "and you kill them."

While normal human beings who didn't think like that were listening in, Tony Ducks Corallo went on to discuss a "crippled" Mafia soldier who needed killing and would be killed despite his disability.

"If it wasn't for me, there wouldn't be no Mafia left. I made all the guys."

"You pick them and you kill them."

That snippet of dialogue spoke volumes about the Mafia Commission.

When the green light was given in 1983 to proceed with the Mafia Commission Case investigation, supervising agent Lin DeVecchio met with Case Agent Pat Marshall and instructed him to listen to every word of every tape and watch every frame of every video that had been gathered in the five separate investigations by five separate squads of the five families under Operation Genus. This task would involve tapes and videos done by the FBI, the NYPD, and the New York State Organized Crime Task Force. Pat Marshall would be listening for evidence that proved the Mafia Commission was a criminal enterprise and that the Commission bosses were the overseers of that enterprise.

"And then," Lin DeVecchio told Pat, "I want you to get with Joe Pistone—but check with Jules first—and get him to give you a full dump on everything he knows about how the bosses work together."

The plan was that the five individual New York family RICO case investigations would continue, but that the Mafia Commission investigation would take priority. There were some who felt that indicting the bosses of each New York family together in one RICO indictment was merely grandstanding, and that it would jeopardize the individual family cases stemming from the individual investigations of each family—investigations that would lead to separate indictments against each family. We had already had the first individual family trial in 1982—the Bonanno family case—and it had been a success and had proven that RICO could be applied to an individual family.

Nevertheless, the vision of a Mafia Commission Case that Jules, Jimmy Kossler, Jimmy Kallstrom, and I had—even before I came out—was not steered off course by anybody who thought we were grandstanding. They were entitled to their opinion, but we still strongly supported getting the Commission all at once in one indictment and one trial.

First, there were interlocking crimes in which several families were partnered, such as the partnerships between the Bonanno family and both the Balistrieri and Trafficante families that I facilitated. Second and more importantly, with all the experience the four of us had with the Mafia, we knew that getting them all at once would have the biggest impact. Getting them piecemeal would still leave a fully functioning Commission in place to replace bosses and assure an orderly succession of any boss who was convicted. But if the Commission bosses were convicted in a single trial, and if the judge did the right thing and banged them good, they would all be quitting at once. There would be no legitimate functioning Commission to assure a bloodless succession. There would be the potential for enormous chaos and disarray.

By the time Pat Marshall was finished, he had assembled the individual strands of evidence that led to a single grand jury indictment against the entire Mafia Commission, several lesser Mafia officials, and the bosses of the five families: Big Paul Castellano (Gambino); Fat Tony Salerno (Genovese); Tony Ducks Corallo (Lucchese); Carmine Persico (Colombo); and Rusty Rastelli (Bonanno).

Believe it or not, during the time of this expensive Mafia Commission investigation—from about 1983 to the indictment in February 1985—there was still an unsettled issue among certain quarters about whether there really was a nation-wide Mafia with a Commission. The Mafia criminals and their allies had long denied it.

In fact, the Mafia put enough pressure on the producers of the 1972 film, *The Godfather*, such that there is not a single mention of the word "Mafia" anywhere in that movie. The Mafia also had influence over even more important people in this regard.

While under indictment in the Mafia Commission Case, and while on trial in a separate Gambino family RICO case, involving stolen luxury cars being shipped to Kuwait, Big Paul Castellano was whacked on December 16, 1985 in front of Sparks Steak House in Manhattan. The very next day, the Democratic Governor of New York, Mario Cuomo, gave a press conference, essentially denying the existence of the Mafia. In a tactic reminiscent of what had been done during the filming of *The Godfather*, Governor Cuomo urged the press and all the media to stop using the word "Mafia" in news reports about the Big Paul Castellano hit. Cuomo said, ". . . every time you say it [Mafia], you suggest to people that organized crime is Italian. It's an ugly stereotype." And then he took the Mafia's 50-year-old party line, saying, "You're telling me that Mafia is an organization, and I'm telling you that's a lot of baloney."

A "lot of baloney"? While we were out there working hard and risking our lives to prove that the Mafia was a criminal organization, Mario Cuomo was campaigning for the press to stop reporting that the Mafia even existed. At the moment he spoke, the newspapers were full of stories about the Pizza Connection trial and the Gambino family trial. Both had been going on for a couple of months at that point. They were huge news, and the Gambino family trial especially so, with the colorful feature story about gay hit man Vic Arena who wanted plastic surgery. Cuomo knew that we were in those and other trials in New York City and around the country, trying to prove to a jury that the Mafia was an organized crime enterprise so that we could put away numerous badguys under the RICO law.

An "ugly stereotype"? At the moment Cuomo chastised the press, the Italian-American Big Paul Castellano had been a key defendant in the Gambino family RICO trial that would continue without him. At the moment Cuomo spoke, Big Paul had been under indictment and facing trial as the star defendant in the well-publicized Mafia Commission trial. I was preparing to testify that a man could not be a made member of the Mafia unless his father was 100% Italian. But then, what did I know?

Why did the governor hold a press conference to use his prestige and the power of his position against what we were doing? What was his reason? Worse than trying to suppress the news and the truth, Cuomo was verbally, at least, undermining his own state investigators. The hard and dangerous work of Ronald Goldstock's New York State Organized Crime Task Force had provided important pieces of the Mafia Commission Case and the other Mafia family RICO cases. And Ronald Goldstock reported up the chain of command to his governor, Cuomo, formerly a New York City lawyer, who was telling the world that RICO did not apply to people like Big Paul and those who would soon whack him and Tommy Bilotti in broad daylight in front of a New York City restaurant nine days before Christmas.

· · ·

On September 8, 1986, almost a year to the day after jury selection had begun in the still-ongoing Pizza Connection trial, the Mafia Commission Case went to trial in the same federal courthouse in Manhattan, in the courtroom right next door. It lasted nine weeks and was concluded while the Pizza Connection trial still had four more months—and two more shootings of defendants—to go.

There were no shootings during the Mafia Commission trial. There had been two deaths of indicted defendants, but they had occurred after the indictment had been handed down and before the trial began. Two weeks before Big Paul Castellano was gunned down (along with Bilotti, his right-hand man and father of nine children), the powerful Gambino underboss Neil Dellacroce died of cancer.

Those deaths meant that the Gambino family would not be represented in the Mafia Commission Case. We'd lose our star defendant, the boss of bosses, and some of the tapes from the bugs at the White House because they were relevant only as to Big Paul. John Gotti immediately took over the Gambino family, but we had no evidence against him, as he had not taken part in any of the Commission's activity during the time of the bugs and taps or during the time that I was under-cover. In fact, while I was undercover, John Gotti was a soldier, a hijacker, and a degenerate gambler who lost huge sums. He and his associates at the Bergin Hunt and Fish Club were also known for being involved in narcotics trafficking.

Prior to trial, lead prosecutor Rudy Giuliani and his appointed trial prosecu-tor Mike Chertoff had made the decision to drop Rusty Rastelli from the case. The Bonanno family had been kicked off the Commission when I surfaced, and Rusty was in jail during the entire time of the investigation. Therefore, Rusty's voice was nowhere to be found on the tapes. But the main reason for dropping Rusty was the ongoing Local 814 case. That case had gone to trial in Brooklyn on May 12, 1986 and was still in trial when the Mafia Commission trial began on September 8, 1986. Rusty couldn't be in two courtrooms at the same time.

It was a shame to lose two of the five families from the indictment. As a con-sequence, the Gambino and Bonanno families, at least for a while, had an orderly succession as far as leadership was concerned.

The principal predicate crime of the Commission trial, besides murder, was extortion—a crime involving something called the Concrete Club. It was an arrangement in which a Colombo soldier and union boss, Ralph Scopo, was the primary player. Ralph Scopo was the president of the New York District Council of Cement and Concrete Workers. His hobby was collecting cars, and he transact-ed Mafia business in them. Unbeknownst to him, bugs were in as many of his cars as were feasible to bug.

The Concrete Club was a small, secret group of seven concrete contractors who reported to Ralph Scopo and made payments to him. Ralph Scopo collect-ed two percent of the gross value of every successful bid for every concrete work valued above two million dollars in every single construction job in New York City. The seven contractors rigged their bids so that they would take turns winning, and the bids would be padded to ensure enough extra money to make the payoffs to Ralph Scopo. No other contractors were permitted to bid or they'd have union trouble, and the seven contractors were not permitted to bid on jobs worth less than 2 million dollars (Ralph Scopo explained to a club member that the family bosses felt the smaller contractors "had to eat, too") Scopo sent the payoffs from the Concrete Club upstream to the bosses of the four remaining families that comprised the Mafia Commission. The fact that Rusty was not on the Commission because of me, cost him a share. Lucky for him, it also bounced him off the Mafia Commission Case indictment prior to trial.

Although Rusty was bounced, there was one Bonanno capo—Bruno Indelicato—added to the indictment in the Mafia Commission Case.

The principal crime of violence in the RICO indictment was the 1979 murder of Carmine Galante. It was believed that the two Zips, Cesare Bonventre and Baldo Amato—Galante's bodyguards—had been active participants in the killings that took place at Joe and Mary's Restaurant. Cesare Bonventre had been murdered shortly after his indictment in the Pizza Connection Case, and Baldo Amato was on trial next-door in that case. However, in addition to Bonventre and Amato's participation in the Galante hit, it was known that there were three masked gunmen who burst in and opened fire. Pat Marshall had an idea how to unmask one of them.

That one was Bruno Indelicato, my contract-murder target. Following the Galante hit in 1979, Bruno had been upped to capo as a reward for his participation in the hit. Two years later, the May 5, 1981 killing of three capos was supposed to have been a killing of four capos, but Bruno never showed up for his own murder. Instead he was around the corner scoring and doing cocaine.

The Ravenite Social Club on Mulberry Street in Manhattan was the semi-official headquarters of the Gambino family. Neil Dellacroce, the old-time underboss, held court there. The NYPD had Dellacroce under video surveillance at the club. About 45 minutes after the hit on Galante in Brooklyn, the NYPD noticed a strange occurrence. Bruno Indelicato, then known to be a Bonanno soldier and the son of capo Sonny Red Indelicato, showed up at the Ravenite. Bruno was

sweating and appeared to have a gun under his shirt. Bruno was greeted in a jubi-
lant way as if he had just hit a game-winning home run and was crossing the plate.
Neil Dellacroce hugged and kissed Bruno. Bonanno consigliere Stevie Beef
Cannone hugged and kissed Bruno.

What were Bonannos and Gambinos doing together at the Gambino headquarters? And what were they celebrating? It very likely had something to do with
the hit on Galante 45 minutes earlier. But what? And even if the NYPD knew,
how could anyone prove it?

When Pat Marshall watched the hugging and kissing in the video, he remembered that the heel of a palm print had been lifted from the right rear door of a
Mercury Montego that had been used in the Galante hit. The car was a stolen
clunker and it had been abandoned and recovered by the NYPD. Eyewitnesses
had reported seeing a man in a ski mask carrying a shotgun get out of the
Mercury from the right rear door of the car and rush into Joe and Mary's Italian
Restaurant. In 1979, the NYPD did not have the capability to take and save what
are called "major case prints," which include a set of prints of the entire palm from
pinky to thumb, including the heel. Bruno Indelicato had been arrested and print-
ed before, but no one had anything more than his fingerprints on file.

After Pat Marshall recalled the palm print, he had Bruno's car followed over
the George Washington Bridge that spans the Hudson River between New York
and New Jersey. Now, I'm not going to accuse Pat Marshall of setting Bruno up
for a bogus traffic stop after crossing the Hudson River. I'm not going to accuse
Pat Marshall of having Bruno followed until he committed a traffic offense that
would have legally justified a stop and frisk. Nope, not me. That tactic might be
against one of the thousands of rules that govern today's police work. But—surprise, surprise—Bruno's car was stopped for a traffic infraction, and a weapon was
found in Bruno's possession, and Bruno was taken in for carrying a concealed
deadly weapon. This time a major case print was taken and, bingo: it matched.

It was Bruno who had exited the rear door of the Mercury and had burst into
Joe and Mary's with a shotgun in his possession. It was Bruno who had blasted
and wasted Carmine Galante and then reported directly to the Gambino family
headquarters, and gotten a big juicy hug and kiss from the boss of bosses' underboss, Neil Dellacroce.

This revelation formed not only a solid case of murder against Bruno; it was a case against the Mafia Commission.

Nothing for nothing, but how's this for a connection: on behalf of Rusty's remaining in place as the Bonanno boss, I had been picked to kill the man who two years earlier had been picked to kill Carmine Galante on behalf of Rusty being restored as the Bonanno boss. "You pick them and you kill them."

• • •

Rusty's family's founding father, Joe Bananas, at 79, came close to being drafted into the Mafia Commission Case by Rudy Giuliani. In 1983, Joe Bananas published his autobiography, *A Man of Honor*. In the book, while he only hinted at his own crimes, Joe Bananas described the formation and the workings of the Commission. When Rudy read the book and saw Joe Bananas promoting it on *60 Minutes*, he said, "If Bonanno can write about a Commission, I can indict it."

Rudy subpoenaed Joe Bananas. Rudy envisioned that he would give Joe Bananas immunity and force the former boss to testify about the things he had written in his book, especially the origin and evolution of the Commission from its roots in 1931 until Joe Bananas got kicked off in the 1960s when he was told to give up his New York crime family and retire to Arizona in exile. This exile was punishment for violating the rules of the Commission, especially the rule that prohibited killing a boss without Commission approval.

In the 1960s, Joe Bananas had plotted to kill two bosses, Tommy Lucchese and Carlo Gambino. His ally in the plot, ailing boss Joe Magliocco, gave the contract to one of his capos, Joe Colombo. Instead of violating Commission rules by carrying out the contract, Colombo exposed the plot, and the Commission rewarded him by making him boss of the newly named Colombo family after Magliocco died of a heart attack. To avoid being killed on orders of the Commission, Joe Bananas staged his own kidnapping and hid out for a couple of years. Or, as he claimed, maybe his cousin, the Buffalo boss in those days, Stefano Magaddino (who, like Joe Bananas, was an original boss on the Commission), may have actually kidnapped Joe Bananas and held him against his will for a couple of years.

The omnipotent Mafia Commission replaced Joe Bananas with one of his capos. Joe Bananas replaced himself with his son, Salvatore Bill Bonanno. This upheaval at the top, which split the family in two, led to the Bonanno War in which several Mafia soldiers were killed on the each side of the Bonanno family. In 1968, Joe Bananas knew he couldn't beat the Commission, threw in the towel, and retired to Arizona.

When Rudy subpoenaed Joe Bananas three months before the Mafia Commission indictment came down, the former boss, then living in style near Tucson, refused to cooperate with the grand jury investigation despite having been granted immunity. Joe Bananas ended up doing 14 months in jail for contempt of court rather than testify in the Mafia Commission trial. At an early point in the sideshow, Joe Bananas told Rudy, "You're doing a good job."

Rudy Giuliani wasn't the only one to see the implications of Joe Bananas, the author, admitting the existence and the functioning of the Commission at a time when RICO was starting to be used against the Mafia.

A tape recorder picked up a March 28, 1983 conversation between Lucchese underboss Tom Mix Santoro and a Lucchese soldier named Sal Avellino, whose Jaguar was bugged by members of Governor Cuomo's New York State Organized Crime Task Force. The Task Force apparently had artistic differences with their boss, the governor. Tom Mix Santoro and Sal Avellino had just seen Joe Bananas' performance on *60 Minutes.*

"I was shocked," said Sal Avellino, "What is he trying to prove, that he's a man of honor? But he's admitting—he, he actually admitted that he has a fam; that he was the boss of a family."

What *was* Joe Bananas trying to prove?

Tom Mix Santoro remarked about Joe Bananas' contention that he was never involved in drugs. "You know, like he says, he ain't never been in narcotics—he's full of shit. His own fucking rule; he was making piles of money. . . ."

One of the many myths perpetrated by many bosses in the Mafia was that they didn't sanction the narcotics trade. This was an important lie for those Mafia bosses to perpetuate. For decades, the Mafia needed to enable corrupt police, like Captain Donahue in Tampa, to rationalize their bribe-taking by believing that the Mafia primarily dealt in "victimless" crimes, like gambling and loan sharking. Once the Mafia's rampant dealing in narcotics was exposed, it would become harder for the Mafia bosses to buy police and political protection.

Nine days after the conversation between Santoro and Avellino, Lucchese boss Tony Ducks Corallo went for a drive in Sal's bugged Jaguar. Avellino told Tony Ducks what Joe Bananas had said on *60 Minutes* about having been the boss "of a family."

"He said that?" Tony Ducks Corallo asked. "They could call him in and lock you up under this act over here."

"This RICO Act," Avellino, who had attended college, said. "He admitted that he was in charge of a family. . . ."

"Now they could call him in," Corallo predicted. "They call him as a witness. . . . What are you going to do then?"

At around the same time in 1983 at the White House, in a bugged conversation about Joe Bananas' revelations in his book, Big Paul Castellano revealed that he understood what was likely to happen as a result of the book. "They're going to make us be one tremendous conspiracy."

Nothing for nothing, but I know these bosses. They never change. In my opinion, Joe Bananas knew when he wrote the book what everyone else instantly knew when they read the book. For sure, the publisher and the publisher's attorneys discussed the legal implications with him before the book went to the printer. Joe Bananas was about to announce what politicians had denounced: the existence of the Mafia as an organization with a ruling Commission. The very year the book came out, there was a Mafia trial in Chicago where the defense was that there was no such thing as the Mafia. The Mafia had been denying its own existence as an organization for fifty years. The penalty for admitting there was a Mafia was death.

This so-called "man of honor," who came to America from Sicily in his twenties, now fifteen years after being banished in disgrace to Arizona, got his revenge on the Commission by admitting its existence and confessing to having been on it from its first day of existence. At the same time, by virtue of his book tour, he became a public relations promoter and instigator of the Mafia Commission indictment that followed his book by two years. In fact, Rudy used the book in his pitch to get approval from Headquarters and from the Justice Department to initiate the expensive Mafia Commission Case investigation. Joe Bananas really meant it when he said to Rudy, "You're doing a good job."

Before trial, Rudy said about the Mafia Commission Case indictment, "The case should be seen as the apex of the family cases. . . . It is an attempt, if we can prove our charges, to dismantle the structure that has been used since the beginning of organized crime in America." Twenty years later, I still get chills reading those words.

. . .

At the Mafia Commission trial, even without Joe Bananas, there were 85 government witnesses and over 100 tapes introduced into evidence.

The defendant lineup at trial was:

1) Boss of the Genovese family and star defendant, Fat Tony Salerno, who had bragged on tape that he "made all the guys."

2) The entire leadership of the Lucchese family: Boss Tony Ducks Corallo, Underboss Tom Mix Santoro, and Consigliere Christy Tick Furnari.

3) The top two-thirds of the Colombo leadership: Boss Carmine Persico and Underboss Gerry Lang Langella.

4) Ralph Scopo, Colombo soldier and Concrete Club operator who was on trial under RICO for carrying out Commission orders.

5) Bruno Indelicato, Bonanno capo, on trial like Ralph Scopo for a RICO charge involving the predicate crime of murder on behalf of the Commission, and not on trial for the murder itself.

In his opening statement to the jury, Mike Chertoff stated the theme he would expound upon throughout the trial. "Mafia families have a single overriding purpose, and that purpose is to make money—to make money illegally, to make money criminally, to make money using corruption, fear and violence."

With the mountain of evidence Mike would introduce, there was no need for breaks going our way, but we got a really big one when Colombo boss Carmine Persico decided to represent himself. This way, Persico got to address the jury directly in an opening statement and in a summation. Persico also got the opportunity to inject his own version of the facts into the questions that he asked. And he got to make all these statements to the jury without testifying directly and subjecting himself to cross-examination. Persico also had the ego that no doubt relished the role of trial lawyer. He loved studying his trial notebook when he questioned a witness; and he loved calling himself "Persico" when he referred to himself in the question; and he loved saying things to the judge like, "My appeal is still pending in the Second Circuit."

It's also likely that Persico saw the handwriting on the wall from his conviction earlier that summer of 1986 in the separate Colombo family case. Aaron Marcu had been the prosecutor in the seven-month trial that nailed eight Colombos, including Persico and his underboss Gerry Lang Langella, when the jury came back with guilty verdicts on Friday the Thirteenth of June, 1986. The seven-month trial must have cost Persico a bundle in legal fees, and he probably thought he'd cut his losses by representing himself.

But he didn't seem to have learned anything from that seven-month RICO trial. Persico clearly did not understand the crime of RICO when he stated in front of the jury in the Mafia Commission Case, "Without the Mafia, there wouldn't even be no case here." Precisely.

The Mafia Commission trial was a history lesson for the jury. It all began with two New York State Troopers who had surprised the Mafia at Apalachin, in New York state, in 1957. Although Joe Bananas could not be forced to testify at the trial, Mike Chertoff did the next best thing and played Joe Bananas' *60 Minutes* interview, where Bananas acknowledged the Commission's existence and gave the history of its formation.

The 75-year-old former underboss of the Cleveland family, Angelo Lonardo, gave live testimony on the Mafia Commission's formation and the lineage of the families—who was boss and when. Lonardo admitted that he was testifying in exchange for leniency and that he had lied on numerous occasions while under oath in trials in the past.

Another turncoat witness was Joe Cantalupo, a Colombo family associate who testified that his apartment was once used for a Mafia Commission meeting. At the time, Cantalupo testified, he was given instructions: "Tomorrow night have your wife make a large pot of black coffee, go out and buy a couple of pounds of Italian cookies, and set the table for five. We'll be over as soon as it gets dark."

One of the lesser, but still significant, predicate crimes in the indictment was loan sharking in Staten Island. On cross-examination, "Clarence Darrow" Persico accused Cantalupo of agreeing to testify because Persico's brother once beat up Cantalupo as punishment for failing to pay a loan-sharking debt. As Persico put it to Cantalupo, "You was angry because you was beat up and you was beat up because you didn't pay back the money?" Precisely.

Cantalupo, like Angelo Lonardo from Cleveland, admitted that he was testifying in exchange for leniency and that he had lied on numerous occasions while under oath in trials in the past. Cantalupo also admitted that, for about a decade, he had been a paid secret informer against his Colombo family friends because he had gotten into money trouble and needed the FBI's paydays.

Although no longer an FBI agent, I couldn't wait to get on the stand and go under oath and answer Mike Chertoff's questions in the case Jules and I had dreamed about. In his book, *The Complete Idiot's Guide to the Mafia,* Jerry Capeci characterized my testimony as follows:

"Hero FBI agent Joe Pistone, who penetrated the Bonanno family by playing the role of a jewel thief, gave the jurors an important overview of the structure and rules that mobsters live by, as well as the function of the Commission, from the witness stand. He also testified about information he gleaned about Galante's killing while working undercover against the Bonannos, as well as the Commission's involvement in the leadership affairs of the Bonanno family. Pistone was a key witness because he didn't have the negative baggage carried by Mafia turncoats."

On cross-examination, all 5'7" of Carmine Persico, with perpetual bags under his eyes, challenged me. Persico had forgotten the time he pulled up with his son Little Allie Boy in his Rolls Royce for an outdoor meeting in Brooklyn with Tony Mirra, and I was present. Persico was already pleased with the idea that his voice was not on any of the tapes, when he asked me, "You never met me, did you?" The defense attorneys all jumped up at once to object, because his question opened the door for me to tell the jury about that meeting that was otherwise irrelevant to this case. Tough break for them, but the smart ones knew it didn't pay to try to cross-examine me. When I testified in this case, I didn't even have the slight baggage of being employed by the government that was doing the prosecuting.

Nothing for nothing, but I've seen many a good case lost because it relied on turncoats' sworn testimony, and the criminality of these turncoats raised a reasonable doubt in the juries' mind about the turncoats' oath to tell the truth. They were cooperators, and there was always the danger that they had a greater motive to cooperate than to tell the truth.

Here, too, in the Mafia Commission Case, there was an abundance of tape recorded conversations and bugs and wiretaps which, as long as they are properly explained, also have no "negative baggage." I appreciate what Jerry Capeci said about me, but for my money the best witness in the courtroom was a tape recorder.

From the Palma Boys Social Club bug, the jury heard Fat Tony Salerno picking the next president of the International Brotherhood of Teamsters. I wondered if it reminded any of the jurors of Jimmy Hoffa's disappearance a few years before that tape, and the statement of Tony Ducks Corallo: "You pick them, and you kill them."

The jury heard Fat Tony Salerno, speaking for the Mafia Commission, avert an impending war over who should be the boss of the Buffalo Mafia family. Buffalo consigliere Joe Pieri was heard complaining about current boss Joe Todaro, who had men "walking around with machine guns." On tape, Pieri said, "I killed a few guys who were against him, and he got to be boss. He's not fit to be boss. He started neglecting me." Instead of referring Pieri to counseling for his abandonment issues, Fat Tony warned him not to take any action and to tell Todaro, "The Commission wants it straightened out. . . . Let the Commission decide. . . . Tell him it's the Commission from New York. Tell him he's dealing with the big boys now."

The jury heard Fat Tony Salerno quote Tony Ducks Corallo regarding the decision to boot the Bonanno family from the Commission: "Tony Ducks told Rusty, he said, 'Listen,' he said, 'take care of your family first. Straighten out your family and when you straighten them out, then we talk about the Commission.'" In another Palma Boys tape, they heard Fat Tony Salerno on the same point regarding Rusty Rastelli: ". . . this guy wants to be the boss. He can be the boss as far as I'm concerned . . . but he cannot be on the Commission. One vote is enough to throw it out. Cause, the Commission thing, it's supposed to be such a sacred thing."

From a bug in one of his cars, Ralph Scopo was recorded talking to one of the contractors about the Concrete Club and about his own vulnerability to the bosses on the Mafia Commission, should he hypothetically ever get arrested.

"Now I get indicted and they're afraid," Ralph Scopo said. "The only guy they got to worry about is me. If I open my mouth they're dead. So to kill the case—bango."

"Really?" the contractor said.

"Yeah. Here I am all my life making them money. I'm taking the fucking chances in the street. I'm willing to go to jail, never gonna open my mouth, but they're not sure of that, see? . . . Say this thing kind of blows up. I'll be one of the first guys to get arrested."

"Why?"

"Because of this club shit. Now when that happens, no matter how much faith they got in you, there's always that little bit. They say, 'Oh, geez, maybe he'll open his fucking mouth.' And then you don't see the guy no more."

•   •   •

Midway through our trial, on October 15, 1986, we got the fantastic news that Rusty Rastelli, Nicky Glasses Marangello, and Big Joey Massino had been convicted in the Local 814 case I testified in across the East River in Brooklyn. Bravo, Laura Brevetti. Mike Chertoff was encouraged by the news, but he was putting in 18-hour days and we couldn't take too much time to celebrate. Our case itself was going extremely well, but the prosecutor's art here was to keep the judge in mind. If we won, we would win little if the bosses did not get substantial jail time at sentencing. The better the judge understood the evil, the more chance there was of that indispensable part of our plan—to put the bosses away a long time.

In our courtroom, the jury saw terrific surveillance photos of bosses leaving a Mafia Commission meeting on May 15, 1984. An informant had told Agent Joseph O'Brien that a Mafia Commission meeting was taking place in the Staten Island home of a relative of a Gambino soldier. O'Brien and his partner, Andris Kurins, staked out the house and took photos of Gambino boss Big Paul

Castellano and many of the Mafia Commission Case defendants as they left the house one at a time, including Genovese boss Fat Tony Salerno, Lucchese underboss Tom Mix Santoro, Lucchese consigliere Christy Tick Furnari, Colombo underboss Gerry Lang Langella, and Ralph Scopo.

It was the first Mafia Commission meeting ever caught on film. We never learned what had been discussed at that meeting, but Ralph Scopo's presence made it clear that some aspect of the Concrete Club had been on the agenda. We knew that normally at these meetings they discussed such things as new members who were being proposed, disputes that had arisen, and contracts—like the one that the Mafia Commission had put out on me at a similar gathering. Ralph Scopo's presence was not needed at any of these meetings. We just managed to get the right meeting for our case. All the photos were put on display in court for the jury to view.

A couple of concrete contractors who had been given immunity testified about how the Concrete Club worked.

The jury heard Lefty tell me on tape: "Now you're going to get straightened out, Donnie." The jury heard Lefty recommend that Sonny Black, as acting boss, should start a war against the Zips, and they heard Sonny's response: "I can't do that. It's Commission rules."

During a recess, the very capable retired NYPD Detective Gene McDonald offered Fat Tony Salerno a granola bar to take the place of the chocolate candy bars he ate. "Who the fuck cares," Fat Tony said, "I'm going to die in the can anyway."

One of my favorite witnesses was Fred DeChristopher. When the indictment came down, Carmine Persico had hid out at DeChristopher's house in Wantagh, Long Island. DeChristopher was an insurance agent whose wife was a cousin of Carmine Persico. She was the sister of Persico's right-hand man and future acting boss, capo Andy the Fat Man Russo.

DeChristopher got to understand what these people were like shortly after he married Andy the Fat Man's sister. One evening, DeChristopher and his wife went out to dinner with Andy the Fat Man and one of Andy's associates. The associate said something Andy the Fat Man didn't like, and so Andy jabbed the associate in the eye with his fork and pressed the fork into the eye, warning the associate that the next time he would take his eye out with the fork.

DeChristopher had no say in the matter of Persico hiding out in his house, and Persico pretty much took over DeChristopher's house. By the time the case went to trial, DeChristopher had divorced his wife. He testified that Persico bragged that he ran his "crime family" from jail through phone calls to his underboss and co-defendant Gerry Lang Langella.

Furthermore, according to DeChristopher, Persico told him, ". . . Ralph Scopo was his front man in the cement and concrete workers' union and that not a yard of concrete was poured in the city of New York where he and his friends didn't get a piece of it." DeChristopher quoted Persico on the Commission's vote to sanction the hit on Carmine Galante. A few years earlier, Persico had shared a cell with Galante and told DeChristopher, "And quite frankly, I voted against him getting hurt." Nevertheless, Carmine Persico voted, and that is the crime of participating in a criminal enterprise. It doesn't matter which way he voted.

Because he chose to represent himself and did not take the stand, the only question Persico answered was one DeChristopher asked from the witness stand. "Wouldn't you like to see me down the sewer altogether?" DeChristopher asked.

"I don't think the judge would permit me to answer that question," Persico answered in front of the jury.

On cross-examination by one of the defense attorneys, DeChristopher explained why he decided to testify against Persico. "I think what they do is despicable. They are the most despicable people on the face of the earth."

The only witness called on behalf of the defense was DeChristopher's ex-wife, Catherine. She tried to do what her brother Andy the Fat Man Russo put her up to do, but as a witness, she bombed. She described Persico's stay at her home as a simple family visit where Persico cooked and they all played Trivial Pursuit. She claimed her ex had meetings with Carmine Galante at a time that Galante was in jail. We never heard that anybody put her eye out with a fork, so her brother must have been satisfied that his sister did her best.

In his summation, Mike Chertoff, reminded the jury about Persico's Mafia comment. "Ladies and gentlemen, it has been said that without the Mafia, there would not be a case here." Mike looked at Persico. "Without the power of the Mafia, these defendants could not have taken control of an industry like New York's cement industry, they could not have authorized the murder of Carmine

Galante, could not have engaged in a loan sharking conspiracy, could not have taken over and dominated labor unions, could not have committed the crimes you have heard about during the course of this case. They could not have done any of these things you have heard about, ladies and gentlemen of the jury, without the Mafia. So that is why there is a Mafia in this case. That is what this case is all about."

In his summation, Carmine Persico complained, "They didn't come here to try a case; they came to persecute people with the word Mafia." Right on.

During their deliberations, the jury asked to review only one piece of evidence. They asked to hear one more time the contemptible conversation recorded at the Palma Boys Social Club between Fat Tony Salerno and Tony Ducks Corallo in 1983:

"If it wasn't for me, there wouldn't be no Mafia left. I made all the guys," Fat Tony said.

"You pick them and you kill them," Tony Ducks replied.

As far as I'm concerned, that snippet should have been played in anti-Mafia ads on New York TV, paid for out of Governor Cuomo's budget. At times during the trial, two of the stars of *The Godfather* movie, James Caan and Robert Duvall, showed up to watch Carmine Persico do his thing. I hope the movie stars were present for that snippet.

James Caan had some kind of close relationship with Persico's capo Jo-Jo Russo, the son of Andy the Fat Man Russo. Jo-Jo was with Persico when Persico was arrested in Fred DeChristopher's house.

On November 19, 1986, after five days of deliberation, the jury returned verdicts of guilty on all 151 counts of the indictment. On January 13, 1987, Judge Richard Owen did the right thing. Judge Owen said, "The sentence has to be fashioned to speak to future [Mafia bosses]." Except as to Bruno Indelicato, Judge Owen handed out the 100-year RICO maximum sentence to every single defendant—even to Fat Tony Salerno, whose only predicate crime was participating in the Concrete Club.

Because Bruno was a capo and not a boss in any of the three leadership positions in the Bonanno family, Judge Owen hit Bruno with a healthy 40 years. Compared to the eye-popping sentences the bosses got, 40 years seemed like a slap on the wrist, but it was a fairly substantial sentence.

Carmine Persico addressed the judge during the sentencing procedure, say-ing, "This case and the attitude of the prosecutor and the court itself is in confor-mance with this mass hysteria, this Mafia mania, that was flying around, and deprived every one of us in this courtroom of our rights to a fair trial and impar-tial jury."

On a purely personal and a very minor note for me, considering what we just accomplished, we still didn't know who killed Sonny Black. Or who did what and where on May 5, 1981 to the three capos. And despite Bruno's conviction, we still did not know for sure who else was in on the Galante hit with him. And because of the Miranda rules, even though Bruno was convicted, we weren't allowed to sit him down and question him about that hit or about anything.

During the sentencing, the judge is required by the federal system to address each defendant individually and recite certain things. Lucchese underboss Tom Mix Santoro got impatient waiting for his turn to come, and said, "Ah, give me the hundred years. I'll go inside now."

Tom Mix Santoro went inside, but he never came out. The Lucchese under-boss died in the can in January, 2000. His boss, Tony Ducks Corallo, died in the can eight months later. Rusty Rastelli had already died in the can in June, 1991. Fat Tony Salerno, as he had predicted for himself, died in the can in July, 1992. And Ralph Scopo died inside in March, 1993.

Colombo boss Carmine Persico, Colombo underboss Gerry Lang Langella, and Lucchese consigliere Christy Tick Furnari are still inside, waiting their turns to get out the only way they can.

CHAPTER 13
THE MAFIA'S WORST YEAR

STARTING WITH THE BONANNO FAMILY verdict against Lefty and Sonny Black's crew in 1982, and continuing through the '80s as jury after jury spoke and judges did the right thing at sentencings, we knew that sooner or later we would slam the door (using RICO) on verbal sabotage by people like Governor Mario Cuomo who claimed the Mafia was not a criminal organization. Eventually, in RICO trials in the years that followed, the defendants themselves got wise and stopped contesting the existence of the Mafia as a criminal organization. They even stopped contesting their positions in the Mafia. The made men and their associates on trial began to restrict their defenses to denying that they committed the predicate crimes. Looking back twenty short years, it seems strange to remember that the Italian Mafia's existence was ever in doubt. But at the time, we knew that when the jury foreman spoke the word "guilty" 151 times in the Mafia Commission Case, we had gone a long way toward accomplishing this important goal.

And make no mistake about it; this goal was not merely a public relations goal. We had crucial practical considerations involved in nailing down the issue of the existence of the Mafia as a criminal organization. To serve the public and get our jobs done, we relied on public officials being willing to spend public money on extremely costly equipment and sufficient personnel to conduct even more costly RICO investigations and prosecutions. RICO was not cheap. The Pizza Connection Trial alone cost the government over $50 million in taxpayer money.

Governor Mario Cuomo was a prominent politician who many people considered for a run at the White House. Senators and Congressmen who controlled our budgets listened to the governor of New York when he spoke about organized crime in New York City. We couldn't financially afford to have a New York governor and Italian-American as influential as him continue to publicly use the ethnic equivalent of the "race card" to blame reporters and others for using the word "Mafia," calling the very word "an ugly stereotype," and worse, publicly declaring at press conferences that the idea of the Mafia as a criminal organization was "a lot of baloney."

I hate to imagine the press conferences if we had lost the Mafia Commission Case. I don't know whether Mario Cuomo, as rumored, had some negative baggage when he decided not to seek his party's nomination for president, but I had no negative baggage when I testified as an Italian-American—as an American first—that the Italian Mafia was a criminal organization and had the rules and the structure that I described. This was vital testimony in, among others, the Bonanno family case, the Local 814 Case, the Pizza Connection Case, and most importantly, the Mafia Commission Case—all within a five-year period after my surfacing.

At the time I testified in the Mafia Commission Case, I felt as if I had been squeezed out of the Bureau before I could qualify for a pension. I personally did not rely on a federal paycheck anymore. I had no financial stake in whether these investigations continued to get the budgetary support they needed or not, but I still knew what side I was on.

My favorite line at one of these press conferences was spoken by another New York Italian-American, Rudy Giuliani. "This [1982] has been the Mafia's worst year. We keep making gains and they keep getting moved backward. If we take back the labor unions, the legitimate businesses, eventually they become just another street gang. Spiritually, psychologically, they've always been just a street gang."

The overriding practical goal of the Mafia Commission Case was to do nothing less than cause the Mafia's stock to go into a severe decline and then crash over time. And like the stock-market crash of 1929, where financiers who lost everything leaped from Wall Street buildings to their deaths, and others trudged to the street corner every morning to sell apples, we looked for devastation and destitution in those three Mafia families whose leadership the case targeted.

When leadership vacuums at the top suddenly appeared, due to previously unheard of 100-year sentences, we hoped for chaos and disarray. In two of the three families whose bosses were eliminated as family leaders by the Mafia Commission Case, we got more than we even hoped for. We got war and frenzy. In the Colombo family we got what Mafia expert Jerry Capeci called a "civil war," and in the Lucchese family we got what he called a "killing frenzy."

Unfortunately, in the Genovese family, the conviction of boss Fat Tony Salerno—which sent him to the can to die eating chocolate candy bars from the commissary—did not lead to anything like a civil war or a killing frenzy. Unlike in Lucchese and Colombo, the boss in the Genovese family was the only Genovese leader convicted. There was still an underboss and a consigliere out there in a social club on Sullivan Street in Greenwich Village who had been untouched by the indictment, the months of trial preparation, the trial itself, and a 100-year banishment to a prison far, far away.

This circumstance enabled a seamless transition of leadership for the Genovese, and gave them plenty of time to prepare for it. Keeping two-thirds of the leadership in place on Sullivan Street discouraged any wannabe capos from making a move to seize power. The new Genovese boss who took over the family's leadership was the manipulative but powerful number-two man: Chin Gigante. In fact, some Mafia historians and some lawmen today say that Gigante had been the boss all along and that Fat Tony Salerno was a front man.

I believe the facts show that Salerno was the boss when we prosecuted him, but either way, the Genovese—often called the Rolls Royce of Mafia families— unlike the Lucchese and Colombo families, did not have any violent reactions to the verdict. That doesn't mean the Genovese didn't suffer irreparably from the Mafia Commission Case. By exposing the Mafia and by beating the Mafia, every family structure was weakened. Those 100-year sentences and the conviction of each boss on every count were lessons that were not going to be lost on the rank-and-file wiseguys when it came time to consider whether to take their chances at trial or to rat and save themselves in the Witness Protection Program.

As Lefty once told me after the Galante hit, "If they can hit a boss, nobody's immune." The "they" was the Commission. That concept of a Commission that was more powerful than one's own dreaded and respected boss kept the troops in line, out of fear. Now we were saying and proving a similar statement to the troops: "If they can convict all the bosses just for being bosses, and send them away for 100 years, nobody's immune." This time, the people of the United States of America were the "they," we were more powerful than all the bosses put together, and we were the ones to be feared in the name of the law.

And the name of that law, RICO, in turn sent Fat Tony Salerno's successor Chin Gigante to the can. The Chin was convicted July 24, 1997, a mere ten years following the initial 100-year sentences.

Chin had been indicted in 1990 but it took seven years to get him to trial, mainly due to his masterful manipulation of renowned psychiatric experts. The boss of the family that controlled the New York Teamsters, various other unions, the Fulton Fish Market, and other businesses, walked around Greenwich Village in a ratty bathrobe, pajamas, and slippers muttering to himself to prove his claim that he was mentally incompetent to stand trial. The Chin was "schizophrenic," according to more than one examining psychiatrist. And if that wasn't enough, according to Dr. Wilfred G. van Gorp, the director of neuropsychology at the prestigious Columbia University Medical School, the former professional boxer's schizophrenia was complicated by "moderate to severe dementia which reflects significant underlying central nervous system dysfunction."

Twelve years earlier, Fat Tony Salerno had been picked up on a bug in the Palma Boys Social Club commenting on the Chin's act: "If he gets pinched, all them years he spent in that fucking asylum would be for nothing."

When the Chin shuffled along in his schizophrenic garb of dementia over to the Italian festival every year (the Feast of San Gennaro) in the company of his brother, the Catholic priest, muttering to himself, he was probably calculating his take. One of the pieces of intelligence Lefty had provided me with was that the Genovese family controlled the Catholic feast. Nobody from the outside had a booth to sell a single sausage and pepper hero sandwich without paying the Genovese for it. Each Mafia family was provided a small section, but even then, if a Bonanno wanted a better location he had to pay the Genovese for it. Lefty paid to have his daughter's watermelon stand moved closer to the action.

Finally in 1997, there were enough turncoats available to testify that Chin was competent enough to stand trial. At that point, he was convicted of being the boss of the Genovese, of illegally controlling the installation of every window in every public housing unit in New York City, and of conspiring to kill John Gotti. The Chin, then 69, continued his incompetence act in court every day. The elderly Judge Jack Weinstein fell for it and gave Chin a mere twelve years, saying, "He is a shadow of his former self—an old man finally brought to bay in his declining years after decades of vicious criminal tyranny."

So, the Chin went to jail, where he continued to drool and act incompetent. He also continued to run the Genovese family from jail via visits from his son, Andrew, a non-made businessman who would communicate with his father using code and hand signals. For years, no Mafia member had been allowed to utter Gigante's name. To refer to the boss, the member had to touch his own chin. Nevertheless, Chin and son were recorded and videotaped, and two Genovese members were prepared to testify. One, a loyal 79-year-old hit man, turned when he discovered he was on Chin's hit list. Another associate flipped after his arrest on a murder conspiracy. This one wore a bug in his Rolex watch and gathered conversations in the social clubs about Chin still running the family.

Long-distance from a federal prison in Fort Worth, Texas, is no way to run a crime family in New York.

Chin's experienced men who did not have bogus schizophrenia and dementia to stall their trials were already in jail thanks to the RICO Genovese family trials. Inexperience at the top led to the guy with the Rolex being able to infiltrate. An undercover NYPD detective working for the FBI known as "Big Frankie" also infiltrated. All this evidence in the new millennium took down six capos and more than seventy men. Cent 'anni, Big Frankie.

I had the pleasure of knowing that I had trained "Big Frankie" in undercover, schooling him in the way of the wiseguy while he was working. I was especially proud of the job he did.

The Chin and son were indicted in 2002. Andrew got two years. The Chin pled guilty to obstruction of justice by faking mental incompetence and stalling his earlier trial for seven years. In open court, as part of the plea bargain, the Chin was forced to admit that he was faking all along and had fooled the psychiatric professionals who had evaluated him. Behaving very competently in court, Chin got another three years on top of the senior-citizen discount of twelve years. Still, Chin died in the can in 2005. They should have made him return the $900 a month he got for years in disability benefits from Social Security based on his mental illness scam.

. . .

Because of underboss Neil Dellacroce's death from cancer while under indictment in the Mafia Commission Case, and boss Big Paul Castellano's murder while under indictment in the case, not a single member of the Gambino family was a part of the Mafia Commission Case. It was obvious that John Gotti was behind Big Paul's murder, and it was soon clear that Gotti was the new boss.

While I had testified in the Mafia Commission Case regarding the friction in the Bonanno family that led to the Galante hit, and that, friction or no friction within a family, a boss could not be killed without Commission approval, it was unclear that Gotti had such approval. But one thing was clear: Big Paul had been rendered vulnerable to a coup and a whack-out by virtue of the Mafia Commission Case investigation and the pending indictment.

Big Paul's White House had been bugged thanks to probable cause gathered from a tap on a phone of a talkative soldier, Angelo Ruggiero. Conversations from that tap were put together with what I had learned as Donnie Brasco, especially from Sonny Black telling me he had gone to Big Paul for approval to kill the three capos on May 5, 1981. Big Paul conducted his business largely from the White House, rarely going to the family's Ravenite social club on Mulberry Street in Little Italy. The White House bug and Big Paul's big mouth produced a ton of incriminating evidence against the Mafia Commission as a criminal organization and against Big Paul and the rest of the Mafia Commission bosses regarding the predicate crimes. But in a strange Mafia way, the thing that made Big Paul even more vulnerable to a capo coup was what the bug revealed about his decadent personal life. With his wife living in the house as his wife, Big Paul kept a live-in maid named Gloria Olarte as his live-in lover and confidante.

While the bosses professed morality and the need to respect wives, they had another motive that went beyond morality. Clearly, wiseguys had girlfriends and mistresses—*cumares*—and Mafia wives accepted that their husbands lived secret lives. But openly flaunting your mistress in front of your wife was forbidden. An irate wife could do a lot of damage, taking revenge by feeding information to the government.

Nevertheless, whatever flaws Big Paul had, they were not obviously self-destructive. On the other hand, the character flaws of John Gotti jumped out at you like one of those surprise snakes in a can that you let your children trick you with. Gotti's character was unchecked by self-control. John Gotti spelled disaster for John Gotti. Gotti was notorious for his tirades, threatening to kill soldiers who were late returning a call. Gotti, the boss of a family in a secret society, was a shameless publicity hound, always ready to flirt with the press and happy to make the covers of *Time*, *People*, *New York* and the *New York Times Magazine*. Gotti was a control freak, demanding that every capo and important soldier show up at the Ravenite Social Club once a week to report directly to him. Gotti was a degenerate gambler who lost tens of thousands every week on sports betting. Gotti bad-mouthed people to their face and behind their back—his own people, the feds, and the lawyers who got him off. Gotti's biggest flaw was the giant ego that drove him, and eventually ran over him.

At the time of the Big Paul hit on December 16, 1985, Gotti was not really known to the public. Of course, we knew him and we knew he was ambitious. From taps and bugs, Bruce Mouw's squad knew that Gotti was in trouble with Big Paul. And it was because of a tap on one of Gotti's crewmember's phones that the Bureau gained probable cause to bug Big Paul. Worse, that crewmember, Angelo Ruggiero, was a heroin trafficker. We figured Gotti struck first. Immediately after Big Paul got whacked, Gotti became front page.

Like O.J. Simpson, Gotti insulted the intelligence of the rest of the Mafia by claiming he had no idea who whacked Big Paul, and claimed that he would hunt for the hit men.

Three months after the Big Paul hit, Gotti went on trial for assault and robbery from an incident that took place while he was planning to hit Big Paul and take over as boss. Gotti had double-parked in front of a bar in Queens. A man on his way home from work beeped. Gotti came out of the bar with another wiseguy. They beat up the car beeper and, while he was down, took $350 from the guy's wallet. In Sonny Black's crew, a soldier who did that would have been punished. The only one I could see doing that in my time with the Mafia was Tony Mirra, but even he would have been smart enough not to take the guy's money and turn a simple assault into a strong-arm robbery. Certainly, no capo I knew—Sonny, Mike Sabella, Big Joey Massino—much less a future boss planning a coup, would do something that stupid.

The man pressed charges and trial was scheduled for March 24, 1986. The victim obviously had read the newspaper after the Big Paul hit. On the stand, he said, "To be perfectly honest, it was so long ago I don't remember." The New York Post headline nailed it: "I FORGOTTI."

Three weeks later, the new underboss that Gotti appointed, Frank DeCicco, was blown to bits in his car in Brooklyn by a remote-control-activated bomb. Gotti was supposed to have been with his underboss at the time. Clearly this was a sign that Gotti did not have the Mafia Commission's approval when he hit Big Paul.

While we were heading into the Mafia Commission trial that September in the federal Southern District in Manhattan under Rudy Giuliani, Gotti was becoming bigger and bigger news. At the same time, the federal Eastern District in Brooklyn decided to prosecute Gotti on RICO charges. Actually, they had revised the original indictment against suddenly deceased underboss, Neil Dellacroce, to target media star Gotti as the primary RICO defendant instead. Like the Mafia Commission trial, this new creation also went to trial in September 1986. But while our trial was over in nine weeks, the Gotti trial took seven months. When our 151 guilty verdicts came down on November 19, 1986, Gotti wisecracked to the press, "That's got nothing to do with me. I'll be home soon."

Diane Giaccolone was the prosecutor on the Eastern District's charges. She was about 30 years old and had had only one jury trial, which she lost. Ron Goldstock, the head of the New York State Organized Crime Task Force, heard that Giaccolone was going to move to revoke Gotti's bail and send him to jail in the months before the trial. Goldstock went to her and asked her not to do that. His outfit had very productive taps and bugs up and running against Gotti at the Bergin Hunt and Fish Club, but the second Gotti went to jail, the law required that the taps and bugs be stopped and pulled down. Let Gotti remain free on bail pending the trial, Goldstock reasoned; he won't flee, and if he decides to flee the taps and bugs will pick that up. Giaccolone denied Goldstock's request, Gotti was jailed pending trial, and our side lost a great opportunity to get quality evidence out of Gotti's own mouth. No prosecutor I ever had the good fortune to work with would have made the decision Giaccolone made.

The next bad decision that Giaccolone was considering, was to publicly expose a Bureau snitch. FBI agents working organized crime are encouraged to develop relationships with Mafia men and to turn these men into informants. To lure the man into becoming an informant, the man might be offered a pass on an arrest for a crime he committed, or he might be paid a regular salary, or be paid for specific information. The idea is to make the wiseguy think you are his friend. You pass along hopefully harmless information to him; you promise never to tell anyone about the wiseguy's cozy relationship with the government; and you promise that he will never be called on to testify. The Bureau had two such invaluable moles inside Gotti's Bergin Hunt and Fish Club.

One of these was Wilfred "Willie Boy" Johnson, a minor defendant in Giaccolone's case. Willie Boy's mother was Italian, but his father was a Mohawk Indian—one of those famous Mohawk ironworkers who have incredible balance and balls. They work on the building of skyscrapers by standing on the top beams and installing new ones. They are proud. They have their own community in Brooklyn with their own bars, and the only competition they have for that dangerous work are the men who come down from Newfoundland in Canada. Because his mother (and not his father) was Italian, Willie Boy could never become a made man. Among other things that Willie Boy didn't like about John Gotti, Willie Boy resented being called a "half-breed" by Gotti. But Willie Boy feared John Gotti and the power of life and death that Gotti wielded in his Bergin crew.

Diane Giaccolone believed that by exposing Willie Boy Johnson as a fifteen-year informant for the FBI it would frighten Willie Boy into leaving the defendants' table and becoming a witness for her in the upcoming trial. The Bureau got on their collective knees begging her not to expose Willie Boy. First, it could get him killed. Second, it would break the promises the Bureau made to Willie Boy. Third, it would send the message to other current and potential informants that the FBI could not be trusted. Fourth, it would end Willie Boy's usefulness as an informant. Fifth, it was no way to show gratitude to a man whose information helped establish probable cause to tap the Bergin crewmember, Angelo Ruggiero, whose conversations helped establish probable cause to bug Big Paul's White House.

Giaccolone denied the Bureau's request and exposed Willie Boy in open court with the press in attendance. But Willie Boy was more afraid of John Gotti than he was of Diane Giaccolone. How could he ever trust that he'd be treated right in this new Witness Protection Program if the government, as it had so often done in the past, broke another treaty with an Indian? Willie Boy stayed at the defense table, doing his best to deny that he had ever been a snitch.

Unfazed, Giaccolone decided to expose the other FBI informant in the Bergin Hunt and Fish Club to try to scare him into turning. His name was Billy Batista, a hijacker and bookmaker. Billy left a good-bye note for his FBI handler, whom he did not blame, and went on the lam. Hopefully, Billy learned his lesson and gave up a life of crime wherever he moved to. If I'd been Billy's FBI handler I'd have given him the money to disappear and get started on a new life. Let the Brooklyn DA prosecute me for obstruction of justice. Giaccolone cost the Bureau another valuable ally in its crusade against the Mafia.

The FBI pulled out of her case altogether, citing "administrative and procedural differences" with Giaccolone. I did not testify. I don't recommend bringing any of this up to Jules unless you want an earful.

The seven-month John Gotti RICO trial involved three murders and depended on the testimony of seven low-level turncoats loaded with the "negative baggage" such witnesses have.

On Friday the Thirteenth of March 1987, the jury after a week of deliberation returned a Not Guilty verdict. It was the first and only RICO victory for a Mafia boss. Gotti, who had been called the "Dapper Don" by the press because of his expensive Italian suits, got a new nickname, the "Teflon Don"—nothing stuck to him. March 1986, not guilty. March 1987, not guilty.

As had become the trend, this jury had been anonymous, its identity kept secret, the way Willie Boy's and Billy's identities were supposed to have been kept secret. But it was later revealed that a juror, George Pape, managed to get word to the wiseguys that he could be bought. He was paid $60,000 to guarantee that he would hold out for a hung jury. Gotti could have saved his $60,000 as the other eleven were unanimous for not guilty, anyway. Pape, meanwhile, would later pay for his sins.

Seventeen months after Gotti's acquittal, Willie Boy Johnson caught nine bullets on his way home from work in Brighton Beach, Brooklyn, and was left dead on the sidewalk as a warning to all informants everywhere. Always ready with a wisecrack, Gotti told the press, "Well, we all gotta go sometime."

Gotti, in his delusions of grandeur, actually believed that by winning cases and rubbing the government's nose in the dirt afterward, the government would eventually give up against the Mafia. Maybe Gotti listened more to the collaborator statements of Mario Cuomo than to the warrior statements of Rudy Giuliani. Gotti was the one, not the Chin, whom the psychiatrists should have evaluated. By his continued course of conduct, Gotti might as well have said to law enforcement, "Please work night and day to shut me down and shut me up."

A very realistic appraisal of how the rest of the Mafia viewed what was going in their world at that time appears in Peter Maas's book, written with the book's subject, and titled, *Underboss: Sammy the Bull Gravano's Story of Life in the Mafia.* In the words of Gravano, John Gotti's former underboss, ". . . here in New York there was the commission case, the pizza connection, on and on. All the old bosses have been put away for a hundred years. . . . A lot of people are saying the whole thing is falling apart. It was unbelievable. Unbelievable what that law professor Blakey did coming up with RICO. And you got to give Rudy Giuliani credit. . . . He showed them how to work this fucking RICO."

• • •

The next trial against Gotti took place in 1990, based on events that had happened a few years earlier. A carpenter's union boss named John O'Connor had busted up a new restaurant owned by a Gambino soldier. During construction, John O'Connor had his hand out for a bribe, but the restaurant owner slapped it down without putting any money in his palm. As it turns out, John O'Connor was connected to the Genovese family but Gotti didn't know it, and John O'Connor didn't know the restaurant was connected to Gotti's Gambino family.

And they call this organized crime.

This was one of Gotti's first matters as the new boss in January 1986. Ronald Goldstock had a bug in Gotti's Bergin club, the bug that was soon to be shut down prematurely by Diane Giaccolone's decision to have Gotti's bail revoked. On a tape from that bug, Gotti seemed to be giving the order to assault John O'Connor. Gotti said, "We're going to bust him up." In short order, rather than beat him up, thugs shot John O'Connor in the legs, presumably as punishment and as a message from Gotti.

Simple case, except for one thing—John O'Connor, the shooting victim, refused to identify anyone and planned to testify for the defense. Twice the case was turned down for prosecution by the federal Eastern District in Brooklyn. Finally, the Manhattan DA's office decided to go with it. The tapes clearly included Gotti's voice seeming to order the assault, but Gotti used words that were subject to interpretation. In addition, there was just one turncoat witness with tons of "negative baggage." He was serving 60 years for RICO, and cooperating was the only prayer he had of ever getting out of jail.

When you consider some of the "negative baggage" some of these Witness Protection guys have, you have to wonder who on the jury would want them to get out in 60 years, much less get out way sooner because of their cooperation. The turncoat witness in this case, a hit man and drug addict with the Irish Westies gang from Manhattan, admitted to the jury, "I killed a guy in a pet store once. I walked into the store and asked the guy if he had any flea collars. He didn't pay me no attention so I shot him in the head. He bounced off the wall so I shot him in the neck."

John O'Connor, Gotti's wounded victim, testified for the defense on Gotti's behalf that Gotti had no reason to have him shot, and that he had many other dangerous enemies who had more of a motive to have him shot. John O'Connor also testified that the police never warned him that they had heard on tape that he was about to take a beating. All law enforcement agencies have a strict policy that any time a tape reveals the threat of violence or death to anyone, detectives or agents will visit that person and the threat will be completely explained to him. If Gotti's words on the tape meant that Gotti was ordering O'Connor's assault, then why wasn't O'Connor warned by the law? Well, the only answer there could be is that

Gotti's words did not convey an order to harm John O'Connor, or the police would have warned him.

In his summation, Gotti's lawyer Bruce Cutler held fast to the 50-year-old party line of the Mafia: "All we ever hear from the government is Mafia! *Cosa Nostra!* . . . Organized crime! . . . But these are pure fantasies. They are constructs of the government. They are imaginary entities they use to categorize people. I say they don't exist. I have never seen one. No one on this jury has ever seen one. . . ."

On February 9, 1990 John Gotti was found not guilty for the third consecutive time in four years.

Jules, knowing something the outside world didn't know yet, gave a quote to the *New York Times* when that Not Guilty verdict came in. "Listen, the FBI hasn't brought a case against Gotti yet. When we do, he can take all the bets he wants, because he's going away to prison for a long time."

The thing that Jules knew when he made that human remark—a remark for which he would have yelled at me if I had made it—was that just two months before that verdict, Special Agent Bruce Mouw's Gambino squad had hit a mother load. They discovered that when Gotti went into the Ravenite Social Club on Mulberry Street in Little Italy, he sometimes took a shortcut to an apartment above the ground-floor hangout. This upstairs apartment belonged to Nettie Cirelli, a 72-year-old widow of a deceased Gambino soldier. When Gotti wanted to talk business, they would arrange for Nettie to leave her apartment. On November 19, 1989, three years to the day after the jury returned 151 guilty verdicts in the Mafia Commission Case, Bruce Mouw had the Ravenite warrant amended to include Nettie's apartment. Jimmy Kallstrom's electronic wizards went right to work and planted bugs in the apartment.

On tape on December 12, 1989 in Nettie's apartment, John Gotti clearly admitted to having three men killed. Gotti bragged that he'd had one of them whacked "because he refused to come in when I called. He didn't do nothing else wrong."

Soon RICO struck again in John Gotti's life. He was indicted, along with his underboss, Sammy "the Bull" Gravano, and his consigliere, Frankie Loc Locasio. This was an indictment crafted with the goal of destroying the entire leadership of the Gambino family all at once, just as the Mafia Commission Case had done to the Lucchese family (leading to a "killing frenzy") and to the Colombo family (leading to a "civil war").

During a hearing on a motion to deny bail to the three Gambino leaders, the Assistant U.S. Attorney in charge of the case, John Gleeson, played the December 12, 1989 tape. The defendants were in the courtroom with their lawyers. Because they had lawyers, neither the prosecutor nor the FBI were permitted to speak any words directly to any of the accused. The only way the government could speak to one of them is if the prosecutor received word from one of them that he wanted to cooperate and waived his lawyer's presence at a meeting. Now I'm not going to say that Gleeson played this tape for Judge Glasser in the presence of Sammy the Bull Gravano as a means of directly communicating certain information to Gravano, but it worked.

Sammy listened to the tape and heard Gotti bad-mouthing Sammy behind his back, making it sound as if Gotti had ordered the three hits because a bloodthirsty Sammy had insisted on the hits. To make the point that Sammy was greedy, Gotti criticized Sammy for having too many construction projects going on. Gotti accused Sammy of working to create "his own family within the family." An underboss who works to build his own power base of men loyal only to him is an underboss intent on whacking his boss and taking over. Gotti had already established such a precedent in the Gambino family of whacking the boss without Mafia Commission approval, but even Gotti had to believe that it wouldn't be real hard to get Mafia Commission approval to whack him.

Shortly after hearing the tapes for the first time ever, Sammy the Bull made the unprecedented decision to turn and testify. The Bull got his wife to contact the two agents that had investigated him, SA Frank Spero and SA Matthew Tricorico. At a confidential meeting with prosecutor John Gleeson and SA Bruce Mouw, Sammy the Bull said, "I want to switch governments."

Jury selection began in January 1992. Judge I. Leo Glasser, the former Dean of the Brooklyn Law School, took Gotti's past jury tampering very seriously. Despite the expense, Judge Glasser sequestered the jurors in separate hotels for the duration of the trial. An anonymous jury did not prevent a crooked juror from reaching out to the Mafia, but sequestration did. The jurors were allowed no visitors, and all their telephone calls were monitored. It was a necessary and bold move. But what a system. You can't direct a single question to a suspect who relies on Miranda when you arrest him, but you can lock up jurors—innocent citizens—for months and deprive them of their loved ones and their privacy on the phone. Maybe because of my years under I'm a little sensitive to what that means to a family. Anyway, later on in the trial, Judge Glasser relented a bit and allowed conjugal visits.

Judge Glasser personally had around-the-clock police protection following numerous death threats. At recess Gotti referred to both Judge Glasser and the federal prosecutor John Gleeson as "faggots." He referred to the Jewish prosecutor James Orenstein as "the Christ killer."

The actors Anthony Quinn and Mickey Rourke attended the trial, waving and giving words of encouragement to Gotti in front of the jury. I wonder what these two celebrities who wished the Don luck against their government thought of the wife and children of John Favara, a supervisor at a Castro convertible sofa factory on Long Island. Favara had accidentally killed John Gotti's 12-year-old son when the boy, driving a mini-bike, darted into Favara's path from behind a dumpster and Favara couldn't stop his car in time. Of course, traffic charges weren't even brought against Favara because he did nothing wrong. Dart-outs happen.

Out of fear of Gotti, and despite the fact that the Favara children played with the Gotti children, the Favaras sold their home to dart out of the neighborhood. But that wasn't good enough for the ego of John Gotti. The last time anyone saw John Favara alive was when an unidentified man sapped him in the Castro factory parking lot, stuffed him into a van, and drove off with him. While it was obvious to everyone, including John Favara's family, that this cruelty was the work of Gotti, no leads ever turned up on that 1980 hit. But today, the 12-year-old deceased mini-biker's sister, Victoria, now has her own hit TV show, all about her own children, on the A&E channel. What a system.

Due to Gotti's whacko and inflexible order that the capos and important soldiers show up at the Ravenite once a week to pay homage, physical surveillance revealed a lot that no one had known about the Gambino family, including the identification of a few capos who had previously remained under the radar. I would have liked to be in the courtroom sitting next to Gotti so I could have gotten a close-up of his face when the surveillance photos and videos—evidence enabled by his own ego—were shown to the jury.

The celebrities in the audience like Anthony Quinn and Mickey Rourke—and earlier James Caan and Robert Duvall attending the Mafia Commission Case—were there as informal character witnesses. By waving to Gotti and wishing him luck, they were telling the jury that they vouched for Gotti without having to take the witness stand and be cross-examined like ordinary character witnesses. It was a form of cheating. They could say he had such good character that they put their reputations on the line for him, and the prosecution could not challenge that. There isn't a wiseguy alive who could afford to call a legitimate character witness and have the witness cross-examined about the wiseguy's bad character, especially not John Gotti. Besides the celebrities in the audience, the defense called one witness, a tax lawyer, and he bombed when he got all the tax law wrong.

On April 7, 1992, the jury found John Gotti and Frankie Loc Locasio guilty on all thirteen counts. On June 23, 1992, Judge I. Leo Glasser sentenced Gotti to life without eligibility for parole. Gotti was sent to the federal prison in Marion, Illinois—the jail that was built to take the place of Alcatraz. Gotti was confined at Marion to lockdown, which meant he stayed alone in a 6 x 8 cell for 21 to 23 hours a day. Gotti died in the can at age 61 on June 10, 2002.

As Special Agent Bruce Mouw said in 1998, "They are in a sad state. They have no real boss, no underboss, and no *consigliere*." And it went downhill from there.

The New York tabloids report that Gotti's young and extremely inexperienced son Junior is the boss of whatever is left. But Junior now claims that he quit the Mafia. When Junior got married and his father was still alive, they had Junior's reception at the Versailles Room of the Helmsley Palace. The hotel flew the Italian flag over the entrance. They should have flown the white flag of surrender. After a couple of mistrials, Junior is still pending trial for ordering a hit on a radio personality, Curtis Sliwa, because Sliwa bad-mouthed Junior's father and sister on the radio. Sliwa was ambushed by gunfire and was wounded, but survived. Every time I hear about a Mafia revenge hit on a person who is outside the Mafia and in an unrelated business, like Curtis Sliwa, I tend to watch my surroundings a little more carefully for a few days.

During Gotti's trial, Sammy the Bull testified for nine days. His reward was a five-year sentence. In addition to testifying against Gotti, Sammy testified against the crooked juror, George Pape, whom Gravano had given $60,000 to ensure a hung jury. Gravano testified at the Chin's competency hearing, and at several other Mafia RICO trials. Sammy also revealed the existence of a crooked cop in the Intelligence section of the NYPD who sold information to the Gambinos. His name was Detective William Piest, and he got seven and a half years in the can.

Eight years after his testimony against Gotti, Sammy the Bull, along with his son Gerard (a/k/a Baby Bull), his daughter and her boyfriend, and his wife, were arrested in Arizona for heavily trafficking in the drug Ecstasy. The Bull got 20 years. He already has Graves' disease, a thyroid disorder, so Sammy will die in the can. The Baby Bull got nine and a half years.

Some critics have written that Sammy the Bull's testimony was not really needed to get Gotti, that the tapes from Nettie's apartment were good enough and that Gravano should not have been given a deal for his testimony. But a lot of sec-ond-guessers today fail to understand that wars are often fought on the level of morale. Destroying the entire Mafia remains the goal, one battle at a time. By the very act of Sammy the Bull turning on his boss, our side inflicted incalculable losses on the Mafia, its supposedly sacred rules, and its structure—not to mention recruitment. Who but the very dumbest among the city's dumb thugs would want the Mafia life as it was now revealed to be?

As Chin Gigante said to John Gotti when Gotti told the Chin that he had "made" his son Junior Gotti, "Jeez, I'm sorry to hear that."

CHAPTER 14
FALLOUT IN PHILLY

"THE COMMISSION WANTS IT STRAIGHTENED OUT. . . . Let the Commission decide. . . . Tell him it's the Commission from New York. Tell him he's dealing with the big boys now."

Those were the words of one of the "big boys," Fat Tony Salerno, boss of the Genovese, spoken in the twilight hours leading up to the nighttime that would descend following the Mafia Commission Case indictment. Fat Tony Salerno, whose words were being secretly bugged, was throwing the weight of a fully functioning Commission around the State of New York. The Buffalo family had a problem over who should lead, and Fat Tony sent the message back to Buffalo that the Commission would "decide" it. The Buffalo boss's men, who were armed with machine guns, were told by Fat Tony to put them away. "The Commission wants it straightened out. . . ." The Commission backed the boss, and there was to be no bloodshed, and there was none.

After the Mafia Commission Case, the "Commission from New York," like an aging wide receiver going out for a pass, began to hear the footsteps of the defensive back. There would still be a Mafia Commission of sorts after Judge Owen got done with them, but there would never be a fully functioning omnipotent Mafia Commission again. This was a huge blow to New York and to the nearby families most associated with the New York families.

The Philly family is a case in point. In 1980, there was an unauthorized coup when boss Angelo Bruno was whacked. Bruno, called the "Docile Don" in the press, had been boss for 21 years. The men who hit the Docile Don with shotguns as he was about to get out of his car, sat down with the Commission after the hit to explain. In fact, they thought they had pre-approval from the Commission. They were wrong. The ringleader was tortured and killed. His co-conspirators were killed. The Commission put in a new boss, an old friend of the murdered Docile Don, Chicken Man Testa. Chicken Man had once owned a fresh chicken store where Italian house-wives selected their live chicken for the evening's meal and had Chicken Man wring its neck and prepare it for pick-up later in the day. In 1981, a year after he became boss, two Philly men decided the "big boys" on the "Commission from New York" had made a mistake in selecting Chicken Man. So they blew Chicken Man up with a bomb planted under his front porch.

Can you imagine the jaws that dropped on "the big boys"—Big Paul, Tony Ducks, Fat Tony, and Carmine Persico—"the Commission from New York?" There were no wires up in 1982, but I can imagine what "the big boys" were say-ing. Don't these people down the Jersey Turnpike get it?

One of the bombers lammed to Florida where he died on his own before he could be whacked. They whacked the other bomber in 1982, a year after Chicken Man got blown up. The Commission made Little Nicky Scarfo boss. Little Nicky was nuts and would kill you as soon as look at you. No doubt the Commission selected him for this trait. The "big boys" on the Commission did not want any more unruliness out of Philly, unless the boss perpetrated it.

That's how a fully functioning Commission is supposed to work in the face of rebellion and the unauthorized killing of a boss.

Despite being nuts, Little Nicky remained boss until a couple of years after the Mafia Commission Case. In 1989 a RICO conviction slammed Little Nicky in the can for the rest of his life. Little Nicky's nephew and underboss, the tall and handsome Phil Leonetti, got 45 years in the same trial.

But by 1989, a lot had changed; night had descended on the Commission. The majority of "the big boys" on the "Commission from New York" were doing 100-year bits in tough prisons. Feeling the weight of a pending 45-year sentence, Phil Leonetti became the first underboss to flip and join the Witness Protection Program. Underboss Phil must not have been impressed with the Lucchese under-boss's old-school Mafia attitude when he was handed a hundred years in the Mafia

Commission Case. "Ah, give me the hundred. I'll go in now."

The Philly underboss ended up testifying all over the New York vicinity and did five years instead of the 45 he had been given. The Philly underboss was a man who had been at his Uncle Nicky's side since his teenage years and who knew a hell of a lot and spilled it all. The Philly underboss even admitted being guilty of a murder he had been found not guilty of.

Would the Philly underboss have turned if Rudy Giuliani had never made a Mafia Commission Case? If there had been a fully functioning Commission in place in 1989? I don't think so. Would he have been scared that the supremely powerful and politically well-connected Commission would eventually catch up to him, penetrate the Witness Protection Program and kill him? I think so.

· · ·

In the Mafia Commission Case we were able to come up with only two turncoats, a 78-year-old from Cleveland who could merely testify about the general history of the Mafia, and a low-level Colombo associate who, because he was not a made man, knew relatively little. In two years, a bumper crop of high-level turncoats had begun to sprout with the turning of the Philly underboss, followed by the turning of Gambino underboss Sammy the Bull Gravano.

In Philly, with Little Nicky in the can and his underboss and nephew gone bad, the family needed a boss. But by 1990 the replacement bosses on the Mafia Commission were either on the run or hearing footsteps.

While the entire Lucchese administration was in jail for 100 years, the new Lucchese boss and underboss were on the lam from a big RICO case, scared to death of getting 100 themselves. The Colombo boss, Carmine Persico, and his underboss Gerry Lang Langella, were in jail for 100-plus years each. But Persico was refusing to surrender leadership and was attempting to rule in New York from a prison in California. The Genovese boss, Chin Gigante, was wandering around Greenwich Village in his bathrobe, trying to avoid the wrath of RICO, not wanting to end up in jail for 100 years like Fat Tony Salerno. The Gambino boss, John Gotti, when he wasn't pandering to the press, was constantly sitting in a courtroom. The Bonanno boss, Rusty Rastelli, was still in jail, but he had been booted off the Commission when I surfaced.

The Mafia Commission was now like a substitute teacher. The class had a license to misbehave.

John Stanfa, a low-echelon figure in the Philly family, in the absence of a fully functioning "Commission from New York," ended up as Philly boss. Sources in the Bureau tell me that Stanfa was appointed Philly boss by John Gotti. Gotti had no real power to do that. Gotti was merely assuming to speak for whatever semblance of the Mafia Commission remained in name only. Stanfa had been the Docile Don's driver and bodyguard in 1980 the night the Docile Don was shotgunned in front of his house. Shooters rushed the car and wounded Stanfa in the shoulder. It looked like Stanfa was part of the plot. But the word around Philly from informants was that Stanfa was so poorly regarded as a soldier that all it took was a shot to the shoulder to neutralize him when his boss was whacked. As soon as Stanfa was named boss—a decade after his boss had been hit on his watch—a revolt broke out in Philly.

Only this time there was no "Commission from New York" to step in; no "big boys now." The Philly family war that followed in the early nineties was not as bloody as it could have been because of the incompetence of the factions, but it was bloody enough. It ended prematurely when the big boys in the U.S. Government stepped in. John Stanfa was hit with a RICO indictment. Bugging, and a number of turncoats diving into the Witness Protection Program like rats from a sinking ship, provided enough evidence against Stanfa for a few consecutive life sentences handed to him in 1994. Stanfa will age and die in Leavenworth, Kansas—a long way from his grandchildren in Philly.

Needing a boss in 1994, what was left of the Philly Mafia had no Mafia Commission to consult, nor "big boys" to fear. A young man whose family went way back in the Philly Mafia, Skinny Joey Merlino, got a brainstorm. Skinny Joey, acting on his own authority, inducted into the Mafia an older man, Ralph Natale, a drug dealer, who had just gotten out of jail in 1994. After giving him his button, Skinny Joey appointed this older man as boss and appointed himself underboss. Skinny Joey now had a figurehead for a boss and the illusion of a fully functioning Philly Mafia family to back up his criminal enterprise. This made his criminal rackets appear more menacing and threatening, and made it easier for Skinny Joey to extort honest businesses and collect gambling and loan-sharking debts.

As soon as the figurehead got himself caught in a crystal meth ring, he did what drug traffickers do. The figurehead, although a boss in name only, became the first boss to turn and testify against his own family. Unfortunately for the prosecutors, the figurehead had very little inside information to offer to a jury. Skinny Joey Merlino, underboss and boss-maker, was acquitted on the most serious charges in July 2001, despite the testimony against him by his own made boss. Skinny Joey Merlino was convicted on gambling and extortion, and did get fourteen years. He will be out in 2011 at the age of 49. Some informants tell us that so-and-so is the new boss; other informants tell us no one wants to be the Mafia boss in Philly in the new century. They call it "the city of rats."

I'll say this for Skinny Joey; he's got good taste in movies. When *Donnie Brasco* came out, some Philly agent friends of mine spotted him and his crew on line to see the flick. From what I hear, the whole Merlino crew gave it thumbs up.

Across the Delaware River from Philly lies New Jersey, the home of the small Sam "the Plumber" DeCavalcante crime family, the model for the Soprano family. When a territorial dispute over Trenton arose in the 1960s between Sam the Plumber's New Jersey family and the Philly family, it was "the big boys" on the "Commission from New York" who sat them down and straightened it out.

Shortly after I came out and the RICO engines began to rev up with the Bonanno family convictions, the other family RICO indictments, the Pizza Connection indictments, and the Mafia Commission indictments, Sam the Plumber DeCavalcante heard the RICO engines roaring and, by 1984, had retired to Florida. He turned the reins over to a new boss. In 1990 the new boss got convicted for simply doing all the things that Sam the Plumber would have been doing if he had not had the sense of self-preservation to retire. No sooner had the new boss been sentenced than his selection as acting boss disappeared. Then an old time capo and former underboss was also whacked. Not only were there no "big boys" on the "Commission from New York" across the Hudson River to straighten out whatever was going on in New Jersey as Fat Tony Salerno had done in Buffalo, but Sam the Plumber DeCavalcante, who was still alive in Florida, had enough good sense not to get involved in trying to mediate any of it. The wise old plumber died peacefully in Florida at age 84 in 1997.

CHAPTER 15

DONNIE BRASCO AT HOME AND ABROAD

WHILE ALL THIS WAS GOING ON—the Mafia Family cases, the Mafia Commission case, and so on—I still had a job to do besides providing background on the Mafia and testifying in court. And that job took me both back to my roots at the FBI training center in Virginia to assist recruits, as well as halfway around the world to bust badguys of all stripes. Whether I was training undercovers, or going back under myself on new operations, I loved my job and was always ready for the next opportunity—whatever it would be.

Here are a few stories of my time away from the Mafia cases, doing what I do best.

"THE RETREAD"

"Who's the old guy?" the kid with the muscles asked.

"Don't you know?" the other recruit answered.

"He looks pretty old to be just joining the FBI."

"He's a retread."

"What's that?

"Dude, I hope you don't expect me to run your mile for you, too."

The kid with the muscles laughed and said, "I guess a retread means he's been through this before."

"Ever heard of Donnie Brasco?"

"Sure, I read the book."

"He's your retread."

"Get out. Way cool. I knew there was something about that old guy. He's got that Corleone look."

"I wouldn't say that to him, dude, if I were you."

I cleared my throat and they turned around. "Break's over, men," I said and headed into the classroom. I had just given them a lesson in the danger of idle chatter.

I took my seat and now I was the pupil.

So here I was in Quantico, Virginia. It was May 1992 and I had become a retread. Normally . . . well, there is no normally. The Bureau lets very few who quit return to duty. But the ones who they did let return, they would just run them through the firearms part of training. Once they qualified on all the weapons, the Bureau would admit them back in. In my case I had to complete the entire sixteen weeks of New Agent Training.

My fame had forced the Bureau to make sure that, for morale purposes, no one could claim I was getting any favoritism. I understood that and I agreed with them because I would have to work alongside my fellow agents and I didn't want anyone thinking I thought I was anything special. I did my job as Donnie Brasco and I would do my job as SA Pistone.

To begin with, my application to return got neglected. I applied, and over a month later I had not even received a confirmation that my application had been received. I didn't want to call Jules or anyone else because I didn't want to start out on the wrong foot. Still I didn't like being ignored. If they didn't want me back all they had to do was say so. Every once in a while I thought of my former supervisor from the southern city. He had been transferred to Headquarters, but he was in a different section and should have had nothing to do with my application.

Finally, I got a call from a buddy who knew I had applied, Agent Steve

Salmeri.

"Your application, Joe," my buddy Steve said to me. "Have you heard any-thing?"

"Not a damn thing. Why? Have you heard something?"

"No, but I had a feeling you deserved a heads up."

It turned out that despite my suspicions, I was merely a victim of inertia. My application sat on the application supervisor's desk. He didn't know what to do with it so he just let it sit there. My buddy Steve had heard it was in the same spot on the desk for weeks so he decided to call me.

With that news I had no choice but to call Jules who, as usual, straightened out the unusual for me.

People ask me why I returned, and yes the pension was a consideration, but I was doing very well from the book and the movie deal. And there were more book offers out there and plenty of ways I could have traded on my fame to make bundles.

I didn't have to rejoin the Bureau to be involved in getting the Mafia. Without being an agent I kept up to date with what was going on in the five families. I was consulted from time to time. Watching from the sidelines and getting the inside scoop from my personal friends and sources was very gratifying. Seeing all the chaos we created paying huge dividends with inferior bosses like Amuso and Gaspipe was something I actually could do better by staying out of the Bureau. I was reachable at all times and for all kinds of information. Back in the Bureau, I would have a certain level and the rules would keep me out of the loop unless I was specifically needed for something. And I'd be less available to my old friends and colleagues. I'd be off on assignments all over the world—posing as an American wiseguy.

Furthermore, I certainly didn't rejoin to work the five families cases. Undercover was my area of expertise and my special talent. That is how I knew I would be used if I rejoined. I was more than washed up as an undercover agent against the five families. Whatever I did to them, and whatever the outcome of what I did would be, was out of my control. This was only troublesome to me with respect to the Bonanno family. The boss, Rusty Rastelli, had ordered the hit on Sonny Black and I could never lift a finger to unravel that hit and bring anyone to justice.

In summing up the consequences the Mafia Commission Case had on each of the five families in New York, Jerry Capeci wrote, "The Bonanno family has had the most stable leadership." Ouch.

The unintended result of my having gotten the Bonanno family kicked off the Commission was that not a single Bonanno boss, underboss, or consigliere was in the Mafia Commission Case. Although, in the can on the local 814 Case, Rusty Rastelli remained boss and groomed his successor, Big Joey Massino, for a smooth nonviolent and legitimate succession. Ouch again. Big Joey got out of jail the year I returned to the Bureau, and while I watched him build the family back up to the number one spot in the city, I would never work the Bonanno family again.

· · ·

They say that gamblers are addicted to adrenaline. The high comes while the coin is in the air, not when it lands on heads or tails. I was accused by an interviewer of running on adrenaline for so long as Donnie Brasco that it was hard for me to give it up. Maybe that's why I returned to the Bureau and put in four more years. Another interviewer suggested I knew the Bureau needed me and that I felt I still had something unique to contribute, something the Bureau couldn't get from anyone else: a ready-made Italian gangster named Donnie. At times like these, I would just nod and say, "You might be right."

But I know the main reason I returned to the Bureau. It was simple, and didn't need any analyzing. I was not finished as an FBI agent. I still had a lot of FBI living to do. I had loved being an agent and I missed it. I also knew that there was a lot of unfinished business for me in the Bureau. I might never be Donnie Brasco again, but I did have that ready-made Italian wiseguy look and all the tools that went with it. I wanted to use them again while I was still young enough—early middle age.

On top of that, my Sicilian nature did not like being forced out one little bit. I could not have that negative memory every time I looked at my souvenirs from my sixteen years of dedicated service to my country.

. . .

The sixteen weeks of New Agent Training amounted to a week for every year I had served from July 1969. The training included classes in the law, both criminal and intelligence gathering; classes in evidence collection, such as fingerprinting; classes in investigative techniques, such as undercover; and far too few classes in interviewing and interrogation.

There was also a lot of emphasis on physical training: running, push-ups, pull-ups, sit-ups, and all kinds of calisthenics and boxing. You had to qualify in a mile run every week, doing it under six-and-a-half minutes. And during untimed running, which was every day, you had to keep up with the Physical Training Instructor's pace. Fortunately, I had always stayed in shape. For years I ran every day. I lifted weights.

Unfortunately, the second day of training I pulled a hamstring. More unfortunately, our PT instructor was an HRT, and this was his first class as an instructor.

An HRT is a Hostage Rescue Team agent, and all they do is train all day long in between missions. I had first run into the HRT shortly after I surfaced in 1981. It was at Quantico. They had a small gym in those days run by a terrific agent, Al Beccacio. Al would sit in a small room behind a glass window and come out if he saw someone using a technique that wasn't quite right. Al was killed in the late 1990s in Bosnia in a helicopter crash.

There were a limited number of exercise benches and machines. In every gym I had ever been in, strangers took turns and shared the machines. I had worked out and done everything but my bench presses. There were two guys on the bench press, but they were just sitting next to it between reps. I brought my stuff over to the bench.

"What do you think you're doing?" one of them asked me.

"I thought I'd take a turn on the bench," I said.

"You can't use the bench."

"Why not?"

"We've got to work out."

"So do I," I said.

"We're HRT."

"I don't know what that is. Are you guys agents?"

"We're hostage rescue agents."

"All right. I was on the first SWAT team in New York. We're going to take turns like people do in a gym."

"No we're not," he said loudly and stood up.

"I'm jumping in," I said just as loudly. I took two 10-pound dumbbells off the rack to warm up.

"The hell you are," he said.

Still louder I said, "If you don't get out of my way right now, I'll crack you with one of these."

Al came running out from behind his window. "I think you better let him use the bench," Al said. "Because he will hit you."

The two HRT guys walked away and stayed away until I finished using the bench.

My next encounter with an HRT was this PT instructor who was none too sympathetic with my pulled hamstring. He kept criticizing me for not keeping up with the other runners and for seeing Jack the trainer to get the hammy wrapped. During the running exercises I lagged behind the men and jogged with the female new agents.

Every timed run saw me missing the mark by 40 to 45 seconds. The HRT complained to Assistant Director Tony Daniels that I shouldn't be allowed to continue. Everybody told the guy to lighten up, but they were talking to a guy who worked out ten hours a day. Unless there was a hostage situation, that's all these HRT guys did. Like a fireman keeping the fire engine in tune in between fires, this guy was obsessed with the physical training part of the job.

Tony Daniels made a point of coming to every timed run and cheering me on, which pissed the instructor off no end. Still, with a pulled hamstring that needs to be wrapped there is only so fast you can go. Jack the trainer was working with me and I was gutting it out, trying to pace myself so I could heal. It was humiliating enough without this guy breaking my balls. I had always been fast as a basketball player, with scholarship offers, and here my instructor was berating me while the Assistant Director cheered loudly.

One day we were out on one of the running exercises and the instructor had one of his HRT buddies running with us. The HRT guy kept running back to the females telling them to get a move on. I was at the back of the pack with the slowest of the females when this HRT guy ran back to me and said, "Come on you pussy, pick it up."

"Did he say what I think he said?" I asked the nearest female.

"Yeah, he did," she said and shook her head in disgust.

I ran up to him. I grabbed him by the shoulder. I turned him around.

We stopped and everybody stopped.

"I don't know who the fuck you are," I said. "You ever talk to me like that again, I'll flatten you."

"Excuse me?" he said.

"I'll say it again," I said. "You don't know why I'm running back here. I don't know who you are. Ever call me a pussy again, I'll lay you out."

He turned around like nothing happened and just started running to the front of the pack.

Nothing for nothing, but what probably scared the guy more than me was his use of the word "pussy." Over the years, that had become a giant no-no. When I trained in 1969 they said anything and everything to us. They humiliated us and kicked our butts. They toughened us up. It was worse than any boot camp. Now with so many women going into the Bureau and the changing times, he would probably rather have taken a shot from me than have to deal with the fallout from his vocabulary.

Finally came the last timed run. As they all were, this one was at the end of a rigorous day. Tony Daniels was on the sidelines cheering me on. I had to make this last mile run under six and a half minutes or I was done.

I missed the run by ten seconds. The HRT instructor made no effort to conceal his pleasure when he announced my time.

"Let him do it again," Tony Daniels said.

"I gave him every chance to qualify," the instructor said. "What if he has to run in the street and people's lives depend on it?"

"When do you want to run again, Joe?" Tony Daniels asked me, ignoring the instructor.

"I'll do it in the morning," I said.

"Sure you don't need a couple more days for the hamstring?" Tony Daniels asked me.

"I'd rather get it over with," I said. "I'll rest up tonight."

I met with the trainer early the next morning.

"Let's try it without the wrap," Jack said. "We'll just keep you in the whirlpool."

"You're the boss, Jack," I said.

Without the wrap putting a slight limp to my gait, I beat it by 35 seconds. Tony Daniels was as happy as I was. Retread, my ass.

SCOTLAND YARD

One day in 1994 I got a call from the Undercover Unit at Scotland Yard. I had worked with them in the past and they extended the courtesy of a direct call to me to see if I was interested before they called my superiors.

Scotland Yard was trying to find the location of a factory in Hong Kong that was making counterfeit American Express cards for the Triad. The Triad is Chinese organized crime. Unlike the American Mafia, which is composed of street guys, the Triad has businessmen, doctors, lawyers, politicians, and other professionals as members, in addition to street guys.

The Triad had a member on the inside at a high level at American Express who was stealing lists of cardholders and their card numbers. The idea was that a card in the name of a real person with that person's real card number could be used for a month until the real person got his bill and saw $20,000 worth of charges he had never made. With 100 such cards, a wiseguy could bring home to his boss a minimum of $2,000,000 worth of merchandise, such as jewelry.

Two Scotland Yard undercovers, one of Italian descent and one of English descent, had penetrated the Triad in England as buyers of these cards. They were buying them piecemeal and could bust the sellers, but that would have gotten them no closer to the factory in Hong Kong, which was their objective. They explained that they wanted me to fly over and pose as a Mafia boss who was interested in buying large quantities of these cards. My objective would be to somehow, during negotiations for a large purchase, get someone in the Triad to reveal a general location of the factory.

I said okay and they called my superiors and made the arrangements.

I flew to London and was met by the two undercovers. We remained in character while in public right from the start. You never know who is watching. At my hotel they explained that I was their Mafia contact in the U.S. who had been backing their purchases. Because everything was working without a hitch on the card scam, I planned on upping the ante. But before I was willing to shell out bigger bucks for more cards, I wanted to meet face-to-face with the people higher up. I wanted to size them up personally. If I got a bad vibe the deal would be off. If I sized them up as solid and reliable, I would put the big money into the operation.

First, however, the two undercovers told me I had to meet with the sergeant in charge of Scotland Yard's Serious Fraud Unit. This was a joint operation between their Undercover and their Serious Fraud Unit.

"Do you have a Not-So-Serious Fraud Unit?" I asked.

I always found the English a pleasure to work with. They had more formalities than we do, but they all had terrific senses of humor and were very dedicated.

They arranged for Sergeant Johnson to meet with me in a safe location. He was in his mid forties, about my height, 6' 1" or so and looked to be in excellent shape. His posture was military. As soon as we shook hands and met he began instructing me.

"These Triads are very keen on being respected. At all times in dealing with them you must pay them deference. Let them set the rules and do the talking. Always keep your tone of voice at a moderate level and keep a serious and respectful demeanor."

At first I thought he was kidding. "You mean I can't smack them around?"

He looked puzzled and said, "Be especially careful not to interrupt them. Sometimes they like to talk and they don't like to be interrupted."

"Look," I said. "Don't try to tell me how to do my job. I'm not telling you how to run your case. I don't tell you how to move the papers around on your desk, so don't try to tell me how to work undercover with criminals. That's what you brought me over to do at no cost to the Metropolitan Police Department.

I assume you brought me over because you trusted that I know how to handle myself."

"Do you know my position in this case?" he said.

"I know who you are. But don't tell me what to do; what I can't do; how to act; how to not act."

Sergeant Johnson was taken back. The two undercovers tried to conceal their smiles. He outranked them both.

"Very well," the sergeant said. "I'm sure you'll know what to do. As long as you know these are very important men you'll be dealing with, if you get that far."

"One more thing," I said. "I need to know where I can buy some ammunition for my gun."

"What do you mean?" The sergeant almost exploded.

"Ammunition. For my gun."

"You have a gun?"

"Sure, I couldn't do undercover without a gun. But I only brought over the rounds in the gun. I like to have extra rounds with me just in case."

"Agent Pistone, I must inform you that police in the U.K. are not permitted to carry guns."

"I never go undercover without a gun," I said.

"You'll have ample protection. I assure you," he said.

"Look," I said shaking my head. "I don't work undercover without my gun."

The sergeant began to stammer. "But, but, but you can't carry a gun in the U.K. It's out of the question."

"I'm sorry," I said. "I can't go undercover without a gun. I'd feel naked."

Finally the two undercovers couldn't contain themselves any longer and exploded in laughter. I burst out laughing too, and when the sergeant saw that I was having some fun with him he joined in the laughter.

"Don't worry," I said. "I've worked undercover here before. I know the rule against guns."

"That's a good one on me," the sergeant said. "Now what will you be wearing?"

Again I thought he was kidding. I said, "What I'm wearing now. A sport jacket, tie, slacks."

"You've got to wear a suit."

"Why."

"Because they do."

"This is all I brought with me."

"I'm afraid that won't do," he said. "These Triads always wear a well-tailored suit. For you to pass yourself off as a high-ranking member of American Organized Crime they would expect you to be well tailored." He hands money to my Scotland Yard contact and says, "Grahm, let's go out and get him a good suit."

I ended up with a Prince Charles plaid suit, a good pair of English shoes, and a couple of expensive shirts and ties. After all, this was "serious" fraud we were investigating.

In the beginning the Triads sent lower-level Chinese businessmen to meet with me, and each time I said, "I want to meet the main guy if I'm going to consummate this deal. Because of my status in the U.S. I don't deal with guys that are that much lower than me."

I used "Donnie" because it was a name I was comfortable with. The movie hadn't been made yet and it was still a safe name. No last names were necessary.

Hotel lobbies are popular meeting places in London. I had two or three lower-level meetings where the Triads were feeling me out. It was a scene out of GQ. Everybody was well dressed. Finally, when I could tell I had convinced them I was the real deal, I told them I was impatient and they had to send the top guy from the Triad in England if we were to go any further with this. "If I'm going to spend millions of dollars," I said, "I've got to know who I'm dealing with."

As I taught my undercover students at Quantico, the goal of the first undercover meeting is the second meeting, and the goal of the second meeting is the third.

The final meeting was set for a fashionable golf resort. I told them I had a suite there and we would meet in my suite. Scotland Yard had everything wired up and were listening in from the room next door. Sergeant Johnson of the Serious Fraud Unit would be there listening.

Right on schedule the Triads arrived. They had the top guy with them. We exchanged pleasantries, and then I began to outline what I was interested in. How much we want to buy. How many he could supply. How long it would take to get them. The more I talked, the more he interrupted me with his own comments.

"Look, you fucker," I said. I could almost hear Sgt. Johnson's jaw drop next door. "I want to tell you something. Why do your sentences begin in the middle of mine? I've shown you respect for a half hour. Why don't you respect me? If you interrupt me one more time when I'm talking we're done talking."

The head Triad, a young man in his thirties, bowed his head and said, "I'm sorry, Mr. Don."

We made the deal and I got the location of the factory. The key to getting information like that is not to seem to want it. It's all about not being interested in what you're interested in. I said, "I've never been to Hong Kong. If things work out on this deal I'd like to take a trip there and see the operation. Is it in a nice part of town?" That sort of thing. Small talk. Narrowing the area. He had no choice now but to politely answer my questions.

In the next room I later heard that the sergeant almost died. "What's he doing? I told him to show respect."

But since I got the factory in one meeting and they had been trying to get it for months, he was really complimentary. "You almost gave me a heart attack," he said. "I thought it was all over. I guess you do know your stuff."

He was a pretty good guy. I would have done just as well without the suit, but I got to keep the suit. They got the factory about a month later with my directions.

MY BLACK AND WHITE WORLD

Before I retired from my FBI world where I saw everything in black and white, I tried to cram as much into the adventure as possible. As with any job it's not all fun and games. There was a particular adventure in a dirt-poor country in the Caribbean that I could have done without. I've told this story before, but never in this depth.

The country was a way station for cocaine coming into the U.S. For security reasons I can't identify the country. The military government was riddled with corruption and stability was not a way of life down there. My partner and I were assigned to pose as American Mafia wiseguys visiting the country to set up trafficking routes. An honest anti-drug Colonel would contact us at our hotel. He was the only one who knew who we were. He would be our only contact on the island and we were not to invoke his name. There would be no one else to trust. The rest of the island would be full of barracudas as far as we would be concerned.

We met with the honest Colonel and he gave me a pearl-handled pistola. Through his contacts he had scheduled a pre-arranged very private meeting for us the next day with a man suspected of being the main drug trafficker on the island. This suspected drug trafficker was also a very high-ranking military officer, and we were going to meet with him at his legitimate military hacienda without a lot of goons with submachine guns guarding him. The honest Colonel assured us that he had taken care of our exit strategy. No one would bother us.

Our job, posing as potential buyers, was to assist the honest Colonel in confirming his suspicions that the target was a drug trafficker. Once it was confirmed they would convince the trafficker to retire from his wicked lifestyle. My partner spoke the language, but the suspected drug lord spoke fluent English.

We paid our scheduled visit to the suspected main drug trafficker. Those who were secretly listening in had their suspicions confirmed. They stepped in to convince the drug lord to go straight, and things got a little out of hand. We slipped out quietly and returned to our downtown hotel.

While my partner was downstairs in the lobby, five soldiers busted the door in, beat me with gun butts and handcuffed me from behind. When my partner came in they did the same to him.

"What do you think you're doing?" I said. "We're American tourists."

The leader of the squad put a key of cocaine in my travel bag and said, "You are drug dealers and assassins. There is cocaine in your luggage."

"We're American tourists," my partner and I said at the same time.

"You are American drug traffickers and you have assassinated" so-and-so. Apparently, they had already discovered that the military drug dealer we had just visited was gone. I had slipped the honest Colonel's gun under the mattress, but they found it and waved it to silence us when we tried to repeat that we were American tourists.

Now without communicating to each other, we knew we had to be in the grasp of the crew of the supposedly assassinated so-and-so. But why didn't they whack us on the spot? Instead they took us out of the hotel and into two jeeps. We got out in front of police headquarters. But that was not necessarily a good sign.

They brought us into a room on the fifth floor and began the accusations again. "You shot" so-and-so. "You are cocaine traffickers." Then they would smack us around. This was followed by our denials. "We're American tourists."

After a long while of this, a big fat Colonel walked in. I guess he was a colonel. They all seemed to be either privates or colonels. By now it was about one in the morning. The big fat Colonel gave the signal and two of the soldiers brought me to the balcony and hoisted me over the side, holding on to my belt.

"We're going to drop you," one of them said.

"You'd better drop me," I said. "Because I don't know what you are talking about."

"You killed" so-and-so.

"I never killed anybody in my life," I said. I tried to stay frozen so they didn't lose their grips. "I'm an American tourist."

We had been well-trained to gut it out, and here it literally was the belt around my gut that was keeping me alive.

The big fat Colonel gave another signal and they hoisted me back inside. My partner and I were standing there when the big fat Colonel looked us up and down and said, "Take them into the jungle and shoot them."

Now I knew why they didn't kill us sooner. In the jungle they would not have to concern themselves about a body. The jungle animals would handle our carcasses.

My partner looked at me and said, "Let's use his name." I nodded in agreement and we invoked the honest Colonel's name. Like the coin in the air—would it be heads, would it be tails—we had a 50-50 chance that these were not enemies of the honest Colonel. But I'm not sure I had any adrenaline left in me while that coin was in the air.

They called the honest Colonel. Bingo, bingo, bingo, they took our cuffs off and drove us back to the hotel as if nothing had happened. We got out of that country on our scheduled flight without sticking around for any sightseeing.

Our honest Colonel was a decent guy. He was trying to do the right thing for his country. We helped him do justice and we never saw him again. He loved pumpkin soup. Two weeks after we flew out of there, they poisoned his pumpkin soup and killed him.

. . .

Each country seems to have its own favorite criminal activity. The U.S. is the capital of the world's narcotics consumption. Mexico had a lot of kidnapping for ransom. Newly emerging countries from the former Soviet Union have a lot of street scams.

The Bureau provides a National Academy for American cops where they come to Quantico and get a certificate in advanced police techniques. The Bureau provides the same service for cops from the former Soviet Union. The Academy is in Budapest, Hungary and cops come to it from places like Russia, Estonia, Slovenia, and Moldova.

I made several trips to Hungary to lecture at the Academy. Budapest is a beautiful city and the food at the restaurants is top notch. The scam in the streets involves money changing. All money changing must be done at banks or legal money changing establishments. The rates are set continually. However, the streets are full of illicit money changers who will give a tourist a better rate. I didn't know how some of them got to deliver a better rate, but they certainly didn't have the overhead of office space,

One evening on a street in Budapest three Hungarian gentlemen stopped another agent and me. They blocked our path.

"Let us examine your money," one of them said.

"Not a chance," I said.

"We just want to look at it."

"You're not getting it," I said.

"We're police. We need to examine your money."

"What for?" I said.

"We saw you exchanging money with people down the street."

"No way," I laughed. "We just left that restaurant down the street. We haven't even talked to anyone."

"Don't lie. We saw you. We need to check your money for markings."

"Okay," I said. "Show us your badges and let's all head to the police station together and we'll look at all the money you want to look at."

All three backed up at once and let us pass. If those con artists had checked our Hungarian money we would have never seen it again. A tourist who had actually exchanged money illegally on the street would have been happy to surrender the money to these phony cops rather than get arrested for it.

Then I realized how some of them got to be able to deliver a better rate of exchange. They stole the money in the first place and re-sold it for American dollars. It was just a form of recycling.

. . .

Speaking of recycling, I was working another case for Scotland Yard. There was a pub in a neighborhood outside of London that the woman owner was suspected of running guns out of. These weapons were being smuggled to Ireland.

A U.K. undercover brought me around to the bar and introduced me as a New York wiseguy. I hung around the pub the way I had done in New York in 1975 posing as a jewel thief to get noticed. I struck up an acquaintance with the frumpy woman who owned and ran the place. She was pale from spending too much time indoors and she relished my company. I sat at the bar and drank draft beer. She would draw a good head on the beer and scrape it off at the top. It was delicious and it made sitting there with the old biddy a lot easier to do.

Finally, after I had expressed an interest in the building a number of times, she took me upstairs to show it off. I hoped I would see some signs that guns were there or had been there, perhaps an odor of gun oil. She showed me the rooms where she housed illegal aliens. The illegals were from Ireland and they worked for her for a pittance and for food and for part of a room. Maybe all she was smuggling was illegal aliens because I saw no sign of guns upstairs.

In a few days I got her to show me the downstairs. Like the upstairs, there were no signs of gun running.

But she was very proud of the downstairs cellar. It was there that she recycled her beer. She had constructed a tube in the drain underneath from where she would draw the drafts of beer for her customers. Any spillage or any beer from the head that she would scrape off would go into the tube. The tube was connected to a keg. She would fill the keg with the spilled beer and sell it as fresh brew. All that time I sat there, who knows what I was drinking. They say your stomach can handle more beer if it's slightly flat because there is less gas content to bloat your belly. So she not only recycled but she sold more of her beer that way. I have to admit, though, it tasted good.

Unfortunately, our effort fell as flat as her beer and I moved on.

SIBERIA

Following my second and final retirement I continued to respond to the Bureau's requests for my unique perspective. I would lecture around the world and advise in general and on specific cases.

But who could have ever thought when it all began in dingy taverns in Brooklyn and Manhattan in 1975 that thirty years later I'd be giving instruction on undercover operations in Siberia?

A couple of years ago I found myself lecturing at a military installation in the natural gas capital of Russia. I had a Russian-born FBI analyst named Nick who translated for me. I also had a "minder" assigned to me named Dimitri. Even today with communism all but gone they still make you travel with a "minder" to keep an eye on your activities.

There were 150 men in uniform in the auditorium. They were a great audience. They sat up straight and hung on every word as if I were lecturing on something they were each about to undertake. Their leader and our main contact was a colonel in the Russian army.

Off to one side there were five guys who were obviously out of place and quite striking in appearance. They were big and tough looking. Hard in every way. They were not in uniform. They wore long black leather coats. They didn't associate with anybody but themselves. And nobody in uniform attempted to talk to them either. They never came to the mess hall for lunch.

Following the second day of instruction, the head guy of the five in black leather coats came up to Nick and me and to my surprise all he wanted was to invite us to dinner.

"Fine," I said through Nick, "We've got to check with the colonel."

"Don't worry about the colonel," the head guy said. "I'll take care of the colonel."

He walked over to the colonel and said a few words and walked back to us. You could tell that the colonel was disappointed, but he appeared to accept the reality that he obviously had no power over this hard case in black.

I called out to my "minder" Dimitri and he started over to join us. But the head guy grunted a word or two in Russian and Dimitri did an about face and did not attempt to join us.

These guys had their own cars out front, two of those little pieces of junk they drive over there. The FBI contingent got in and we drove off. The black leather jackets pulled up in front of the best restaurant in the Siberian city, but only one guy made a move to get out. The rest of us sat there in the two cars while he went into the restaurant.

Soon we began to see an unusual volume of people coming out of the restaurant. We got out of the cars and went into the restaurant and they locked the doors behind us. The restaurant was empty. People had been in the restaurant eating their dinners and they had been cleared out. That was spooky.

We sat at a big round table and were introduced to each guy by his first name only. We were told none of their ranks. I do remember the head guy's name but it is not something I am free to reveal.

It turned out from talking to them that these guys were all decorated veterans of the war in Chechnya. They were selected for their current assignment on the basis of their courage and toughness. These five guys in black leather were part of an anti-Mafia unit that reports directly to the President of Russia through some minister. They have unlimited authority and can go anywhere in Russia in pursuit of the Russian Mafia.

We were the first Americans they had ever had contact with.

After dinner they took us to an old military base that they were having rebuilt for their special needs. We saw their arsenal of weapons; it was enough to take over a Third World country.

At the end of the visit the head guy said to Nick, "Tell Joe I am sorry to tell him there are three Russian Mafia spies in the audience at his lecture."

"Nick," I said. "I don't want to insult the guy, but is there anything else we should know? And how does he know there are three spies in the audience?"

The head guy laughed as if I had just told the funniest joke in the world. To begin with, whenever you ask a Russian a question they answer by telling a story. He continued to laugh and finally said in so many words, "Everything is not what it seems to look like. Tell Joe we do our homework."

"Well," I said. "Tell him we'll tell the colonel tomorrow about the three spies."

"Joe doesn't have to tell the colonel anything," he said. "We will solve the problem."

The hell with it, I thought. It's their problem, not mine. If he doesn't want me to say anything to the colonel I won't. As far as I know I'm not teaching anything that would be of value to the Russian Mafia anyway.

The next morning and for every day's lecture thereafter, I looked out at three empty seats where before there had been men in uniform. No one else ever sat in those vacated seats.

These five men in black were very good company. They took us out for dinner a couple more times, picking my brain on undercover work. But they never said a word about the three empty seats and we never asked.

CHAPTER 16
THE LUCCHESE FAMILY

TRIAL TESTIMONY OF JOSEPH D. PISTONE IN THE MAFIA COM-MISSION CASE:

MICHAEL CHERTOFF: When he said Tony Ducks, did you know who he was referring to?

JOSEPH D. PISTONE: Tony Ducks Corallo.

MC: Had you at any point ever met Mr. Corallo in the course of your undercover operation?

JP: Sure did.

MC: Who did you understand Mr. Corallo to be at that time?

JP: At that time I understood him to be a boss.

MC: Did you know then which specific family?

JP: Lucchese family.

That testimony may not sound like a big deal today, but it sure did the afternoon when the Mafia Commission Case jury heard it. It was crucial to our case that we establish Tony Ducks Corallo as the boss of a crime family known as the Lucchese crime family. Without it, we had no case. The moment I said, "Sure did," the jury knew that as a Bonanno family member I had met Tony Ducks Corallo in the capacity of the boss of the Lucchese family. I was an eyewitness to that indispensable proof in a RICO trial. And the source of that proof brought no "negative baggage" to the witness stand that would inject doubt or cause a jury to wonder about the truth of it. I was not facing a life term. I had sold heroin to no one. I had killed no one while trying to buy a flea collar in a pet store. I was an undercover FBI agent who had put his life on the line to gather this information, and the jury understood that.

The Lucchese family had been a very stable family ever since the formation of the Commission in 1931. The existence of the Lucchese family was not known to the public until 1963 when Joe Valachi turned and became the first made man in history to violate the Mafia's sacred oath of *omerta*. That code of silence required Mafia members and associates to: deny the existence of the Mafia; admit nothing; never speak about family matters to outsiders; and certainly never provide information, evidence, or testimony to the law. Valachi, at the time he turned, was a Genovese family soldier who believed that the boss of the family, Vito Genovese, had ordered his murder while they were in federal prison together in Atlanta serving lengthy sentences for heroin trafficking. Vito Genovese was the Mafia enforcer for Italian dictator Mussolini. Genovese ordered Carmine Galante to murder the New York anti-Mussolini newspaperman Carlo Tresca.

At a nationally televised Senate hearing in 1963, Joe Valachi identified the Lucchese family as one of the five New York Mafia families. Joe Valachi identified Tommy Lucchese as the boss of the family that had been started by Tommy Gagliano in 1931, with Tommy Lucchese then as the underboss.

Tony Ducks Corallo was only the third boss the family had ever had from 1931 until the Mafia Commission Case in 1986. There had been no upheavals; this was a well-oiled machine. Gagliano died of natural causes in 1954, and Lucchese the understudy underboss took over and was boss when Valachi testified. Lucchese died of natural causes in 1967 and Tony Ducks Corallo took over.

After the 100-year sentences in 1986, believing it likely that his entire administration would never get out of jail alive, Tony Ducks Corallo appointed Vic Amuso as boss and Anthony "Gaspipe" Casso as underboss of the Lucchese family.

In his *Complete Idiot's Guide to the Mafia*, Jerry Capeci succinctly summed up the effects the Mafia Commission Case convictions and Judge Owen's 100-year sentences had on the Lucchese family: "The conviction of Lucchese boss Tony 'Ducks' Corallo and his underboss and consigliere brought chaos to that family.

Vittorio 'Vic' Amuso and Anthony 'Gaspipe' Casso began a family killing frenzy that left dozens of mobsters and associates dead."

Then that "killing frenzy" left dozens of made men with no choice but to cooperate and go into the Witness Protection Program to keep from getting whacked by Amuso and Gaspipe. But for Judge Owen stepping up to the plate and sending a strong message to current and future Mafia bosses, the Lucchese family would not have begun a journey into impotency that was fueled by cooperation with the FBI at every level of the family.

Jerry Capeci wrote that Amuso and Gaspipe "were totally out of their league when it came to the subtleties of running such an operation." The family had many capos that would not have been out of their league, men who had been made decades ago. Amuso and Gaspipe's initiation as made men had only occurred in 1974.

That Gaspipe was never considered a powerful man in the Mafia before he was made underboss can be seen by an attempt to whack him that took place in September 1986, the month we began picking the jury for the Mafia Commission Case.

Gaspipe had a beef with a Gambino capo, Mickey Boy Paradiso. The beef was over money, naturally—who was entitled to what on a heroin deal. Normally, the Mafia Commission would mediate a money dispute between members of two different families. There'd be a sit-down presided over by the Commission. But at that time, the Mafia Commission was indisposed in a federal courtroom. They could not afford to get photographed conducting sit-downs and giving Mike Chertoff more evidence against them.

So Mickey Boy, not respecting Gaspipe's power, not thinking a soldier like Gaspipe could generate a backlash if he were eliminated, dispatched four hit men. Gaspipe was lured to a meeting and, while parking his Lincoln on a street in the Flatlands section of Brooklyn, a car pulled alongside and four men began firing. A shotgun blast went through the driver's window. Gaspipe was hit twice, but managed to get into a restaurant and then to a hospital.

In processing Gaspipe's Lincoln, the NYPD found a highly classified list of license plate numbers. They were the numbers of the unmarked cars used by the NYPD in physical surveillance and tails. The only thing Gaspipe would tell the

NYPD is, "There's nobody who don't like me. I don't know nothing about organized crime."

Besides all this, Amuso and Gaspipe had another black mark. They were primarily drug traffickers. Tony Ducks claimed to be against drugs. Yet Amuso had served four years for heroin trafficking and Gaspipe had beaten drug trafficking charges, almost getting himself whacked in a drug dispute with Mickey Boy Paradiso. I couldn't even get made in Sonny Black's crew if I took a drug bust. Both Lefty and Sonny warned me on this subject when they told me I was going to be made that December of 1981. And I was in the Bonanno family, the family with the reputation for heroin smuggling. One of the Palma Boys Social Club tapes that were used in the Mafia Commission Case included Fat Tony Salerno's disapproving critique of the Bonannos' involvement in narcotics: "Yeah, they took too many junkies in there, the Bonannos."

If Tony Ducks was searching for quality leadership, like Donald Trump he'd have excluded drug traffickers. Because of the extremely long sentences and the difficulty of beating the charges, drug traffickers, more likely than, say, hijackers, have a tendency not to stand up. The drug policy of the bosses while I was under should really have been expressed this way: "We love drug trafficking and we appreciate the large sums of money you send upstream, but if you get caught on a serious drug charge, we will whack you."

It was a heroin trafficker, Joe Valachi, who had exposed the Lucchese family to the public to begin with. Valachi feared being hit by his heroin trafficking boss, Vito Genovese, who suspected that Valachi would rat to shave time off his heroin sentence.

So why did Tony Ducks Corallo appoint two drug traffickers with very little leadership experience to the top spots in the family? Gaspipe had never served as a capo and had never even led a crew. Gaspipe, a soldier, was so little regarded in the Mafia that he got no respect from Gambino capo Mickey Boy Paradiso. What made them qualified?

The way I see it, unlike Donald Trump, Tony Ducks' primary consideration was not finding the most qualified leaders. The primary consideration now was the Lucchese leaders' court appeal and the slim hope of getting their convictions overturned.

If a miracle happened and they won their appeals, appeals of a pretty much untested RICO law, these three bosses would need loyal men as acting boss and underboss, men who lacked ambition, men who would treat them with respect when they returned from jail.

Gaspipe Casso led the league in oily displays of loyalty and lack of ambition. Earlier in his career Gaspipe had turned down the job of capo and suggested Vic Amuso for the job. This was a foxy show of loyalty and lack of ambition. It happened when Christy Tick Furnari got upped and was made consigliere. Christy Tick offered the capo spot of his former crew to Gaspipe. In turning it down, Gaspipe said that he'd rather stick to Christy Tick's side, since a consigliere is allowed to keep one soldier as an aide de camp. Then after the 100-year sentences, Amuso and Gaspipe were told by Christy Tick that they were each being considered for boss. Again Gaspipe deferred to Amuso, asking to be underboss. This subservient act by Gaspipe fooled Christy Tick Furnari.

But once in as underboss, Gaspipe wasted no time in proving that he was full of what Mario Cuomo might call "a lot of baloney" when he had played the humble role with Christy Tick Furnari. My sources in the Bureau assured me that Gaspipe was the true dominant force of the two new leaders—the brains, the strategist, the master manipulator. As second fiddle, Gaspipe was the one who orchestrated things. And under Gaspipe's baton, Amuso began to seize the reins of power with a vengeance.

Jerry Capeci wrote: "Their main idea of management was to kill anyone who displeased them in any way. Their secondary plank was to kill anyone whom they thought might displease them."

They just banged them out. They killed one capo just because Tony Ducks Corallo had been considering the guy for boss before he settled on Amuso. They killed another capo thinking he might be a potential challenger, but really, they ended up getting the dead capo's loanshark book which was worth seven million dollars. Whoever owed money to the recently departed capo now paid that vig to Amuso and Gaspipe. They cremated one guy in a funeral parlor that they used to dispose of bodies. He was a long-time made man who was being replaced by a non-made man in a garment industry racket. This was not how wiseguys were supposed to be treated. The made man protested the loss of his position to a non-made man. What was the value of your button if a non-made man could replace you? The guy referred to his replacement as "a Jew bastard," and was promptly whacked.

One poor guy saw the handwriting on the wall and fled to California. Gaspipe tracked him down and sent a four-man hit team to gun him down. This hit, even more than the others, illustrated how much of an act Gaspipe had put on for Christy Tick. The man who had fled to California was former underboss Tom Mix Santoro's nephew.

In one hit, the guy smelled trouble while he was walking into an auto body shop garage with his friends who were going to kill him. The guy bolted and ran for the exit. Soldier Louis "Bagels" Daidone had been a quarterback on Brooklyn's New Utrecht High School football team and had a short stay at Indiana State on a football scholarship. Louis Bagels made an open-field tackle and brought the guy deeper into the garage where they whacked him. Louis Bagels had killed and frozen a canary, saving it for the occasion. He stuffed the canary in the deceased's mouth and that was the way he was found. The idea of the canary was that the guy had begun to sing to the feds. The guy had committed another sin, too. He had failed to visit Gaspipe when Gaspipe was recuperating from the attempted hit in September 1986. Gaspipe kept score his own special way.

With all of these hits, and many others, there was a certain amount of "cleaning the house" that had to be done. It is accepted that if you whack a guy you need to "clean the house." You need to be sure to whack whoever you believe will seek vengeance. It was partly "cleaning the house" that caused Sonny Black to give me the hit on Bruno after they whacked his father Sonny Red. The guy who Louie Bagels tackled had two good buddies. The three of them were jewel thieves together. For obvious reasons, I hate to see jewel thieves get whacked. But these two were gunned down. One of them was suspected of having homosexual tendencies, so he was shot in the groin a few times.

Any time there was a federal investigation, Amuso and Gaspipe did not wait to see who might be indicted. They just whacked out people. They hit a Democrat Party district leader and former union leader as he left his mistress's apartment. They hit another leader of a union that was being investigated. The man was wounded with the first surprise shot and, before he was finished off, he looked up at the shooters, his friends, and said in disbelief, "I'm not a rat."

Gaspipe ordered a hit on the architect of his $1.2 million house. The reason given was always the same—suspicion of informing. The architect had been tortured with bullet wounds, stabbings, and cigarette burns before being finished off. There was a rumor that the architect had had an affair with Gaspipe's wife.

They killed another guy who had allowed Bonanno family associate Gus Farace to hide out in his apartment. Gus Farace had shot and killed a DEA agent, Everett Hatcher. After Gus Farace gunned down Hatcher in the street, certain law enforcement authorities had visited the bosses and demanded Farace's head. The guy who hid Farace was told to kill Farace right there in his apartment and failed to do it, no doubt not wanting to kill someone in his own apartment, but his excuse was not accepted and he was whacked.

One of Gaspipe's neighbors made the mistake of griping to Gaspipe that the neighbor's daughter's ex-boyfriend couldn't take no for an answer and still came around to the house despite the fact that his daughter was now engaged to another man. Gaspipe had the forlorn lover whacked as an act of neighborliness.

There were also many murder attempts that went awry. Gaspipe paid 400-pound Fat Pete Chiodo $40,000 to go to Florida to whack a soldier. Fat Pete fired two bullets into the soldier, but the guy lived. Gaspipe complained, "Petey cost me $20,000 a bullet."

• • •

But for the success of the Mafia Commission Case, these killings and many others would not have happened. You can't feel good about hits like these, but not because it's wrong. I mean, who really cares when they kill each other? It's just an excuse to arrest them for murder and put them away. The reason you can't feel good when the job you did has led to hits like these, is that you know that there were others also, innocents, who were killed "but for" the job you did.

In the Mafia Commission Case there was a bug on Sal Avellino's Jaguar. That bug led to incriminating comments by Lucchese underboss Tom Mix Santoro and by Lucchese boss Tony Ducks Corallo. Those taped statements were introduced into evidence against the Lucchese family at the trial. Sal Avellino was embarrassed and lost face over the bugging of his Jaguar. To reclaim his self-respect he asked Gaspipe to whack the businessman who had given the New York State Organized Crime Task Force information that helped provide probable cause to authorize the bug.

Robert Kubecka, age 40, had been determined not to pay tribute to the Mafia or to let the Mafia drive him out of his family business as a waste hauler on Long Island. Kubecka cooperated with the New York State authorities. On August 10, 1989, Kubecka and his brother-in-law Donald Barstow showed up for work at 6 a.m. Within minutes these two valiant men were gunned down by two of Gaspipe's cowards. Kubecka and Barstow left behind wives and children. Kubecka's father, Jerry, missed being killed by staying home from work that day. I can't even imagine what that family has lived with.

Donald Barstow died instantly, but the courageous Kubecka, before he succumbed to his mortal wounds, had managed to reach one of the two shooters and injure him in some unknown way and to such an extent that the shooter left a trail of blood.

In the days before they were killed, these true American heroes had asked the state to provide security cameras for their office and to have a cop car sit out front off and on as a warning. They were denied any support. Because the state failed to protect them, their families sued for negligence and at least got a monetary settlement.

• • •

In May 1990, three years after taking over, Gaspipe got inside information from what he called his Crystal Ball, that he and Amuso were about to be indicted with a number of bosses from the other families in what came to be known as the Windows Case. It was a RICO case involving the Mafia's control of the installation of windows in all public housing in New York.

Amuso and Gaspipe met with Lucchese capo Little Al D'Arco, a Korean War veteran, and told him they were going on the lam. Amuso and Gaspipe said that they wanted the RICO Windows Case to proceed to trial without them. That way, when they returned, their lawyers would have the benefit of the trial transcript and they would stand a better chance of beating the case in court. This was the same successful tactic used by Big Joey Massino in the Bonanno family trial when he hid out at Goldie Leisenheimer's parents' vacation house in the Poconos.

Amuso and Gaspipe told Little Al D'Arco that he would be appointed acting boss in their absence, but that they would still control the Lucchese family. Gaspipe detailed an elaborate code and system of communication using pay phones. Little Al D'Arco had been a made man for only eight years and had spent four of those years in jail on heroin trafficking charges. Little Al had been a capo for only a couple of years and functioned primarily as Amuso and Gaspipe's personal bagman for operations like the Lucchese bosses' control of the Hunts Point wholesale produce market. Little Al had his own son made and installed him in heroin deals, and the son became a junky. And now Little Al D'Arco was acting boss. How much things had changed in three short years since Judge Owen sent his message. A succession such as this would have been impossible with a strong Commission in place.

Gaspipe called Little Al frequently. Little Al would follow orders and the killings would continue. In one phone conversation, Gaspipe went on a tirade about ten particular soldiers, saying, "I'm going to kill them all because they took advantage of me while I was on the lam."

Before Amuso and Gaspipe went on the lam, they were embroiled in a dispute with the long-time head of the Lucchese family in New Jersey, capo Tumac Accetturo. When Tony Ducks Corallo was boss, he had accepted $50,000 a year from Tumac regardless of how much the New Jersey family earned. Gaspipe wanted to change that arrangement and demanded half of whatever New Jersey earned. Tumac said no. Gaspipe labeled Tumac a rat, stripped him as capo and issued a contract to Fat Pete Chiodo and Little Al D'Arco. They were to kill Tumac, his wife Geraldine, and his son Anthony. But Tumac was nobody's fool. Tumac traveled between New Jersey and Florida. While he was deserted by all but seven trusted men, those who deserted him still were not likely to kill him despite his outlaw status.

Little Al even went so far as to distribute photos of Tumac like the Bureau has in the post office. Little Al told everyone, "Accetturo is an outlaw and you have to make all efforts to kill him and his son and whoever sticks by him.

One day Fat Pete Chiodo, who had cost "Gaspipe $20,000 a bullet" in a failed hit in Florida, took Little Al aside and said, "These guys have a pattern of calling people rats and they are making guys rats and killing them. I got information that you and I are going to be killed and hurt."

Little Al had some information of his own: Gaspipe told him to hit Fat Pete. The reason given was that Fat Pete had arranged a plea bargain for a ten-year sentence in two RICO cases, including the Windows Case, without first getting Amuso and Gaspipe's approval even though Amuso and Gaspipe were on the lam and communication was not all that convenient. "Kill Fat Pete," was Gaspipe's order. Little Al tapped Fat Pete's phone to track his movement, and sent a crew including Little Al's junky son. They found Fat Pete in Staten Island and shot him twelve times without killing him. His body fat served him well; the bullets were slowed down and stopped by the fat. While not killed, he would be partially paralyzed and confined to a wheelchair.

On May 8, 1991 Fat Pete joined a number of other Lucchese family would-be targets and enrolled in the Witness Protection Program.

Fat Pete had been Gaspipe Casso's right hand. He had participated in a number of the hits launched by Gaspipe's paranoia. When Fat Pete turned, the Bureau learned for the first time about a good portion of the murderous rampage of Amuso and Gaspipe.

Gaspipe told Little Al to whisper to Fat Pete's parents that if Fat Pete testified or cooperated, they would be killed. The parents scurried into the Witness Protection Program. Gaspipe then had Fat Pete's uncle whacked. The lowest moment in all of this was when Fat Pete's sister, Patricia, dropped her kids off at school, drove home, and was greeted as she pulled up by a masked shooter who opened fire with a pistol with a silencer, seriously wounding but not killing her. I would have loved to visit Tony Ducks Corallo to be the one to tell him about this botched hit on an innocent mother of three children.

Amuso and Gaspipe would sometimes secretly return to New York for a meeting. Such a meeting was held in Staten Island in July 1991. At that meeting Little Al was relieved of command as acting boss. He had botched the hit on Fat Pete and the hit on Fat Pete's sister, and now Fat Pete was in the program. A committee of four capos, which included Little Al, replaced Little Al.

At a committee meeting in September 1991 at a New York hotel, Little Al went to the bathroom and noticed a bulletproof vest and a gun on a driver for one of the other capos. Little Al ran out and kept on running until he got home. The next morning Little Al's parole officer called him to warn him that the FBI had learned that there was a contract out on him. Little Al was afraid that Gaspipe's inside information, his Crystal Ball, had been coming from the FBI office in Manhattan and he was afraid to go there. So he packed up his wife, his son, and a few close relatives and drove north to the suburb of New Rochelle, where he turned himself in to the FBI office up there.

Now with Little Al's debriefing, the Bureau really learned about Amuso and Gaspipe's "killing frenzy." In 1992, when Sammy the Bull Gravano hammered out a deal to turn and testify against John Gotti, he got a special Gaspipe clause in the agreement. Because Gaspipe killed relatives, Gravano could not be forced to provide evidence of any kind against Gaspipe.

And then Vic Amuso was caught. An informant gave details of where Amuso would be at a certain time on a certain day. Amuso would be at a particular pay phone at a shopping mall in Scranton, Pennsylvania. Amuso was at the phone as part of the elaborate communication scheme that very few people knew the details of.

While he was on the lam, the RICO Windows case against Amuso had mushroomed to include many predicate murders that Little Al and Fat Pete squealed about. In January 1993, with Gaspipe still on the lam, Vic Amuso, age 62, was found guilty in a major RICO indictment and got life without the chance of parole.

Meanwhile, although the Lucchese family was now so weakened and preoccupied that it had not been able to rein in the outlaw Tumac Accetturo, law enforcement had been able to. Tumac went to trial in 1993 and was found guilty in a RICO extortion case. Little Al had testified against Tumac, and after the trial Tumac threw in the towel and joined the Witness Protection Program.

I have to figure that Tumac did not like the idea of being cornered in a prison population where it would be easy for Gaspipe to finally have him killed. In fact, two Lucchese soldiers who sat at the defense table during trial and were convicted with Tumac were allied with Gaspipe and had been out looking for Tumac to kill him.

Tumac's decision to flip brought three other Lucchese solders into the Witness Protection Program. This avalanche of ready-made witnesses caused guilty pleas from eleven other Lucchese members in a Lucchese family RICO case that included nine murders.

Speaking about the changes in the Mafia and in law enforcement agencies over the years, Tumac later told Selwyn Raab, the *New York Times* reporter, Mafia authority, and author of *Five Families*: "In those days, we were disciplined, coordinated and better organized than they were and we took advantage of that. Now it's just the reverse. These guys are coordinated together and we're trying to murder one another."

On January 19, 1993, Gaspipe's show closed on the road. Tracing the cell phone of a Lucchese member, Gaspipe was located at his girlfriend's house in Mount Olive, New Jersey. He had pocket change with him totaling $340,000 and a large collection of police and FBI reports.

The Windows RICO Case for Gaspipe now, thanks to Little Al, Fat Pete, and Tumac, included 25 murders.

In his book *Five Families*, Selwyn Raab wrote that the Lucchese family was "more seriously affected than any other" family by the Mafia Commission Case.

Sure was.

CHAPTER 17
GASPIPE IMPLODES

IT TOOK HIM A WHILE, but eventually it dawned on Vic Amuso that his little road partner Gaspipe Casso had been a bit of a troublemaker all along. Amuso finally figured out that Gaspipe was the only one who could have tipped the authorities to the pay phone at the shopping mall in Scranton, Pennsylvania. While they were both in the can, Amuso stripped Gaspipe of the position of underboss. Amuso then stuck the rat label on the prince of rat labelers and spread the word in prison.

But before he was stripped, Gaspipe took the liberty of inducting into the Mafia a new member. It was the masked inept shooter of Fat Pete's sister Patricia. The sacred ceremony was conducted in the john with the use of burning toilet paper to take the place of a card with a saint's image on it. Of course there was no gun, no knife, just burning toilet paper and kissing in the shithouse. It works for me.

In February 1994, two weeks before his RICO and murder trial on the Windows Case, Gaspipe Casso looked at the list of cooperating witnesses against him. Gaspipe realized that Amuso had already tagged him with the rat label. Being stripped of power meant that Gaspipe could no longer engage in his favorite pastime, ordering hits. Gaspipe could not order a single beating from prison. Gaspipe flipped.

On March 1, 1994, Gaspipe pled guilty to fourteen murders, each carrying a potential sentence of life without the possibility of parole. His sentencing would be delayed while he cooperated and testified. If he did a good job on the witness stand, he would be accepted into the Witness Protection Program; the prosecutor would go to bat for him at sentencing; and the judge would be influenced to give him a break of some kind. It was a typical one, two, three deal. It all depended on what Gaspipe accomplished as a government witness.

Gaspipe was taken to what they call the Valachi Suite in La Tuna, Texas to be debriefed. The suite had been built for Joe Valachi at a time when there was no Witness Protection Program, to house the witness and his FBI agent protectors. Immediately, Gaspipe coughed up 22 more murders for which he had not been suspected. That made a total of 36 murders the government knew that their new star witness had committed.

One of these newly revealed hits was the bombing murder of John Gotti underboss Frank DeCicco in April 1986. The plan had been to kill both Gotti and DeCicco. Unknown to the bombers, Gotti was not there. Another wiseguy who looked like Gotti was with DeCicco. The bomber, Blue Eyes Pate, carried grocery bags past DeCicco's car, dropped something, bent down to pick it up and slipped a bag with plastic explosives under the car. When DeCicco and the Gotti looka-like got to the car, a remote control device from a toy car detonated the bomb. The other guy had his toes blown off and DeCicco had everything blown off. Gaspipe was at the scene in a lookout car with a police scanner. Gaspipe said that Chin Gigante and Tony Ducks Corallo had ordered the hit as punishment for Gotti's unsanctioned hit on Big Paul Castellano.

Another newly revealed killing by Gaspipe occurred in 1978 during the hey-day of his drug trafficking. The Coast Guard had seized a shipment of 23 tons of marijuana and a half million Quaaludes. Gaspipe was concerned that the boat cap-tain's son might flip and identify Gaspipe as the owner of the drugs. Gaspipe invit-ed the young man to go fishing. When the fellow showed up, Gaspipe promptly shot him in the face. Gaspipe put him in a grave he had dug, but the boy wasn't dead. Gaspipe smacked him with the shovel and buried him alive. When asked by the prosecutors debriefing him if he felt bad about burying the boy alive, Gaspipe said, "No, it had to be done."

Assistant United States Attorney George Stamboulidis, who put together a tremendous RICO case against the Colombo family, said that Gaspipe Casso had "more horrendous baggage than virtually any cooperating witness the government has ever signed up."

And Gaspipe added to his "horrendous baggage" by attacking two inmates in a special section of the Manhattan Correctional Center for cooperating witnesses. He surprised and attacked one guy who was stepping out of the shower. Ever the paranoid, he suspected that guy had ratted him out for bribing guards for special food, vodka, and other favors. Gaspipe attacked another guy with a rolled-up magazine while that guy was playing cards. To call Gaspipe a loose cannon would be an insult to loose cannons. Meanwhile, never mind the attacks, what was he doing breaking the law by bribing guards?

With these attacks on other cooperating inmates, as cases went to trial, Gaspipe was not being used. This spelled disaster in his mind. The only way he could get leniency was by having a track record of cooperation. But how could he cooperate if the government wouldn't call him? The last opportunity he had to testify was against the Chin in the case that finally ended Chin Gigante's one-man play as a schizophrenic punch-drunk senile collector of Social Security disability payments. But although he was listed as a witness, the government didn't call Gaspipe.

The prosecutor Gregory O'Connell said that "using him would be like putting Adolph Hitler on the stand."

Gaspipe lashed out and wrote a letter to the judge, accusing the government's star turncoat witnesses of lying under oath in Chin Gigante's RICO trial that had finished off the Chin. Now this was not what government prosecutors had in mind when they asked for Gaspipe's cooperation. The letter Gaspipe wrote was the letter-equivalent of a bomb in a paper bag. If the government's star witnesses had lied under oath, then the Chin, and many others, were entitled to a reversal of conviction.

Gaspipe wrote the judge that Little Al D'Arco was guilty of résumé inflation when he testified that he had been acting boss of the Lucchese family. Gaspipe wrote that Little Al had never achieved that height. This was a minor point of no real legal significance. The big deal was that Gaspipe claimed that Sammy the Bull Gravano lied when he testified that he had never dealt drugs. Gaspipe said that he had sold large amounts of marijuana to Gravano in the 1970s and that Gravano had offered to sell him heroin from China. This claim had the ring of truth, and of course, years later Gravano got caught heading a Gravano family Ecstasy ring in Arizona.

However Gaspipe, as was his way, had gone a little overboard; had crossed the line into frenzy in his letter to the judge. Gaspipe claimed that the day after the Reverend Al Sharpton was stabbed, he and Gravano were chatting in a schoolyard in Brooklyn. Gaspipe wrote to the judge that Gravano told him he had ordered the stabbing of Sharpton. There were problems with that story. One, on that day, Gaspipe was on the lam and nowhere near a schoolyard in Brooklyn. Two, on that day, Gravano was in jail. Strike three—as a government witness, you don't get to lie, not even once. Gaspipe, unable to get his murderous hands on others, had finally killed himself off.

The government prosecutors accused Gaspipe of violating the terms of his cooperation agreement by making false statements, bribing guards, and attacking fellow inmates. Gaspipe lost whatever deal he had, and in July 1998 he was sentenced to 455 years.

For his own protection, since he was a publicly exposed rat, Gaspipe—who had spent three and a half years in kinder, gentler prisons reserved for cooperating witnesses—would now be housed in the new "Alcatraz of the Rockies" in Florence, Colorado. It had been built to replace the maximum-security prison in which John Gotti died in Marion, Illinois, that had been built to replace Alcatraz. Gaspipe would be on lockdown while, by contrast, Little Al and Fat Pete would spend not a day in jail. Tumac would get a manageable 20-year sentence. He would be released in 2002 and settle down at age 63 somewhere in the South.

At the age of 56 and with 455 years to serve, Gaspipe would have plenty of time to write letters to judges and the media for attention until the day he died in the can along with his new archenemy, Vic Amuso. *60 Minutes* paid attention to his allegations, which by now included a claim that he was double-crossed by the prosecution. *60 Minutes* sent a film crew and interviewed him for a show. It didn't do Gaspipe any good; the world seemed done with him.

Gregory O'Connell and his co-prosecutor Charles Rose had used the code name "Lucifer" for Gaspipe. O'Connell said about Gaspipe, "He had boundless enthusiasm for conspiracies and for murder. . . . Gaspipe was more dangerous than Amuso and more responsible for the mayhem that fortunately for us ruined the family."

My sources told me that in 1992, when I was getting ready to return to the Bureau as an agent, the Lucchese family had been cut in half as a result of the Mafia Commission Case. In five years, half its made men were in jail, murdered, or had turned. Better believe we were never going to give the Lucchese or any other family a chance to rally. My last testimony against the Lucchese family was in the summer of 1993. Little Al and I testified in a RICO and murder case against Joey Bang Bang Massaro, whom I had met a few times while I was under.

But Little Al continued to testify over the years. Little Al even went against other families. In 1997 Little Al helped take down the Genovese boss Chin Gigante. Next, Little Al moved down the line and helped take down the Genovese *consigliere* James the Little Guy Ida. The Little Guy had turned down a plea bargain for fifteen years and got mandatory life at trial. Little Al was still testifying at trials in 2006. Having been through it, I'm not so sure jail wouldn't be preferable to fifteen years of testifying.

In the mid 1990s, Little Joe Defede took over the Lucchese family as acting boss, the job Little Al had held in the early 1990s. By 2002, following a RICO conviction, Little Joe Defede followed Little Al and became a cooperating witness. From jail, Vic Amuso replaced the turncoat Little Joe Defede as acting boss with Louie Bagels Daidone, the former Indiana State football player who had tackled the escaping murder victim and stuffed a canary in his mouth. Along with Little Al, in 2004 Little Joe testified against his successor, Louie Bagels, and they helped tackle Louie Bagels and bring him to the ground for life for RICO and murder, including the murder of the tackled victim. Ironically, Little Al and Louie Bagels had been made on the same day in 1982, around the time I would have been made. The Mafia Commission Case launched Amuso and Gaspipe, and these two incapable and weird leaders gave us the gift that kept on giving.

By his "mayhem" Gaspipe had done far more to bring ruin to the Lucchese family before he was caught and turned than he ever did after he was caught and turned. When the decision was made not to use Gaspipe as a government witness—at first on a case-by-case basis, and then finally and forever after the poison pen letter about Sammy and Little Al—a number of prosecutions had to be dropped or plea-bargained way down.

The two shooters of Robert Kubecka and Donald Barstow, whom Gaspipe had fingered in his debriefing, were plea-bargained considerably. One despicable killer got four years. There was no physical evidence even linking him to having been in the state of New York on that day, much less linking him to the crime scene. The other coldblooded killer, the one who had been injured by Robert Kubecka in the struggle and whose blood was finally matched when he was caught in 2002, got fifteen years, but by then he was 76 years old and so that was a life sentence.

CHAPTER 18
THE MAFIA COPS

THE INVESTIGATION NOBODY in law enforcement wanted to lose as a result of Gaspipe's self-destruction as a halfway-credible witness was Gaspipe Casso's "Crystal Ball." As Gaspipe, while in prison, heaped more and more "horrendous baggage" onto his future role as a witness, potentially the crown jewel of his cooperation—the fingering of two NYPD detectives, Lou Eppolito and Steve Caracappa, as being his Crystal Ball—got tossed to the curb. It was his word against theirs, and Gaspipe had no word left. Moreover, Gaspipe had never dealt directly with the two cops, and claimed to have only seen them once in a Toys 'R' Us parking lot and that glimpse was from afar. Gaspipe claimed that he recognized the cops when Detective Louis Eppolito and co-author Bob Drury published a book about Eppolito's life, *Mafia Cop: The Story of an Honest Cop Whose Family Was the Mob*. The book had lots of photos of Eppolito, and one photo of Eppolito and Caracappa together in the Brooklyn Robbery Squad where they met and had been partners. Lou Eppolito was a very large flamboyant man with a big head of hair. He had been a bodybuilder and was a former Mr. New York City. Steve Caracappa had very short hair, a neat mustache, and was so skinny they called him The Stick.

Clearly, Gaspipe did have a Crystal Ball. From his days as a drug dealer when the list of license plates from unmarked surveillance cars was found in his car the night he was shot, to the day he and Amuso went on the lam, it was apparent that Gaspipe had his own information pipeline into law enforcement. But were these two detectives that Crystal Ball? Gaspipe had said in his *60 Minutes* interview that the two detectives "wanted to kill for me."

In his very first round of debriefing at the Valachi Suite, Gaspipe told prosecutor Charles Rose that while he was on the lam, through his intermediary, he had passed along a contract to Eppolito and Caracappa to tap Charles Rose's phone and whack him. Gaspipe explained that he suspected the prosecutor had been the one who leaked a story to the press that Gaspipe had tortured and killed his architect for having an affair with Gaspipe's wife. Charles Rose, whom we later lost to cancer, God bless him, just looked at Gaspipe and said, "I forgive you, Anthony, let's continue."

The fingered detectives clearly ignored that nutty opportunity to hit a federal prosecutor. But Gaspipe claimed there were many other opportunities the NYPD partners grabbed. According to Gaspipe, in addition to supplying information for a price, they supplied victims. Gaspipe alleged that the Mafia Cops used confidential police computer banks to identify the whereabouts of men that Gaspipe wanted hit. As is often the case in the Mafia, you might know a guy for years and pull score after score, even hits, with him, and not know his name. You would know his nickname or maybe his first name. But you would not know his full name or where he lived. The only reason Lefty got to know my last name of Brasco is because I was best man at his City Hall marriage and he needed my full name for the certificate.

The intermediary Gaspipe used in dealing with the detectives was an old-time gambler, garment-industry guy, and drug trafficker named Burton Kaplan. It was Kaplan and only Kaplan who dealt directly with the detectives, and only Kaplan who knew their names. Kaplan was no dummy. Once he revealed the names of the crooked cops, Kaplan would have become disposable goods.

As the story goes, in 1982 Kaplan had been turned on to them in jail in Allenwood, Pennsylvania, by Frank Junior Santora, a Gambino family soldier and Eppolito's cousin. Santora highly recommended his cousin and his cousin's partner, Caracappa, as potential collaborators in crime. When Burton Kaplan got out of jail he told Gaspipe about the crooked cops.

And that began the criminal enterprise among Gaspipe, Kaplan, Santora, Eppolito, and Caracappa. In the beginning, according to Gaspipe, Kaplan dealt through cousin Junior Santora. But when cousin Junior was whacked by mistake in 1987, Kaplan began dealing directly with the two cops.

Gaspipe admitted he was hellbent on using the cops to help him discover who had tried to kill him on September 8, 1986. They say the most dangerous animal is a wounded animal. Gaspipe had recognized one of the shooters as 28 year-old Gambino associate Jimmy Hydell, but did not know where Hydell lived or hung out.

Gaspipe explained during debriefing at the Valachi Suite that the dirty cops brought Jimmy Hydell to a Toys 'R' Us parking lot in Brooklyn on September 14, 1986—six days after the attempt on Gaspipe's life. Hydell was in the trunk of a car. The car was dropped in the lot by the cops, who were then driven away by Kaplan. Gaspipe was some distance away, but saw the cops' faces. Jimmy Hydell was taken to a basement where Gaspipe personally tortured him until Hydell gave up the names of his three partners in the attempted hit. Hydell was then whacked. His body was never found.

There was a lot more that Gaspipe claimed about Eppolito and Caracappa, but what good was it? The key to prosecuting them would have been Burton Kaplan's indispensable testimony. After all, he was the man who gave the cops their assignments and paid them afterwards. But despite a 27-year sentence in 1997 for cocaine and marijuana trafficking, and getting a full-court press from several law enforcement agencies, Burton Kaplan, old school that he was, refused to cooperate and corroborate this outrageous story of police corruption that Gaspipe had given the government prosecutors during his debriefing in 1994.

Eppolito had retired from the NYPD in February 1990, and Caracappa had retired in November 1992, both with full pensions, years before Gaspipe publicly identified them as hit men. Nothing for nothing, but Caracappa retired the same month Big Joey Massino got out of jail (on Friday the Thirteenth of November 1992) and took over as boss of the Bonanno family.

Without Kaplan, and with Gaspipe unusable as a witness, the investigation sputtered and died.

• • •

Betty Hydell had two grown sons who still lived at home in Staten Island. They could never be made men because, while she was Italian, their father was not. On September 16, 1986, her son Frank walked in the door and told his mother that a blue car with two men in it had been following him and he thought that the blue car was now parked out front keeping an eye on their mother's house. Frank had been driving his brother Jimmy's car.

Betty Hydell went out and got in her car to confront the situation. She spotted the blue car with the two men in it. She pulled alongside the car and asked them what they were up to. Both of the men appeared to be of Italian descent. The driver was a big guy with a full head of hair, a white shirt, and a necklace. The passenger was a skinny guy with very short hair and a mustache. The big guy flashed an NYPD badge at her.

"You should let people know who you are and what you're doing," Betty Hydell said.

And that was the end of that. Except that the last contact she had with her son Jimmy was when he called her that day from a pay phone across the harbor in Brooklyn. Jimmy went missing and, for people tied in with the Mafia, that means that he was dead. Still, for a while, anyway, Betty Hydell had the thin hope that he would simply walk in the door one night and tell her where he'd been and why he hadn't called.

One afternoon six years later, when all hope of her son's return was gone, Betty Hydell was sitting at home watching daytime talk TV. The *Sally Jesse Raphael* show had a retired cop on who had just published a book, *Mafia Cop*. The author, Lou Eppolito, had had a bit part as a gangster in the movie *Goodfellas*, and was launching an acting, producing, and screenwriting career. Betty recognized him immediately as the distinctive-looking cop who had flashed a badge and had followed her son Jimmy's car to their Staten Island home.

Retired NYPD Detective Lou Eppolito told the viewers that his father's side of the family was heavily into the Mafia. His grandfather, known as Luigi the Napolitan, had been a friend and Mafia associate of Lucky Luciano. The Gambino underboss, Joe N. Gallo, attended Luigi's funeral in 1978. Luigi had three sons who went into the Mafia. Eppolito's father, before he died of natural causes, had been a Gambino family soldier known as Fat the Gangster. Eppolito's uncle Freddy was very high up in the Gambino family; he'd been at Apalachin in 1957. Uncle Freddy drank himself to death from alcohol poisoning while he was holed up and hiding out from a Mafia contract on his life. He'd rather die from Chivas Regal than go out on the street and meet his certain fate.

Eppolito's other uncle was a Gambino family soldier named Jimmy the Clam. His cousin Jim-Jim, Jimmy the Clam's son, had set up a phony charity for the hungry children of the world called the International Children's Appeal. Jim-Jim had gotten public endorsements from President Jimmy Carter's wife and from Senator Edward Kennedy. Jim-Jim's scam was exposed on TV and it made Carter and Kennedy look bad. The publicity also mentioned that Jim-Jim was with the Gambino family and was the son of Jimmy the Clam. It was 1979, while I was still under and before President Reagan declared war on organized crime in his 1982 speech. In 1979 Big Paul Castellano did not need the president of the United States to authorize him to seek revenge against anyone in the Mafia. Uncle Jimmy the Clam and Jim-Jim were found shot to death in a car in Brooklyn in October 1979.

As his father used to say to Lou Eppolito, "Nobody never gets killed for no reason."

Except that years later Jimmy the Clam's former bodyguard, cousin Frank Junior Santora, the Gambino soldier who'd been in Allenwood Prison in 1982 with Burton Kaplan, was whacked by mistake on September 3, 1987. The shooter mistook cousin Junior for Carmine Variale, with whom Junior was walking. So, almost "nobody never gets killed for no reason." But then maybe it all worked out in the end when the shooter, or maybe the finger man who pointed out the wrong target, or both, ended up getting killed for a good reason.

Betty Hydell instinctively knew looking at the TV that she couldn't breathe a word about her shock of recognition. It was bad enough the guy was a cop and they all stick together, but he was a Mafia cop who claimed that he was the white sheep in a family of black sheep. Baa. Betty wasn't born yesterday. She'd like nothing better than to stick a pin in that "baloney" that was coming out of the side of his mouth. But she had her son Frank to think about. Frank would be a sitting duck the moment she went to the police with this.

And if Betty needed any more motive to clam up, Lou Eppolito was telling

Sally Jessey about the time in 1984 that he was "wrongfully" accused of leaking confidential NYPD information to Rosario Gambino. This was the heroin trafficking nephew of the deceased boss, Don Carlo Gambino, and a member of the same Mafia family as Luigi the Napolitan, Fat the Gangster, Uncle Jimmy the Clam, Jim-Jim, and cousin Junior Santora. When the FBI executed a search warrant on Rosario Gambino's home in New Jersey, they found a photocopy of Gambino's highly classified NYPD folder. The copy machine at Eppolito's precinct had been used to copy the folder's contents. Eppolito was the last person to sign the folder out from the ultra-secure Intelligence Division, the heart of organized crime data, where you have to give your fingerprint to enter. When the New York press reported the story, two wiseguys were picked up on a tape saying they couldn't call on their cop source for something "because he's in trouble now." But Eppolito had a reason for having the folder. In fact, he had been ordered to get it. With the help of his union and his record of commendations, Eppolito beat the charges at a departmental hearing.

In hindsight, had Eppolito been like the crooked cop who responds to an elderly lady's apartment, finds her dead, and removes her diamond ring and pockets it? He didn't kill her; he just seized the opportunity. Had Eppolito found himself in possession of a Gambino family folder for a legitimate reason and seized the opportunity? Cousin Junior was still alive then to facilitate.

To the nose of an honest cop, and with rare exception that means the rest of the NYPD, Eppolito's book itself smelled rotten. Eppolito charged that he had been the victim of bias because of his family tree, that old "ugly stereotype" argument again that Governor Cuomo was so fond of. "As frightening as it may sound," Eppolito wrote, "I found more loyalty, more honor, in the wiseguy neighborhoods and hangouts than I did in police headquarters."

There were many other things that were more frightening in the book, although not intended. Eppolito talked about how he would go into a social club, throw his weight around, and demand answers on a wiseguy homicide investigation. He would know that the room was bugged, so he said he would "be nodding and winking to show that it was all a big joke." Although he doesn't point this out to the reader, by "nodding and winking" he is giving away the existence of a secret bug. He does tell the reader, however, why he wasn't taking the investigation seriously. "For all my time on the job, I never really lost sight of my old man's credo that nobody got killed for no reason." In other words, while under oath as a cop he conducted organized crime homicide investigations as if it were perfectly okay for the Mafia to murder its own.

In another episode described in the book, Eppolito charged into a social club and put a sawed-off shotgun into the mouth of a wiseguy who had threatened him on the phone. Eppolito admitted, "Suddenly, I knew what it felt like to be my father. I was walking like a wiseguy, talking like a wiseguy. The power surge was what I had felt at times as a cop, yet somehow different." But the most powerful surge came from what Eppolito told the wiseguy with the shotgun in his mouth. It was the confluence of two powerful rivers coming together to form an even more powerful river, the power of the wiseguy combining with the power of the cop, the very idea behind the Mafia cop when he said, "Guess whose job it's going to be to find out who killed you? Mine, Frankie."

The strangest episode was a meeting Eppolito described that he had with Big Paul Castellano at the White House in 1979. After Uncle Jimmy the Clam and Jim-Jim had been whacked, Eppolito was asked by his cousin Junior Santora to attend a meeting with Big Paul. Eppolito claimed that Big Paul had called for the sit-down to make sure that there were no hard feelings. Eppolito admits that when it was his turn to speak, he called Big Paul "Godfather" like out of the movies. Big Paul laughed at the gesture and said, "I am not Don Corleone."

At the meeting, Big Paul tacitly admitted that he was behind the hits on Uncle Jimmy and Jim-Jim, and Big Paul hoped that Lou Eppolito understood. Why the feelings of Lou Eppolito had to be dealt with at the level of the boss, and why the boss spoke so freely to a supposed cop are mysteries to me. Eppolito claims that Big Paul seized the opportunity to offer to put Eppolito on the Gambino family payroll. Eppolito claims to have been insulted by the offer.

None of this, if it happened at this meeting, was ever reported by Eppolito to the NYPD as is required by the most basic principles of police work. I don't know what happened at that meeting. I do know that it took place in 1979, and 1979 was the first time Eppolito had been caught cooperating with a wiseguy. Eppolito had supplied the wiseguy mug shots of criminals who looked like the wiseguy so that they could be used at trial to cast doubt on an eyewitness identification.

Eppolito was let off with a warning. That was also the year that Eppolito and Caracappa met and became partners in the Brooklyn Robbery Squad. Whatever happened at this meeting at the White House, we do know that according to Lou Eppolito, he met with the boss and the boss treated him with respect. It appears that the future Hollywood wannabe cop began playing a new role the night he was treated with respect by Big Paul.

The book quotes Eppolito's wife, Fran, at length about the "weird" personality changes in Eppolito following his meeting with Big Paul Castellano at the White House. Fran said, "From that day on Louie was a different person. It was like he now had a little more pride in what his uncle was. . . . Then I noticed that he began picking up some Italian mannerisms that he never had before. . . . He started talking with his hands. . . . Then I noticed that he also began talking about his Italian heritage all the time. Bragging about how Italians did this, Italians did that. . . . I used to laugh as he sat the girls on his knees and told them . . . about how important family ties were. The kids were babies and they looked at him like he was nuts."

Fran admitted that she found "Lou's new persona a little weird. I mean when Steve Caracappa came over you'd think there were two godfathers sitting at our kitchen table. The talking with the hands. The drinking of the double espressos. 'Salud'ing each other to death after every sip. And now Louie was starting to kiss everybody on the cheek. . . . Now it was kiss city."

Kiss of death city.

Mafia Cop: The Story of an Honest Cop Whose Family Was the Mob came out two years before Gaspipe identified Eppolito and Caracappa as his Crystal Ball. Jerry Capeci, in an article for the *New York Daily News*, broke the story in 1994 and named names. Betty Hydell's identification was now confirmed in her mind. Both Betty and Gaspipe had identified the corrupt cops from the same photo of them in Eppolito's book. But still Betty remained silent. After all, her son Frank was out there on the street.

Burton Kaplan was soaking in his bathtub when he heard the news that Gaspipe had identified Eppolito and Caracappa as his Crystal Ball. Kaplan had the drug trafficking charges hanging over him that would eventually send him to jail. And now Gaspipe had turned and was providing evidence against the cops, and no doubt against him.

Burton Kaplan kissed his wife and daughter goodbye and, at 61, went on the lam with his girlfriend. He went to San Diego, Mexico, Oregon, and Las Vegas.

Eppolito and Caracappa had moved to Las Vegas in December 1994, following the heat from the Jerry Capeci story. Maybe their arrogant brains figured: out of sight, out of mind. The two men were living across the street from each other in a gated community. Caracappa was doing some private investigating stuff and selling George Foreman boxing machines on the QVC channel. Eppolito, wearing rings on every finger and often dressing in black with a white tie, was doing his Hollywood wannabe stuff. Eppolito had grabbed $45,000 from a former Las Vegas hooker. He agreed to write a screenplay about her experiences and get a movie made from it. She complained later on that he had scammed her because he had no skill in writing a screenplay. In the screenplay, Eppolito had written that this woman who had once had an affair with Frank Sinatra slept one night with a 300-pound man. She was outraged. "He wrote himself a part in my movie," she complained.

Burton Kaplan contacted Eppolito and asked for a couple of meetings at a Smith's supermarket to touch base with them to see if they were getting any heat from the feds. Eppolito said that they were feeling heat from the press and he had hired a lawyer, but they had not heard anything from the law.

In 1996 Kaplan returned to New York and was arrested. Refusing to cooperate, he lost his trial, got a 27-year sentence, went to jail, and there he lingered.

In April 1998 Betty Hydell's other son, Frank, was gunned down on the sidewalk outside a Staten Island strip club. In July 1998 Gaspipe had been officially declared unusable as a witness and been sentenced to 455 years.

In September 2003 Betty Hydell tested the waters. Betty told NYPD Detective Tommy Dades about her identification of Eppolito from the *Sally Jesse Raphael* TV show, and her identification of Caracappa from a photo in Eppolito's book. It was a dream come true for Dades, who shortly thereafter retired from the NYPD. Later Dades would refer to Betty Hydell as "the missing link."

In 2004 Dades took a job as an investigator with the office of Charles J. Hynes, the Brooklyn DA. There he could work the case more closely with Joseph J. Ponzi, the DA's seasoned chief investigator. The two of them put together a small team in a War Room to review every word in the mounds of material that was on record about Gaspipe, Kaplan, Santora, Eppolito, Caracappa, and all the Mafia Cop murders Gaspipe had talked about in his 1994 debriefing. The team of investigators that holed up in the War Room also included: former undercover Douglas Le Vien; William Oldham, a federal investigator with Brooklyn United States Attorney Roslynn R. Mauskopf; and Robert Intartaglio, who had investigated a gang of safecrackers and burglars known as the Bypass Gang (for their ability to bypass alarms). Intartaglio had a wired informant within the Bypass Gang. That informant was outed from inside the NYPD, and he was whacked.

First draft choice of the first round for the new team was Burton Kaplan. He had been in jail a long time and had had a lot of opportunity to think about the aging process and dream about life on the outside. There was no statute of limitations problem because murder is never time-barred. However, in order to sweeten the pot for Kaplan, they needed to be able to offer Kaplan the federal Witness Protection Program. For that they needed a federal RICO case. But for RICO, the last criminal act done to further the criminal enterprise, even if it's a murder, had to have been committed within five years of the indictment. I've got to hand it to the investigators; they were thinking every step of the way. They decided to go fishing in the desert. They went out to Las Vegas to fish for some new crimes to extend the criminal enterprise from 1979 to practically the present.

In 2004 they went to jail and met with the short, balding, nearsighted 71-year-old Kaplan. They laid it out, did their magic, and with Joe Ponzi's "skills of persuasion" they got the old swindler to agree to turn. It seems that all the hard work that a cast of thousands had performed over the years to bring down the Mafia continued to pay off—over and over again. As Burton Kaplan later explained his reason to flip: "I was in jail nine straight years. I was on the lam two and a half years before that. In that period I seen an awful lot of guys I thought were stand-up go bad, turn and become informants."

He sure did.

For their fishing trip to Las Vegas to solve the RICO statute-of-limitations problem, they baited the hook with a wired accountant with a gambling addiction who was working off his charges. He had gotten caught for embezzling $5.4 million from his clients. The baited hook went right for Eppolito's weak spot—

Hollywood. Former CPA Steven Corso, working off his own unrelated charges, posed as a moneyman with Mafia drug money that he was intent on laundering in feature film investments. Corso paid Eppolito $14,000 that he said on tape had come from a Mafia drug deal. It was to jump start a script of Eppolito's called "Murder in Youngstown." I guess we'll next see that script on eBay.

Eppolito bragged on tape to the accountant that he and his wife Fran hid a lot of income from the IRS. (Probably including that $45,000 he grabbed from the Vegas call girl.) Eppolito claimed on tape that even though he was retired he still had a mole within the NYPD should they ever need that resource. The fishing was spectacular.

One more thing the accountant needed was some crystal meth to entertain some "Hollywood punks." Eppolito said, "No problem, I'll have my son set it up. Tony can handle that for you." And Tony did, delivering an ounce of crystal meth to Corso and receiving $900 from Corso. All on tape. The Mafia cops had now bridged the time gap from Gaspipe's Crystal Ball to Corso's crystal meth. They had made a federal case out of their lives.

Eppolito, his 24-year-old son Tony, his wife Fran, a friend of Tony's who was in on the crystal meth transaction, and Caracappa were arrested in Las Vegas on March 9, 2005. At his arrest, Tony was found to be in possession of an additional ounce of crystal meth that he had planned to sell. Tony and his friend were indicted on Nevada drug charges. Eppolito and his wife were indicted on income tax evasion charges. Eppolito was found in possession of an old NYPD case folder involving a murder of a prostitute that ended in the conviction of a postal worker named Barry Gibbs who had admitted smoking crack with the prostitute and having sex with her but denied strangling her. Finding it strange that Eppolito had this piece of NYPD property, they did some investigating and talked to the eyewitness who had identified Barry Gibbs as the man who dumped the prostitute's body. The witness, an ex-Marine and recovering drug addict, quickly recanted his identification and said that Eppolito had intimidated him into making it. Barry Gibbs, at 57, after seventeen years in jail, was freed by the Brooklyn DA's office.

The indictment against Eppolito and Caracappa alleged that the rogue cops were engaged in a criminal enterprise with the Lucchese family as a secret asset of that crime family. Judge Jack Weinstein, then 85 years old and still nobody you would want to run into in a dark alley, warned the prosecutors that their case was "weak" and they should consider dropping their indictment and bringing state murder charges that had no statute of limitations. The judge saw that the Lucchese family participation had ended eleven years earlier in 1994 when Gaspipe gave the cops up. The Brooklyn United States Attorney's office, still thinking every step of the way, re-indicted the cops, this time alleging that the long-standing partnership of Eppolito and Caracappa was its own criminal enterprise and corrupt organization under RICO. The partnership predated the association with Gaspipe, and it had begun in 1979 with cousin Junior and the Gambino family. After all, when Junior told Burton Kaplan about the dirty cops in Allenwood in 1982, the two-man partnership had already "done things" and were recommended by Junior as "capable guys."

That new indictment was cake.

The day after the arrests in this case, coincidentally, there were sweeping arrests of thirty-two members and associates of the Gambino family, including one of the last of the old-time powerful Gambino capos, Greg DePalma. DePalma was one of a group of Mafia dignitaries that included Don Carlo Gambino and future turncoat Jimmy the Weasel Frattiano who had all posed in a famous backstage photograph with Frank Sinatra. The arrests came as a result of what the press called a "two-year Donnie Brasco operation" pulled off by an undercover agent who went by the name of Falcone. An undercover and his little friend RICO had struck again.

And once again, I had special pride in having trained Falcone in the way of the wiseguy.

CHAPTER 19
THE MAFIA COPS' POSITION

IN HIS SIX MONTHS OF DEBRIEFING, Burton Kaplan had come up with ten provable murders the Mafia Cops had knowingly facilitated. One for Kaplan and nine for Gaspipe, whom Kaplan called "a homicidal maniac." To solve the problem of Burton Kaplan's enormous "negative baggage," the investigators and prosecutors did an outstanding job of digging up corroborative witnesses and one dead body.

The first murder victim was Israel Greenwald. He was a diamond merchant and a launderer of money for the Mafia. Burton Kaplan, like the undercover ex-CPA Steven Corso, got into trouble to begin with because of his severe gambling addiction. "I got sick with it," Kaplan said. He placed his bets with future Lucchese consigliere and Gaspipe Casso's "rabbi," Christy Tick Furnari. Burton Kaplan always needed money that he had no way to earn legitimately in the garment industry. Soon, to pay off vig, Kaplan began doing favors for Christy Tick—a slippery slope that led him to launch his own life of criminal deals and schemes. These schemes included dealing in Peruvian passports, counterfeiting designer clothes, and selling hot appliances. In one of his schemes, Kaplan involved Israel Greenwald. It involved trafficking in U.S. Treasury Bonds. When an investigation was initiated, Kaplan became afraid that Greenwald would not stand up and would "go bad and turn."

On February 10, 1986, Greenwald was pulled over and arrested on suspicion of a hit-and-run. The police asked Greenwald to accompany them to an auto body shop for an identification. If the witness cleared the bearded Greenwald he'd be released. Wearing a yarmulke and a pinstriped suit he was escorted into the body shop garage by Steve Caracappa, where Junior Santora shot him twice. Lou Eppolito waited in the car as lookout. Santora, Eppolito, and Caracappa split $30,000. Kaplan had no idea where the body ended up. Greenwald left behind a wife and eight-year-old daughter Yael who, in vain, expected her daddy to come home that night for dinner and many nights thereafter.

The Mafia Cops investigators followed up phone numbers from cousin Junior Santora's 20-year-old address book. They came up with a 5' 4" tow truck operator who owned a parking lot near an auto body shop. He confessed to them that he had befriended Santora, and that one day Santora called him over from his parking lot stall. The witness walked into a one-car garage and saw a man in a yarmulke who he had seen enter with a man who looked like Caracappa. Only now the man was dead. Santora tossed the tow truck operator a spade and ordered him to help dig a five-foot grave, throw the dead body in it, cement it over, and keep his mouth shut. The tow truck operator quoted Santora on that subject: "He said that if I told anybody he'd kill me and my family."

On top of that, the man said he had met the lookout before. He said he knew him as a cop, Lou Eppolito. Put a cop into the crime and where does a citizen turn? He added, "I was afraid of Lou Eppolito." In April 2005, based on the witness' information, Israel Greenwald's skeletal remains were recovered along with his yarmulke and pinstriped suit. I can only imagine the elation that Tommy Dades, Joe Ponzi, and the prosecution team must have felt.

The investigators interviewed cousin Junior Santora's 33-year-old daughter, Tammy Ahmed, and she positively identified Kaplan and the Mafia Cops as men who occasionally came to her family's home to meet with her father before he was gunned down by mistake when Tammy was 16.

On September 14, 1986, Jimmy Hydell was arrested in front of a coin laundry in Brooklyn. At a safe spot that provided privacy, Jimmy was transferred into the trunk of a car. With Jimmy kicking inside the trunk, the cops dropped the car off at the Toys 'R' Us parking lot in Flatbush and Gaspipe took over from there. In the basement of a house in Marine Park, Brooklyn, Gaspipe shot Hydell 15 times to torture out of him the names of his accomplices on the failed hit on

Gaspipe. Hydell gave up the names of the rest of the Gambino shooters—Nicky Guido, Bobby Boriello, and Eddie Lino. Knowing he was about to be killed, Jimmy begged Gaspipe to "throw me in the street" so his body would be found and his mother Betty could collect on his life insurance policy. Gaspipe promised he would, then fatally shot Jimmy and threw his body anyplace but the street. About the Hydell hit for which the two detectives received $30,000, Eppolito remarked to Burton Kaplan, "We're just doing our job."

Later on, when the new investigation that was started by Betty Hydell became public, Gaspipe, never one to disappoint, offered to lead the investigators to Jimmy Hydell's body in exchange for a twenty-year cap on his sentence. I'm not sure they even answered his letter. At any rate, as their case came together they dropped his name from the witness list. Who would a prosecutor rather have as a witness to corroborate Kaplan—the 33-year-old daughter of Junior Santora, or Gaspipe Casso?

On Christmas Day 1986, Nicky Guido's mother Pauline had cooked home-made manicotti for her family, including her sons Nicky and Mike. After dinner 26-year-old Nicky, who worked for the phone company and was on the list for the New York Fire Department, asked his uncle Anthony to go out and take a look at his new red Nissan Maxima, which was parked on the block. Nicky got behind the wheel and Anthony got in the passenger seat when gunmen opened fire. Nicky threw his body across his uncle's to protect him. No doubt the gunmen chose Christmas Day to lay in wait for Nicky because there wouldn't be a lot of people on the street. Tragically, they had picked the wrong Nicky Guido. The one they wanted lived a few blocks away and was three years older.

Pauline was doing the dishes when Anthony ran in to say that Nicky had been shot. Pauline ran outside and saw her son covered in blood. She said, "I touched his fingers and he had just died. His fingers were cold." Nicky's older brother Mike said he had been inside with his parents digesting his dinner when "we heard the pops." Every Christmas Day after that for the Guido family was the anniversary of Nicky's murder in a certain parking spot in front of their house. Nicky's father died three years later of a broken heart from unceasing grief. Until the case was broken nearly twenty years later, the family lived with the suspicion that neighbors thought that somehow Nicky had gotten involved in something bad with the Mafia. Nicky was buried in the nearby Green Wood cemetery; the oldest in the city, where such murdered Mafia figures as Crazy Joey Gallo are buried.

Steve Caracappa had made the mistake that killed a young innocent boy when he used his own ID to go into the police computer to get an address for the Nicholas Guido whose name had been given up by the tortured Jimmy Hydell. Despite their error, the Mafia Cops split $4,000.

A couple of weeks after Christmas 2005, Steve Caracappa appeared on *60 Minutes*. Caracappa was asked about the charges and said, "Totally ridiculous. It's ludicrous. Anybody that knows me knows I love the police department." Even though it was an investigation that originated out of the NYPD and the Brooklyn DAs office, Caracappa blamed the feds. I guess he agreed with his lawyer Eddie Hayes, who said, "After the FBI blew 9/11, want to trust them now?"

Before trial the prosecutors offered a list of over 100 witnesses. Judge Jack Weinstein told them to forget that idea and pare their list to a manageable size. As a result, the government dropped two of the ten murders in the indictment, leaving seven murders that the two Mafia Cops had facilitated together and one more that was Eppolito's alone. The two that were dropped were Bobby Boriello and Jim Bishop.

Jim Bishop was a Democratic Party District Leader and former head of the painters' union. The Mafia Cops learned that Bishop had begun secretly cooperating with the Manhattan DA in an investigation of a painting contracting scheme. They passed that intelligence to Kaplan, who passed it to Gaspipe, and Bishop was whacked in May 1990.

Initially, the Mafia Cops had been given the contract to kill Gambino soldier Bobby Boriello. But when another detective questioned why they were looking for Boriello, Eppolito and Caracappa decided to back off the direct kill and opt for the indirect kill. They provided Boriello's address to Kaplan, who gave it to Gaspipe. In 1991, just before *Mafia Cop* hit the bookstores, Bobby Boriello was hit outside his house in Brooklyn. Boriello had been John Gotti's driver and he was one of the shooters that Jimmy Hydell had given up during his terrifying time with Gaspipe.

When it was announced that the Bishop and Boriello murders were being dropped due to the judge's pressure, Caracappa's lawyer Eddie Hayes said, "It doesn't make any real difference; Steve Caracappa's position is he didn't kill anyone." Nothing for nothing, but the use of the word "position" makes me wonder. Imagine telling your wife that your "position" is you didn't do it; it just wouldn't fly.

Eddie Hayes and Eppolito's lawyer, Bruce Cutler, while not partners, have been longtime friends. Cutler is Hayes's daughter's godfather. Cutler, far more than Hayes, is well known as a Mafia lawyer. Cutler represented John Gotti in those cases that earned Gotti the nickname of the Teflon Don. Judge I. Leo Glasser did not permit Cutler to represent Gotti in Gotti's last case because Cutler had begun to pal around with Gotti, as if he were on the fringes of the criminal enterprise himself. Cutler was frequently seen in surveillance tapes of the Ravenite Social Club and appeared to be house counsel for the Gambino family.

Cutler was famous at trial for denying that the Mafia exists, a defense strategy that we beat into the ground in RICO cases beginning with the Bonanno family trial in 1982. Eddie Hayes, not too shy when it came to speaking to the press, said about Cutler, "When we got into this, I called him up and told him, 'Bruce, you got to say there is a Mafia and you hate them.'" Easy enough if all you are interested in, as you should be, is the client you have and not the next client you want to get. Hayes did very little Mafia defense work. His clients were people like Sean Combs and Robert DeNiro. Like Eppolito, Hayes had a part in *Goodfellas* as DeNiro's Lawyer. Hayes could afford to say he hates the Mafia.

Maybe it's my turn to question Mafia defense attorneys after all that I had to put up with from them. You've got to wonder why Eppolito hired Cutler to begin with. Eppolito is fighting accusations that he's with the Mafia, and he goes out and hires the one lawyer in New York with the loudest and biggest reputation for defending the Mafia. I would say that the personality change that Fran Eppolito saw in her husband after his sit-down with Big Paul Castellano at the White House led him to hire Cutler. Lou Eppolito was now not just talking with his hands, he was thinking with them. The wannabe actor who'd had bit parts in a dozen Mafia movies lost himself in the starring role of a lifetime. It reminds me of the movie that Ronald Colman won the Academy Award for when I was a kid, *A Double Life*, where he plays a stage actor who loses his own personality in the roles he plays. Come to think of it, an old Hooverite accused me of "going native" in my Mafia role as Donnie Brasco.

Jury selection in the Mafia Cops Case began on March 6, 2006, almost exactly a year after the sensational news of their arrest. It's a sad sign of our times that, of the first thirty jurors questioned, five of them were excluded because a close friend or relative had been killed or been a killer.

The Mafia Cops Case was packed with writers. Eppolito's book had been reissued by Pocket Star publishers. The two defense lawyers, Eddie Hayes and Bruce Cutler, in addition to having their own Court TV show, each had a book out. Tommy Dades had a book deal with Warner. Investigator William Oldham had signed a contract with Simon and Schuster for a book called, *The Brotherhoods: A True Story of Two NYPD Detectives Who Murdered for the Mafia.* Nicholas Pileggi, the author of the true crime book, *Wiseguy,* was writing a fictional account of the Mafia Cops based on the true facts of this case. Jimmy Breslin was in court to take notes for his book on the Mafia Cops. I don't think any of these writers were disappointed by what they were about to hear.

Before the trial, defense attorney Eddie Hayes pointed out that investigators Tommy Dades and Bill Oldham, as witnesses, had "a direct financial interest in the conviction." Hayes later said, "The question is whether the government witnesses told Dades and Oldham what happened, or Dades and Oldham told the government informer what to say so they could sell the story."

The U.S. Attorney's office didn't need that cross-examination theme to blow a fog of smoke all over the integrity of their case, and so they dropped both Dades and Oldham from the witness list. The prosecutors' biggest challenge was to remove "baggage" from their star witness, the very tainted Burton Kaplan, by finding corroborating witnesses, not by calling witnesses with their own "baggage."

Besides, there was plenty of evidence without Dades' and Oldham's testimony. As Dades said before trial, "It's basically a slam dunk case. Unless they know where Osama bin Laden is, they're not striking a deal."

• • •

In his opening statement, Assistant U.S. Attorney Robert Henoch, who ran a tight trial throughout, wasted no words. Henoch knew that the only weakness he had in a case that Tommy Dades also described to the press as "airtight" was the statute of limitations issue. Was the Mafia Cops' partnership a criminal enterprise that began before the time of Gaspipe and rolled right along through the supermarket meetings with Kaplan in Las Vegas to last year's Mafia drug money laundering? Henoch told the jury that the government would prove that Lou Eppolito "began seeking bribes in exchange for information as early as the late-seventies." You've got to wonder about that meeting with Big Paul in 1979.

Mitra Hormozi, the next federal prosecutor to address the jury, moved briskly from crime to crime, from murder to murder, sticking to the facts and the issues. "For years," she said, Eppolito and Caracappa "armed one Mafia family—and one treacherous man within that family—with the power of the City of New York." I'll bet she read his book about that "power surge" Eppolito got from walking and talking like a wiseguy while at the same time kicking ass and taking names like a cop.

In his opening statement, Bruce Cutler ignored Eddie Hayes's advice and performed his one-man tribute to a romantic Hollywood vision of the Mafia. Cutler used words and phrases that any Mafia boss would have sanctioned. Cutler bellowed to the jury about our nation's "moral and spiritual cancer" that had decimated the ranks of men of honor to "a few true believers in the outlaw life." Cutler mentioned John Gotti by name. Cutler condemned those who "call each other tough guys, goodfellas, until the jail door is shut. Then they wet their pants and call their mommy, the government." In the 1980s at Fran Eppolito's kitchen table, if the two godfathers Steve Caracappa and Lou Eppolito had read that in the paper, they would have raised their double espressos and said "Salud!"

My man Little Al, now 73 and in the Witness Protection Program for fifteen honorable years, was the first witness for the prosecution. Fat Pete Chiodo had been on the witness list but didn't make the cut. Little Al testified that as acting boss of the Lucchese family he knew that Gaspipe had two NYPD detectives on the payroll, but he didn't know their names. On cross-examination, Bruce Cutler instigated a shouting match and wanted to know why Little Al hadn't said anything before now about Gaspipe having two "bulls" on the payroll. "Maybe I have," Little Al shouted back, "I've been around longer than you, you loudmouth." A little later Little Al told Cutler, "I wouldn't agree with you on anything."

Providing an insider's insight into the way of the wiseguy, Little Al, in the personal "baggage" section of his cross-examination, told about one of his own hits. "He got himself killed," Little Al said, "even though I killed him."

CHAPTER 20
THE MAFIA COPS CONVICTED

THE GOLDEN MOMENT, the payoff for all the hard work and skillful case preparation, came when Burton Kaplan testified. In hindsight, my guess is that the investigators and prosecutors were not overly concerned with Kaplan being able to hold up under a tough cross by Cutler and Hayes. They knew they had a ton of corroborating witnesses. The investigators had gone out and found several strong "baggage handlers" to handle Kaplan's "baggage."

Before Kaplan took the stand, both Little Al and the 5' 4" tow truck operator and frightened gravedigger had already given Kaplan a good jolt of credibility. Israel Greenwald's remains alone should have been enough to handle Kaplan's "baggage."

Kaplan detailed the steady relationship of a $4,000-a-month retainer as payment for information on "wiretaps, phone taps, informants, ongoing investigations, and imminent arrests." That's a mouthful. A lot of mayhem could flow from ongoing betrayal like that. But of course, it didn't stop there. These two godfathers of the kitchen table were hands-on wiseguys. It was "kiss city."

Kaplan described how the Mafia Cops helped "kiss" the first three victims, Israel Greenwald, Jimmy Hydell, and the wrong Nicky Guido. These three victims were victims that had been designated for death by Gaspipe and Kaplan.

Eppolito put the fourth victim on the executioner's block. This is the one murder that Caracappa was not charged with. On St. Valentine's Day 1987, Pasquale Varialle, age 26, was gunned down on a sidewalk a stone's throw from where Israel Greenwald's remains rested under five feet of concrete. Eppolito had picked up word that Varialle was an informant. Trying to be worthy of his $4,000-a-month, he passed that information to Kaplan who passed it to the "homicidal maniac."

Around Columbus Day on October 8, 1987, Otto Heidel, age 30, was changing his tire on E. 35th Street in Brooklyn. Giving a guy a flat tire makes it easier to come up behind him and whack him. Otto was a burglar with the Bypass Gang. Otto was also a secret police informant. Bob Intartaglio's people had fixed Otto up with a wire. Eppolito learned about it and exposed the fact that Otto was an informant to Kaplan. But that wasn't good enough. Eppolito provided a cassette tape recording that Otto had secretly made. This proved to Gaspipe that Otto was a wired rat. The hit on Otto took place a month after Eppolito had lost his cousin Junior Santora on a Brooklyn street in a hit, so Eppolito didn't have to split any of this money with Junior.

Shot to death in a garage apartment in Los Angeles on February 4, 1990 was Anthony Dilapi, 53. He was the nephew of Tom Mix Santora. Dilapi is the former Teamsters official and Lucchese soldier who tried to get away from Gaspipe's "killing frenzy" by disappearing to Los Angeles. Kaplan explained that Eppolito and Caracappa brazenly reached out to the Los Angeles Police Department for help in locating Dilapi. They got his address and passed it to Kaplan. Gaspipe handled it from there.

In May 1990, the month of the hit on Jim Bishop of the Painters Union investigation, Gaspipe Casso and Vic Amuso went on the lam based on insider information about a pending indictment in the Windows Case. As suspected, the Mafia Cops had provided that leaked information.

While on the lam Gaspipe kept in contact with Kaplan. On August 30, 1990, Lucchese capo Bruno Facciola, age 54, was tackled in a garage, killed and had a canary stuffed in his mouth by Louie Bagels Daidone, the ex-Indiana State quarterback, future acting boss, and future lifer who was thrown for a loss in 2004 by Little Al and Little Joe and our little friend RICO. As suspected, Eppolito and Caracappa had informed Kaplan that Bruno the capo was an informant.

By now Caracappa had been transferred to the newly formed Organized Crime Homicide Unit and had easier access to the kinds of information that would earn blood money for their criminal enterprise. The very idea of forming a unit to focus on Mafia hits was revolutionary. For the first ninety years of the twentieth century the NYPD despaired of ever solving a Mafia hit. Not even the victims cooperated with the police. Now there was a unit that specialized in the still enormously difficult job.

Finally, building up to it by degrees, Eppolito and Caracappa got the chance to feel the mother of all power surges. They actually "kissed" a wiseguy themselves for a fee of $65,000. On November 7, 1990, on the Belt Parkway in Brooklyn, they activated the police flashers on what appeared to be a typical unmarked police car. They pulled over the black Mercedes of Eddie Lino, a Gambino capo. They had followed Lino from his social club and had waited for an appropriate spot on the Belt Parkway to get Lino on to the parkway's berm. Eddie Lino, a cousin of the Bonanno family capo Frank Lino, had been one of John Gotti's shooters in the hit on Big Paul Castellano and Tommy Bilotti. More importantly to Gaspipe Casso, Eddie Lino was also one of the three shooters who wounded him that Jimmy Hydell had given up.

Eppolito asked Eddie Lino, "What's on the floor?" When Eddie Lino turned to look at the floor on the passenger side, Caracappa shot him in the back of the head. At ten o'clock that night Eppolito visited Kaplan in the hospital. Kaplan was recovering from eye surgery. Eppolito announced with pride, "I got good news. We got Eddie Lino." When Kaplan asked why Caracappa did the shooting and not Eppolito, the son of Fat the Gangster said, "Steve's a much better shot." Come on, the skinny Caracappa must have fired six inches from Lino's head. In fact, Eppolito couldn't admit that his partner had a personal stake in killing Lino because any personal satisfaction in making the hit might have lowered the price. Caracappa's revenge had to do with Lino's hit on Tommy Bilotti. Turns out Caracappa and Bilotti were bosom buddies growing up together on Staten Island. Small world.

Kaplan testified that "Gaspipe purchased a copy of Lou's book, which is the source of our problems."

Gaspipe making the Mafia Cops from the photo in the book would be easy for a jury to believe. The two crooked cops are individually distinctive in appearance, and unforgettable as partners—the Stick and the former Mr. New York City. These two were on the street together working undercover in reverse for years. A lot of people, like Betty Hydell, had seen them doing a lot of little things that could be trouble for them if they ever got identified, but they couldn't resist putting their picture in Lou's book.

Burton Kaplan testified about his decision to leave his wife and daughter Dolores—grown now and a Criminal Court judge—and go on the lam. He testified about his meetings with the Mafia Cops in a Smith's supermarket in Las Vegas. Caracappa's lawyer Eddie Hayes asked Kaplan on cross-examination if Kaplan hadn't been afraid of the detectives when he met with them. "Believe me," Kaplan said, "that was on my mind. . . ." Why else was he meeting with them in a supermarket?

At one point Kaplan told Hayes, "I'm being honest. I'm a criminal." At the end of the day, outside of court, Eppolito said, "He doesn't bother me."

· · ·

Next came the rest of the prosecution's "baggage handlers."

A Las Vegas resident testified that he had observed Kaplan and the distinctive-looking Eppolito and Caracappa appearing to be having a meeting and conducting business on two occasions at the Smith's supermarket. Investigators, if they are extremely lucky, find that kind of witness by wearing out the soles of their shoes.

An NYPD officer at the Eddie Lino crime scene had found a Pulsar watch with a black face lying near the curb 100 feet from Eddie Lino's black Mercedes on November 6, 1990. Eddie Lino still had his watch on, and the Belt Parkway is not a place where people dump perfectly good watches. A year before Lino got hit, there had been a promotion at the Major Case Squad and the man promoted, Sgt. Joseph Piraino, had a homemade video of the occasion. Sgt. Piraino came to court with a still photo from that video. It showed Steve Caracappa with a cigarette dangling from his mouth like Humphrey Bogart. On his wrist was a Pulsar watch with a black face.

Burton Kaplan's former personal assistant in various legitimate and illegitimate matters, Thomas Galpine, testified that on two occasions he delivered cash to Eppolito. One of those occasions was a trip to either Martinique or St. Marten's; Galpine wasn't sure. But he was sure that Eppolito and his wife were on vacation in the Caribbean and Eppolito needed cash. Galpine delivered ten thousand in hundred-dollar bills.

Galpine testified that Kaplan told him that Eppolito and his partner were on the Lucchese family payroll for information. Kaplan's old address book was introduced. It had the Mafia Cops' unlisted phone numbers under the name "Marco." I hope that using an Italian code name like that wasn't another instance of an "ugly stereotype."

In all, the Mafia Cops had received $375,000 from Gaspipe and Kaplan. Who knows what they got from the Gambino family. Who knows the full extent of what they did for the Gambino family besides supplying Rosario Gambino with a copy of his classified NYPD folder.

. . .

Lou Eppolito had to have been extremely bothered by one particular corroborating witness. Her name was Cabrini Cama. She testified that between 1983 and 1989 she had been Eppolito's mistress—what the wiseguys call his *cumare*. "He was a nice guy," she said. She also said that during their time together Eppolito, Caracappa, and Burton Kaplan used her apartment for meetings where the cops exchanged confidential information for cash. Wife Fran Eppolito sat in the front row and listened to every bit of that. Eppolito was playing every part of that new wiseguy role of his, *cumare* and all. If I had been technical advisor on the movie version of this story, I'd have advised that the only thing missing to go along with the espressos and the talking with hands was a *cumare*—until Cabrini the *cumare* opened her mouth and put closure on her relationship with her ex.

The most heartwarming corroborating witness, though, was Judd Burstein, a hero who deserves a lot of credit. He had been Kaplan's lawyer in 1994 when Jerry Capeci broke the news that Gaspipe had turned and had fingered two dirty NYPD detectives. Kaplan waved his attorney-client privilege so that Burstein could testify in this trial about confidential communications between them. Burstein testified that after Kaplan learned the news in 1994, he called Burstein "in a panic. . . . He said, 'This is a big problem for me. I was the go-between for Gaspipe and these two cops.'"

Burstein gave a seldom-heard explanation for his motive in contacting the prosecutors and telling them what he remembered Kaplan had said to him just before Kaplan went on the lam ten years earlier. "I thought it was my obligation as a citizen to come forward. This is the right thing to do."

It looked like the Mafia Cops were about to be buried under five feet of concrete witnesses when Gaspipe reared his ugly head. Gaspipe wrote a letter saying that he had "information favorable to the defense." Hayes and Cutler demanded a mistrial. Instead, Judge Jack Weinstein gave them an opportunity to talk to Gaspipe on the phone from his prison in Florence, Colorado. If they chose, they would be permitted to call him as a defense witness.

On the phone, Gaspipe told the lawyers and their clients that he and Kaplan had made the whole thing up about the Mafia Cops. Gaspipe had gotten their names for the Rembrandt (a frame up) from his "real" Crystal Ball, an FBI agent. "Let me tell you something," Gaspipe told a captive audience, "Burton Kaplan is saying on the stand what I want him to say on the stand. I was supposed to be part of this." Gaspipe said that he and a couple of Lucchese soldiers had done the Eddie Lino hit. The Mafia Cops never gave any information to him and he never gave them any money. Any inside tips he ever got he got from a rogue federal agent, and that agent wanted these cops framed. The Mafia Cops did not deliver Jimmy Hydell to him at a Toys 'R' Us parking lot or anywhere else. They were not involved in the hit on Israel Greenwald; Burton Kaplan had done that hit.

Gaspipe explained that his late wife Lillian, and Kaplan's wife Eleanor, coordinated the details and carried messages between the men during inmate visits. "My wife convinced him that this will work. I told Kaplan if we bring this case to the government we'll both get our freedom."

"Anthony, this is Lou Eppolito, thank you very much." At least Lou Eppolito had learned enough over the years not to call Gaspipe "Godfather."

Hayes and Cutler, however, had heard enough from Gaspipe to know that they were listening to preposterous lies. In the end, Gaspipe had too much "horrendous baggage" for either side to call him as a witness. Unless he breaks out of jail some day, I've got to think that we have finally heard the last from Gaspipe Casso.

When it was time for the defense to begin, Eddie Hayes went on the lam, so to speak. An associate of Hayes's showed up for court, but no Eddie Hayes. When Judge Weinstein asked where Hayes was as the defense was about to begin, the associate explained that Hayes had an important meeting on a case in Los Angeles and was, at that moment, at the luxurious Hotel Bel-Air. "He's not in California with my permission," Judge Weinstein responded and ordered the lawyer to return to Brooklyn.

Neither defendant took the stand. They had sat through the trial as motionless as an oil painting. Maybe their defense was to try to present themselves to the jury as if they were sitting in a frame like a Rembrandt. The complete defense lasted one measly hour. Hayes called a couple of witnesses on a minor point. Cutler opened a shoebox full of commendations for the eleventh most decorated officer in the history of the NYPD—a cop who before he smeared himself, his family, and his badge with slime and blood had been accustomed to newspaper headlines like this one from 1973: "Eppolito Does It Again."

Eppolito was quoted outside of court saying, "I don't think there was much of a defense because that's not what he was supposed to be doing. I have faith in Bruce and always will." Always is a long time. That was April 1, 2006—April Fools Day. Was Eppolito only fooling?

In his summation, federal prosecutor Dan Wenner put to rest the idea of a frame by Burton Kaplan. "Think how dangerous it is to frame a cop. Cops have paperwork. They have time cards. Burton Kaplan testified about things that happened on certain days. How would he know that the cops weren't somewhere else on those days?"

The trial had lasted twelve days; it was supposed to have taken eight weeks. The government ended up paring its witness list from over 100 to 34 who actually testified.

On April 6, 2006 the Mafia Cops were convicted on all seventy counts of the RICO indictment. As if he had won instead of lost, Eppolito embraced and backslapped Cutler like Gotti did when he was acquitted. Eppolito forgot that he was starring in a different movie.

"My mother is feeling pretty good today," Mike Guido said. "More at ease. . . . Me, I feel like an anchor has been lifted off my chest. Someone is paying for killing my kid brother. Finally."

Thomas Repetto, author and NYPD historian of a police department that he loves, spoke as if his heart ached. "In the 160-year history of the police department, there have been shocking cases, but nothing like this where police officers committed murders for gangsters."

Eppolito's 29-year-old daughter, Andrea, a marketing specialist in Las Vegas, took to the microphones outside the courthouse and said, "People have called this the worst case of corruption that New York has ever seen. And I agree with them, but it was not on the part of my father. It was not on the part of Steve Caracappa. The corruption came from the government." Andrea wrote a letter to Judge Weinstein asking him to overturn the jury's verdict and not force her father "to pay for the sins of his father and the family that came before him."

Andrea's brother Tony will pay for his own sins. But doesn't it sound like Tony was brought up "like the family that came before him"? Remember what his father said about the crystal meth—"No problem, I'll have my son set it up. Tony can handle that for you."

A week later, Bernardo Provenzano—boss of all bosses of the Sicilian Mafia— was captured after forty-four years on the lam.

Ten days after the verdict, by telephone from jail, Lou Eppolito gave an interview to a reporter for the *New York Daily News*. "I wanted to take the stand," he said. "I begged them. I said, 'Put me up there. This is my life I'm fighting for. . . .' I just don't know what they were thinking."

It turned out that Eppolito had only been fooling on April Fools Day. He said, "We were abandoned by our lawyers. They put up no defense for our lives. I believe you have to fight."

As for the verdict, Eppolito said, "It was a perfect frame. There's no more perfect a frame than this." He blamed the 1984 accusation over the classified folder and said, "I was the most perfect scapegoat in history." He blamed prejudice over his Mafia family ties and said, "It was a perfect stigma." Perfect four times. As somebody in the business of reading scripts, I could see why the Vegas call girl thought Eppolito was a lousy writer. Too repetitive.

"I would not have been arrested if I had not written the book," Eppolito said. "Still, there are no regrets, not a one. . . ."

. . .

On a personal note, following this case reinforced in me how grateful I was to have had Jules protecting me when I was under for six years. The Mafia Cops illustrate why no one outside our immediate little group, not even my supervisor in the field office in the South to which I was assigned, could be trusted to know much about me or my activities out of concern that I could have ended up like Otto Heidel, changing a tire and landing in the gutter in my own blood.

When I got a call with news of the jury's verdict, I looked back over twenty years and reflected on Bob Blakey's RICO statute and the Witness Protection statute; Rudy Giuliani's appointment to U.S. Attorney in July 1983; the technical advances in electronic bugging equipment; the use of the anonymous jury; and the Mafia Commission Case and Judge Richard Owen's 100-year sentences for each boss across the board.

But for the clean sweep in the Lucchese family, its top leadership would have continued to be stable; there would have been no "killing frenzy" and no reason for the likes of Little Al to ever turn; and the paranoid hotheaded Gaspipe Casso would no doubt have gotten himself whacked in some other drug dispute along the way with the likes of Mickey Boy Paradiso.

Eppolito's book came out in 1992, the year I returned to the Bureau. I could live with Eppolito's assessment in his book of what he called "low-life FBI agents who trailed these mobsters. . . . They all had tunnel vision. They saw things one way, in black and white." Fuggeddaboudit. In the end it was a detective in his own proud department, Tommy Dades, who saw things one way—in black and white.

CHAPTER 21

THE COLOMBO FAMILY AND THE SCARPA DEFENSE

IN NEW YORK CITY, except for the Lucchese family losing all three bosses, no family was as affected by RICO and the Mafia Commission Case as directly as the Colombo family. Their downfall had a special meaning to me since the Colombos were my original entrée into the Mafia as Donnie Brasco in the early seventies.

Jerry Capeci pointed out in the *Complete Idiot's Guide to the Mafia,* that the result of Colombo boss Carmine Persico's guilty verdicts in the Colombo family case and the Mafia Commission Case was that "Carmine Persico's permanent incarceration led to a civil war within his family."

And unlike in Buffalo a few short years earlier, there was no fully functioning Commission, no "big boys," in a position to do a thing about the bloody Colombo civil war.

Persico was the youngest of the convicted Mafia Commission bosses at 53. Maybe that's why he was the only boss convicted in the case who refused to relinquish power when he went to jail. Or maybe it was his ego and his desire to build a dynasty with his son, Little Allie Boy, who was in his early twenties at the time and not yet ready to take over. At any rate, there was no fully functioning Mafia Commission in a position to insist that Persico step down.

· · ·

Historically, the Colombos had been the first New York family since the Commission was formed in 1931 to engage in an internal war. The crew belonging to Larry Gallo and his brothers, Crazy Joey Gallo and Kid Blast, started a war in 1961 against boss Joe Profaci. Carmine Persico was with the Gallos at the start, but quickly defected and began killing his former combat brothers. Behind his back he earned the nickname, "The Snake." The ineptitude exhibited during the war prompted a book by Jimmy Breslin, and a movie of the same name, *The Gang That Couldn't Shoot Straight*.

Because boss Joe Profaci seemed to have it under control, the Mafia Commission did not offer to help in the Gallo War. During the war, Larry Gallo was almost killed by a garrote in a bar. He was saved when a cop walked into the bar to check on a door that was ajar and interrupted his murder. (That incident, by the way, was copied in *The Godfather*.) Larry Gallo refused to cooperate with the NYPD, but it was known that Persico was part of the hit squad. Persico got shot up when the back door of a truck opened and a rifleman, Larry Gallo, fired at Persico's car. Persico sustained permanent damage to his left hand. Persico also did not cooperate with the NYPD.

Nevertheless, the NYPD ended the war. The Gallo side lost Crazy Joey to a lengthy jail sentence. Seventeen other Gallos were indicted.

The war killed 12. During the war, boss Joe Profaci died of natural causes in 1962; his successor did the same a year later. The Mafia Commission installed Joe Colombo as the new boss and all seemed settled until Crazy Joey got out of jail in March 1971.

Boss Joe Colombo founded the Italian-American Civil Rights League. Its purpose was to persuade the public into believing there was no Mafia. At a League rally at New York's Columbus Circle in June 1971, a black man posing as a photographer shot Colombo. The shooter was immediately killed. Fingers pointed at Crazy Joey as the orderer of the hit. Nine months later, in March 1972, Crazy Joey was whacked in Umberto's Clam House in Little Italy. Gallo was shot while celebrating his birthday with a small group including the late *Law and Order* actor,

Jerry Orbach. Orbach refused to answer a single question posed by the founder of the NYPD organized crime homicide unit, Detective Joe Coffey.

Thirty years later, my co-writer Charles Brandt revealed in the book *I Heard You Paint Houses* that Frank Sheeran—the right-hand man of Colombo's dear friend, Pennsylvania boss Russell Bufalino—had shot Gallo. When I was under I used to see Bufalino and Sheeran in Bufalino's New York restaurant, the Vesuvio. By then Sheeran was drinking heavily. Before his death, Sheeran confessed the Gallo hit to Brandt. A civilian eyewitness later corroborated it. That eyewitness, a *New York Times* editor, was at the next table and positively identified Sheeran as the shooter. It was Detective Joe Coffey's case and Jerry Capeci covered it as a young reporter. Both agreed that Sheeran was the shooter on behalf of Bufalino. And Bufalino could not have ordered the hit unless he knew it would meet with the Commission's approval.

Shortly after the hit on Crazy Joey, the Gallos retaliated. Intending to kill Persico's brother Allie Boy and three others in a New York restaurant called the Neopolitan Noodle, their hit man killed two innocent Jewish businessmen instead.

In the midst of this mess, with Colombo in a coma and Persico in jail, the "big boys" stepped in and moved the entire Gallo crew into the Genovese family. You can almost hear the Commission say in unison, "Enough already." The Gallo crew was not heard from again. I have it on good authority that the surviving brother, Kid Blast, now owns a piece of Mike Sabella's former restaurant CaSa Bella's, a short stroll down Mulberry Street from where his brother Crazy Joey got hit.

Colombo never came out of his coma and died in 1978 while I was under. I had already left Jilly Greca's crew in the Colombo family and switched over to Tony Mirra and Lefty in the Bonannos.

Persico went to jail in 1972 for 14 years for a hijacking charge that was eleven years old by the time he started his sentence. Persico's father had been a legal stenographer. That might be one reason Persico played lawyer in the Mafia Commission Case. It might also explain how he played the legal system from 1959 until he went to jail in 1972. In 1959 Persico turned down a plea bargain that would have had him out of jail in a year. In 1961 he went to trial on a hijacking charge and there was a hung jury. In 1962 he was convicted, but on appeal he got a new trial. In 1963 he got a mistrial for medical reasons so he could recover from the bullet wounds inflicted when a rifleman opened up at him from the back of a truck. In 1964 he was convicted, but again on appeal he got a new trial. Meanwhile, Joe Valachi, the first made Mafia soldier ever to do so, had turned and agreed to testify. Valachi had appeared on television before the U.S. Senate, and now the judges, the juries, the FBI, and the media were taking the Mafia seriously. In 1968 Persico was convicted for the third time, but this time the appeals court left it alone. In this 1968 trial, Joe Valachi testified as a witness for the first and only time in court. When the conviction was upheld, "Clarence Darrow" Persico had turned a one-year bit into a 14-year sentence.

Persico exercised control over the Colombo family from prison using his two brothers and his cousin, Andy the Fat Man Russo. The Fat Man's son Jo-Jo still has some kind of relationship with one of the actors who showed up at the Mafia Commission trial, James Caan.

After serving almost twelve years of his fourteen-year sentence, Persico got out in 1979, the year Galante got whacked at Joe and Mary's and the year Tony Mirra introduced me to Persico and his son Little Allie Boy outside Persico's Rolls Royce one night on a dark street corner in Brooklyn. With Colombo dead after seven years in a coma, it was common knowledge among my Mafia crewmembers that Persico was now officially the boss of the Colombos and was grooming his son Little Allie Boy to take over someday.

Persico enjoyed almost a year of freedom, spending time at his Nesta Social Club in Brooklyn, his Long Island home, and his horse farm in upstate New York.

In November 1980 Persico was indicted for having his cousin Andy the Fat Man bribe an undercover IRS agent to get Persico special treatment in jail and to squelch the tax problems of Persico and commercial realtor John The Redhead Francis—the Russell Bufalino associate who drove Frank Sheeran the night Sheeran whacked Crazy Joey Gallo. Even though I experienced first-hand how these wiseguys keep showing up in connected dots, these connections never cease to amaze me. Persico got a five-year sentence out of this bribery charge and was back in jail until 1984.

Since 1971, Persico had been out of jail less than three years when his convictions for the Colombo family case and the Mafia Commission case put him back in for 139 years. Would anybody in his right mind want a job like that, with that kind of downside?

Persico's son and heir apparent, Little Allie Boy, was convicted in the Colombo family trial and got 12 years.

In 2001 Little Allie Boy got another 13, and in a plea bargain, admitted that he was acting boss of the Colombo Mafia family. This admission would have been unimaginable when there was a fully functioning Commission. Little Allie Boy's co-defendant, an old-school wiseguy and underboss, refused to plea bargain if he had to admit to the existence of the Mafia. He went to trial without Little Allie Boy at his table. The old-school wiseguy beat the major charge and went down on a minor count, puffing out his chest the whole way. Nothing for nothing, but you've got to admire that in your enemy. This was the kind of tough made man that Lefty and Sonny Black were.

• • •

After getting banged for 139 years, Carmine Persico installed a short, chubby 54-year-old capo named Little Vic Orena as acting boss. Little Vic had been a soldier in Little Allie Boy's crew, and when Little Allie Boy went to jail, Little Vic had been appointed capo to run the crew. Upped to acting boss, Little Vic was to follow orders from Persico in prison and warm the boss's seat until Little Allie Boy got out.

Carmine Persico, who looked like a man with a Napoleon complex in the Commission Case, and who would get out of jail at the age of 109, insisted on long-distance rule and repeatedly made personnel changes in the family. Without a fully functioning Mafia Commission to fear, Little Vic decided this arrangement made no sense.

Worst of all, Carmine Persico began to negotiate with a film company for the TV rights to his life story. The Mafia had had a bite out of that banana before with the Joe Bananas book, *A Man of Honor*. At that time, the Mafia Commission couldn't stop Joe Bananas because he was no longer on the Commission and couldn't be threatened with being booted off. The Mafia Commission couldn't stop Carmine Persico, either, because it no longer had the capability or potency to do so.

Little Vic didn't want to hand the top job over to Little Allie Boy, when the time came. Little Vic asked the family consigliere, Carmine Sessa, to poll the family capos to vote Little Vic in as boss instead. But Carmine Sessa ratted out Little Vic to Carmine Persico in jail in California.

Thus began the two-year "civil war" between the forces of Persico and the forces of Little Vic. On June 20, 1991, a little over four years after Persico got his hundred years, Little Vic spotted a car full of hit men, including Carmine Sessa, waiting for him near his home. Little Vic did a U-turn and sped away.

At the beginning of the civil war, the Little Vic faction had about 100 made men while the Persicos numbered around 25. Joe Colombo's four sons sided with Little Vic. Capo Wild Bill Cutolo was Little Vic's strongest ally with the toughest crew.

Jersey Sal Profaci, son of the family founder Joe Profaci, sided with Little Vic. Jersey Sal complained to Philly boss John Stanfa, ". . . Persico is losing his mind . . . calling press conferences. . . . He wants to go on *60 Minutes*, Barbara Walters interview. . . . A hundred people say it's not right what he's doing, and he's got a hundred-year sentence."

By far the deadliest Persico ally was capo Greg Scarpa. Scarpa had bravely fought alongside Persico in the Gallo War and was known to have said, "I love the smell of gunpowder." When a soldier criticized the performance of Scarpa's son on a bank robbery, Scarpa whacked the man where he stood.

My sources told me that Scarpa envisioned himself as a James Bond type with 007's license to kill. Scarpa's favorite TV show was *Mission Impossible*. In 1986 Scarpa had hernia surgery and refused the hospital's blood. Scarpa wanted blood only from the made men in his crew. One of those who gave blood unknowingly had AIDS, and Scarpa got it and knew it. So while he was engaged in this bloody "civil war," he was even more fearless than normal because he knew his days were numbered anyway.

While the Colombo civil war was winding down, and with Scarpa in jail for murders he committed during the war, it came out that Scarpa, beginning around 1960, had been a secret informer for the FBI. In exchange for payment, he fed the Bureau invaluable information that led to arrests, indictments, and convictions of his pals.

Can you imagine how Carmine the Snake Persico must have writhed inside his cage when it was confirmed that his toughest ally, a brother he had fought alongside in the Gallo War, had made a fool of him and was betraying his family's every move for over three decades? Persico had to be stewing and seething that Scarpa's information led to indictments that put him and others away and cost the family a ton of money. But how do you get revenge? How do you get your cousin Andy the Fat Man Russo to stick a fork into the eyes of a man dying of AIDS in a prison?

Persico had to have felt much worse than Rusty Rastelli and the Mafia Commission felt about Sonny Black, Lefty, and me when it ordered hits on the three of us.

There was a secret story about Scarpa that Jerry Capeci first broke in 1994 in the *New York Daily News*. I have it on excellent authority that the story is true. In 1964 the KKK kidnapped and murdered three civil rights workers in Philadelphia, Mississippi: Michael Schwermer, Andrew Goodman, and James Chaney. These three civil rights heroes disappeared completely. Two days later their burned-out station wagon was pulled out of a nearby swamp. The FBI conducted a massive hunt in rural Mississippi for 44 days, using sailors and a helicopter, but turned up no bodies.

There was a nervous Klansman who owned an appliance store, but while he looked to the trained investigator as if he had guilty knowledge, he refused to cooperate in any way. The Bureau flew Scarpa to Mississippi. Scarpa bought a TV from the nervous man and said he'd return at closing time to get it. While the man was helping Scarpa get the TV into his car, Scarpa sapped him and took the Klansman to a shack deep in the woods. Scarpa tied him to a chair while agents waited outside. Scarpa came outside twice to report the Klansman's answers, and each time the agents knew that he was lying because they had already checked those particular locations for the bodies. Scarpa asked an agent for a gun, went back in, stuck the gun in the Klansman's mouth and yelled, "Tell me the fucking truth or I'll blow your fucking brains out!" Not only did the Klansman give up the location of the bodies—buried seventeen-feet deep in red clay at an earthen dam—but he also gave up the names of the Klan killers, leading to seven civil rights convictions.

. . .

Because he was so tough and fearless and no one knew he was an informant, it made perfect sense that the first shots fired in the Colombo civil war would be fired at Greg Scarpa. Getting him out of the way would go a long way toward a Little Vic victory. On November 18, 1991, Scarpa was a passenger in a car being driven by his daughter. Scarpa's two-year-old granddaughter was also a passenger in that car. Suddenly, a drive-by shooter opened fire. The flying bullets hurt only bystanders, but Scarpa was now more dangerous than a wounded animal; he was a disrespected psychopath.

Little Vic's shooters struck again five days later when Wild Bill Cutola's crew hit Hank the Bank Smurra outside a donut shop. Fifteen days later, Little Vic's shooters went to a bagel shop owned by Persico allies. They panicked and killed an 18-year-old kid working in the shop for minimum wage, Matteo Speranza, who died not having any idea why.

That wasn't the only bad hit in the war. Persico shooters raided a Little Vic social club and killed 78-year-old Tommy Scars Amato, a retired Genovese old-timer who happened to be in the wrong place at the wrong time. Naturally, the Persico people apologized to the Genovese people. No doubt, the Chin was more interested in preserving his own assets and avoiding his own trial with his dementia routine than in trying to put an end to this war. In fact, the war's headlines took heat off of him.

In December 1991 five Colombo family members were whacked, including one that Scarpa shot while the man was hanging a Christmas wreath on his front door.

Before Christmas the Brooklyn DA, Charles J. Hynes, in an effort to throw cold water on the war, subpoenaed 28 Colombos before a grand jury. But they all dummied up. Hynes said, "They've turned this into a class B movie. We're not going to allow this county to become a shooting gallery where innocent people are being gunned down."

There is no way the Commission that ruled the Mafia when I was under would have ever allowed things to reach the point where a grand jury was convened for the killing of an innocent 18-year-old. The heat caused by the spotlight of a grand jury would have led "the big boys" to insist that the Colombo family troubles be straightened out at once. Persico would have been forcibly retired.

The "civil war" raged for two years. They had done hits at a donut shop and a bagel shop, and in 1992 they moved on to something completely different, a pastry shop. James Caan's buddy Jo-Jo Russo and two other Persicos shot John Minerva and another Little Vic man in front of Minerva's Massapequa, Long Island pastry shop. No wonder so many of them have nicknames like "Fat" and "Big."

• • •

In the absence of a true ruling Commission, the people of the United States of America stepped in to end the violence. On April 1, 1992, Little Vic was indicted on RICO and an old murder that pre-dated the war. Little Vic at 58 got life without parole. With their own boss in jail, Little Vic's faction could no longer protest the fact that Persico was in jail, and they made peace. At the end, there were thirteen dead with two of the dead not involved in the war. Four of the dead were Persico's, and six were Little Vic's.

The last murder occurred on October 20, 1993. An 18-year-old Persico triggerman and two accomplices hit Joe Scopo, the son of the Concrete Club bagman, Ralph Scopo. When the 18-year old heard that his two accomplices were bragging that they had done the hit themselves, he whacked them both. The teenage triggerman was convicted of those murders and got four life sentences plus 45 years. Across his back the 18-year-old has a tattoo in Italian that translates: "Death Before Dishonor." You have to wonder who filled a young kid's head with that kind of horseshit.

After the war, to cement relations between the two factions, Persico appointed Wild Bill Cutolo underboss of the newly unified Colombo family. In May 1999, six years after the Colombo civil war ended, Wild Bill disappeared. His body was never found. Is there any doubt that the Snake seethed in jail, bided his time, and finally got Wild Bill?

Persico's son Little Allie Boy, now 52, was indicted for his role in the Wild Bill murder and, at the time of this writing, is scheduled to go to trial. The two-year war brought an onslaught of defectors trying to save their skins, including two capos and the former *consigliere* Carmine Sessa who started the war by warning Persico about Little Vic. It brought 73 capos, soldiers, and associates under indictment for war crimes. Fifteen Little Vics were convicted. Forty-one Persicos were convicted, including Jo-Jo Russo, who got life for the hits in front of Minerva's pastry shop.

This "civil war" was a gift that kept on giving. After Jo-Jo's conviction, his father, the acting boss Andy the Fat Man Russo, attempted to get to a juror. The idea was to manufacture false legal grounds for an appeal. It was unique appellate jury tampering. If the juror would come forward on her own to reveal improper jury conduct, such as one juror referring derogatively to "dagos" and "wops," then Jo-Jo would get a new trial with the luxury of having heard the government's entire case. Andy the Fat Man used his *cumare*, the lawyer Dorothy Fiorenza, to try to reach out to the anonymous juror that Jo-Jo's *cumare* had recognized from childhood when she visited the trial. The lovely Dorothy Fiorenza—now married to Tattoo Fiorenza, who is serving life for murder and is dying of AIDS—copped to obstruction of justice and testified against Andy the Fat Man. At his own sentencing, the Fat Man told the prosecutor, Daniel Dorsky, "You ended up getting me a life sentence with this Mickey Mouse case."

Thirteen Little Vics were acquitted after a controversy arose when it was revealed that Scarpa had been a Bureau informant for decades before the civil war and for the two years the war raged. By the time of the war, the supervisor of the Mafia Commission Case, Lin DeVecchio, was handling Scarpa. Allegations were made that Lin DeVecchio was supplying information to Scarpa that Scarpa then used to gain tactical advantage for Persico against Little Vic. It became known as "The Scarpa Defense." Basically, the Little Vics' defense was that the government and Scarpa attacked the Little Vics and they merely defended themselves.

This defense led to a two-year investigation by the Department of Justice, which concluded not only that there were no grounds to indict Lin DeVecchio, but also that there was insufficient evidence to bring Lin up on internal Bureau violations. A later investigation launched by Judge Jack Weinstein reached the same conclusion. Weinstein got it right when he wrote, "DeVecchio and Scarpa's relationship reflects, to a degree, the manner in which the FBI and other investigative agencies conduct business with top-echelon informants and the hazards associated with doing so. . . . That DeVecchio conspired with Scarpa on the side of the Persico faction or that he stirred up the war is not [likely]."

Many Colombo turncoats who were in positions to know gave statements that contradicted the allegations against DeVecchio. Before he died of AIDS in 1994 at 66, Scarpa, who had been convicted of wartime murders, was interviewed in jail and said that Lin DeVecchio had not provided him any confidential information that he used in the war or to kill anyone. Scarpa had killed three Little Vics, but he admitted that he never divulged that fact to Lin.

Nevertheless, in March 2006, over twelve years after the war ended and on referral from a Massachusetts Congressman, Brooklyn DA Charles J. Hynes—who had convened a wartime grand jury in December 1991 and had talked about a "class B movie"—indicted Lin DeVecchio on four state murder charges. News of this state indictment came out during the Mafia Cops trial in federal court, and DA Hynes managed to grab his share of headlines and face-time on TV. Hynes got to call his case "the most stunning example of official corruption I have ever seen."

The indictment alleged that Lin DeVecchio aided Scarpa's war effort with confidential information knowing Scarpa would use it to kill people, and that before the war Lin had provided information that led to Scarpa murdering informants. The DA added the allegation that Lin got weekly payments from Scarpa for this information totaling $66,000.

After Lin helped to bring down the Mafia Commission, and by degrees the Mafia itself, as this book went to press Lin DeVecchio faced life in the can, doing hard time alongside the people he helped put there.

Jimmy Kossler, Pat Marshall, Jules, myself, and others—who worked with Lin in our tireless effort to destroy the Mafia—are helping him raise money for his defense. Damon Taylor, the agent who worked with Scarpa before Lin got involved with him, said about Scarpa, "He was the crown jewel, for all his faults. I would give credibility to anything he said." Damon is helping raise money for Lin's defense. Jimmy Kallstrom, who is now the senior counter-terrorism adviser to New York's Governor George Pataki, said, "Lin DeVecchio is not guilty and he did not partake in what he's being charged with. It's as simple as that."

However, one agent who worked under Lin—an agent named Christopher

Favo—helped keep the allegations alive with a story about the time Favo walked into Lin's office and told him that two of the Little Vic faction had just been hit. "As I started into that he slapped his hand on the desk and he said, 'We're going to win this thing,' and he seemed excited about it. He seemed like he didn't know who we were—the FBI. It seemed like a line had been blurred. I thought there was something wrong. He was compromised. He had lost track of who he was."

Nothing for nothing, but the phrases "He seemed," "He seemed like," and "It seemed like" are not words an investigator uses. That's not "the facts, just the facts." That sort of wishy-washy language is more like what you might expect from Doctor Phil than from an FBI agent. The only "fact" in all of that is that Lin heard the tremendous news about two of Little Vic's supporters getting whacked, slapped his desk, and said openly to anyone who wanted to hear it, "We're going to win this thing."

Can you imagine that a supervisor and seasoned agent who had gone bad for money and was secretly helping Greg Scarpa commit murder in exchange for weekly payola, would openly cheer for the wiseguys in front of a subordinate?

Lin explained the obvious. "What I meant was that the fighting inside the Colombo family was going to help us—the FBI—win the war against the Colombos by providing us with tons of defectors and intelligence."

When I think of that prosecutor, Diane Giaccolone, getting Willie Boy Johnson murdered by exposing him as our informant, then losing her case against Gotti and going on with her legal career unscathed, I feel even worse for Lin.

In addition to supervising the Mafia Commission Case, Lin had headed the Colombo family squad and the Bonanno family squad—my two Mafia families. Maybe they ought to charge the rest of us in the case as all being a part of and furthering Lin's criminal enterprise.

That would include the terrific Colombo family prosecutor, George Stamboulidis, who praised all the murdering that resulted from the "civil war" and what that murdering produced. "The war helped us destroy the family from within. Instead of pulling together in the face of government investigations, they were worrying about saving their lives and that gave them incentives to become cooperating witnesses." Let the butchery begin, Stamboulidis is all but saying.

That also would include the terrific Lucchese family prosecutor, Gregory

O'Connell, who praised the "killing frenzy" that Amuso and Gaspipe produced. "Gaspipe was more dangerous than Amuso and more responsible for the mayhem that fortunately for us ruined the family." Let the "mayhem" begin, O'Connell is saying.

An opinion by one of the judges who granted a motion for a new trial to Jo-Jo Russo for the Minerva pastry murder based on one aspect of the "Scarpa defense"—the government's failure to disclose that Scarpa often blamed others for hits he did—illustrates how little the amateur knows about what the professional needs to do to get the job done. It is comments like the following from Judge Charles Sifton that make me shy away from revealing everything about my under-cover duties. Here's what a federal judge, a political appointee, wrote about a ded-icated agent, Lin DeVecchio: "Scarpa emerges as sinister and violent and at the same time manipulative and deceptive with everyone, including DeVecchio. . . . DeVecchio emerges as arrogant or stupid, or easily manipulated, but at the same time, caught up in the complex and difficult task of trying to make the best use of Scarpa's information to bring the war to a close."

Well now, the judge's anti-war position is the exact opposite of George Stamboulidis's or Gregory O'Connell's. Or mine, when I learned that Sonny Black had been whacked on account of me. To begin with, but for the dedicated good guys like Lin working on the Mafia Commission Case, there wouldn't have been a Colombo family "civil war" in the first place. Once started, where does it say that it was Lin's job to use "Scarpa's information to bring the war to a close?" Were we supposed to save the Colombo family from its own self-destruction or were we supposed to harvest the cooperating witnesses that were refugees from that war?

Judge Sifton allowed the conviction of one of the Minerva pastry murderers to stand because a Parliament cigarette found at the scene corroborated it. Of course, Sifton neglected to mention that the Parliament also corroborated Scarpa. Sifton went on to write that he was not going to let the defendants get away com-pletely. He was only ordering a new trial because the government did not cross over the line into a "level of uncivilized and indecent behavior." At the next appel-late level, Sifton's grant of a new trial was overturned. Jo-Jo Russo's murder con-viction was reinstated and he remains in jail for life. So far.

When I teach undercovers, I tell them to know who they are dealing with at all times. This is the same Colombo family that, in March 1987, two months after Persico got his hundred-year sentence, whacked 78-year-old George Aronwald while he was picking up his shirts in a Chinese laundry in Queens. The Colombo shooters followed him into the laundry and shot him twice in the head and five times in the body. They mistook him for their actual target, his son, the former federal prosecutor William Aronwald.

Don't be fooled by who they claim to be. Two months before the Aronwald family's tragedy, Carmine the Snake Persico's wife (and Little Allie Boy's mother, Joyce) wrote a letter to the Long Island newspaper *Newsday*. Believe me, Joyce had to have had the boss's approval before she sent this letter about the ". . . years of excessive punishment the government has inflicted on us. We survived the ordeal, Carmine came home, and just when we thought it was safe to resume our lives again, along came RICO and Giuliani."

Twenty years after the Mafia Commission Case, a jailhouse informant revealed that he had been Carmine Persico's "legal secretary" for years. Persico, the son of a legal stenographer, had his own letters to his lawyers typed for him by the informant. According to the rules that our prisons are saddled with, the authorities are not permitted to open and read any letters addressed to lawyers, including those that the informant typed. The shit-stained lawyers who got the letters from Persico passed them on to his acting bosses, like his cousin Andy the Fat Man Russo, the father of Jo-Jo, the convicted murderer, and the friend of James Caan. That scheme involving letters to lawyers enabled Persico to continue to conduct family business and order hits from the can.

Once the FBI learned of this from the jailhouse informant, they created a "lawyer" mail drop for the snitch. The drop revealed that an enraged Carmine Persico, who had nothing to lose because he could get no more time, attempted to order hits on Rudy Giuliani, prosecutors Aaron Marcu and Bruce Baird, and FBI agents Denis Maduro and Damon Taylor. Just like he no doubt ordered the hit on former federal prosecutor William Aronwald that caused the mistaken murder of his father George in a Chinese laundry.

After the announcement of the murder indictment against Lin DeVecchio, the actor James Caan wrote a letter to Brooklyn DA Charles J. Hynes thanking him for "undertaking such an extensive and malignant corruption case"; praising the DA for "taking the time to evaluate the situation to correct the wrongs that have affected so many lives"; and reasserting his own friendship with Jo-Jo Russo. "Joseph Russo is a dear friend of mine," Caan wrote, "and I cannot express enough how pleased I am that your office has taken interest and is in pursuit of correcting this problem."

This letter from James Caan could not have been written on behalf of a "dear friend" in the Mafia unless Caan had that friend's permission. It takes about an hour of dear friendship with a made man to learn that you do not interfere in his business, legal or otherwise, even to help him, unless he allows you to do so.

Nothing for nothing, but James Caan is well known in law enforcement for his "dear friendships" of some kind with high-end bookmakers. In fact, James Caan's "dear friend"—Jo-Jo's father Andy the Fat Man Russo, who supplied his own sister, Jo-Jo's aunt, as the lone pathetic witness for their cousin Carmine Persico in the Mafia Commission Case—was the acting boss of a family of book-makers.

Friends do favors for their friends when they are called upon to do so.

This letter from James Caan is a gift. It reveals the seething thinking and well-worn tactics of Carmine the Snake Persico and his cousins and loyalists. It is reminiscent of the letter Persico's wife Joyce wrote to *Newsday* about how, just when they thought it was safe to resume their lives again, "along came RICO and Giuliani."

In James Caan's letter, the "Scarpa defense" rides again. Lin helped put Caan's "dear friend" and the Snake's cousin Jo-Jo Russo away. Jo-Jo's father Andy the Fat Man went to jail trying to fix a juror to create grounds for an appeal for Jo-Jo. Then making use of "the Scarpa defense" with Judge Charles Sifton, Jo-Jo came oh-so-close to skating on appeal. Why not try again on appeal—only this time with a lot more ammunition against Lin, this time getting Lin banged for what Judge Sifton called a "level of uncivilized and indecent behavior."

By their twisted legal theory, if Lin is convicted of corruption on other murders done by Scarpa on behalf of Persico, then those men Lin helped put away for the Minerva pastry murder done on behalf of Persico should get away. Fortunately, despite what Judge Sifton said about "uncivilized and indecent behavior," the law doesn't work that way.

DA Hynes' witnesses against Lin include three Persico loyalists in the civil war. One is the loyal Carmine Sessa, the consigliere who informed on Little Vic and started the war, and who has already given sworn testimony inconsistent with the indictment against Lin.

The chief DA witness is the former *cumare* of Greg Scarpa, Linda Schiro. Although she stated differently in the past, Linda Schiro now claims that over the years she sat in her kitchen with Scarpa and Lin and watched Scarpa hand Lin money in exchange for information. Imagine anyone as intelligent as Lin openly accepting money in front of her. Fuggeddaboudit.

In the past, Linda Schiro denied that she had seen any such thing. "I stay out of the kitchen," she had said. One of the three Persico loyalists who are now providing testimony against Lin is a Colombo family soldier that Linda Schiro recruited into the Mafia by sexually seducing him when he was a grocery delivery boy. The information that led to Lin's indictment was provided to the DA by the effort of Sandy Harmon, a woman with whom Linda Schiro is collaborating on a book. I'm experienced enough in the publishing field to know that if Linda Schiro wants a publisher to accept what she is writing, then it is in her interest to have Lin DeVecchio at least stand trial.

A few years ago, when Linda Schiro self-righteously emoted during the sentencing of a man who had killed Linda Schiro's hit-man son in a drug-dealing dispute, the convicted killer's mother was heard to say, "She's such an actress. She should get an Academy Award. Look at those tears."

Is the indictment of Lin DeVecchio then a kind of legal hit, ordered by the son of a legal stenographer who in 1959 "cleverly" manipulated a one-year sentence into a 14-year sentence, and who in 1986 represented himself in the Mafia Commission Case like a man with a Napoleon complex, and who in 1994 had to sit in his cell and seethe with undying hatred toward Greg Scarpa and his handler, Lin DeVecchio?

At this point, what I've said here is just a theory. But if there's one thing in this world that I do know, it is how these people think.

If by some lapse in today's system—where FBI agents are prize trophy defendants for DAs—Lin's trial goes the way Persico wants it to go, Persico the Snake can then once again hold his evil little head up high. If he gets his way, he might say, "I wasn't made a fool of by Greg Scarpa. My trusted right-hand man and fox-hole buddy wasn't really on the government payroll selling out the great Carmine Persico. Get it, my fellow inmates, and my Colombo family supporters? Greg Scarpa had the G on his payroll. The Colombo family owned the FBI; they didn't own us. My blood brother Greg Scarpa didn't fool me; he fooled the government—you know, those same people I conspire to kill every chance I get."

If Satan wins and things go the Snake's way, Carmine Persico will then get a chance to slap his hand on the prison desk that he still uses to write letters, and shout out loud, "We're going to win this thing."

CHAPTER 22
HOORAY FOR HOLLYWOOD

WHEN MY FRIEND LIN DEVECCHIO was indicted for murder in Brooklyn, he hopped a Delta flight from his home in Sarasota, Florida to surrender to the DA's office in Brooklyn. "I'm surrendering tonight," Lin told a reporter, "but I certainly would feel better if this wasn't so." Lin spent the night on a cot in the DA's office and the next day he appeared in court for the setting of bail.

In the Brooklyn courthouse the next day, the real world was left behind at the door and the events inside the courtroom took on the form of a bad Hollywood movie.

The producer of the melodrama was Michael F. Vecchione, a prosecutor in the DA's investigations division. Vecchione had invested heavily in the script. He bought the stinker—hook, line, and sinker. Vecchione opposed bail of any kind for Lin. Vecchione wanted Lin to rot in jail from that day until the trial many months later. Even though Lin had turned himself in, Vecchione argued that Lin was a risk to run away to a foreign land. After all, Vecchione told the judge, Lin had support from retired FBI agents, some of whom had once worked overseas and could assist Lin in his getaway.

There were 45 retired agents sitting like extras in the courtroom to show our support for Lin. The retired agents groaned as one at this ridiculous plot twist. Sitting in that room, who could understand what would make this Vecchione guy think like that?

The plot thickened. Vecchione argued to the judge that Lin's gray-haired retired FBI supporters had already gone out and attempted to intimidate prosecution witnesses against Lin. This band of witness intimidators would help Lin flee the country.

Lin's lawyer's only explanation for this bizarre tale, other than to call it absurd, was to tell the judge that Vecchione's office was not used to making organized crime cases and didn't know how to evaluate them.

Nothing for nothing, but I knew it wasn't just that. There was something else going on here. The indictment claimed that Lin helped his secret informer Greg Scarpa in eliminating his enemies before and during the bloody Colombo Family War. The star witness against Lin was going to be Scarpa's longtime live-in *cumare* Linda Schiro.

It was Linda Schiro's team that had brought the case to Vecchione 13 months earlier. Linda Schiro and her co-writer Sandy Harmon were trying unsuccessfully to sell a book to a publisher. They added Angela Clemente to their team, an unlicensed self-styled private investigator from across the Hudson River in New Jersey. Angela first attempted to get a congressman to conduct congressional hearings—hearings that would have been a publicity platform—with no real cross-examination. The congressman declined and recommended that Angela take the package to the Brooklyn DA's office.

However, Linda and company's package—chock full of cooperating Mafia witness statements—had one serious flaw. Twelve years prior, FBI agents had interviewed the witnesses, including Linda Schiro, when the charges against Lin first surfaced. All the witnesses denied any knowledge of any transactions of any kind between Lin the handler and his informer, Greg Scarpa. Linda Schiro said she'd seen Lin about ten times in twelve years and that "she was not close enough to hear the contents of their discussions." Which, if you know anything at all about handling high-level informers, makes sense.

So now how do you explain the complete about-face by Linda and her cast of characters—from knowing nothing to knowing everything? Easy. Linda and her company of players were intimidated by the FBI twelve years earlier. And guess what, here today in 2006 those same intimidating agents are still attempting to intimidate witnesses. See? Nice and neat. And totally fictitious.

Still that's only half a pizza. It explains why Linda and company would claim that intimidation was still occurring in order to boost their claim that intimidation had once occurred. But why would Vecchione believe Linda and company's pitch that FBI interviewers had once intimidated them into mass perjury and that retired agents are still attempting to intimidate witnesses? Why couldn't Vecchione see the obvious self-interest these people had to change their earlier statements? Why would Vecchione greenlight this project?

Nothing for nothing, but could Vecchione also have been bitten by the Hollywood potential for this story with all its plot twists and the FBI as the villain? You don't have to win a case to make a big score. Marcia Clark pocketed a $5 million book advance for bungling the open-and-shut O.J. Simpson case. Could Vecchione have his own self-interest that blinded him to theirs?

Fortunately, the judge wasn't biting. He was not convinced by Vecchione's arguments and reality was restored. Lin was released on bail and five retired FBI agents co-signed the bail. Retired agent Chris Mattiace said, "We believe that the charges are frivolous." The movie should be called "Frivolous and Frivolouser."

And the "Frivolouser" part was about to begin.

Linda Schiro and company are in it for a book deal and a ticket to Hollywood. But Persico and company could not possibly care a little bit about the traitor Scarpa's former mistress and her book deal. The Colombo family Mafia witnesses would "cooperate" with Linda, Sandy, and Angela only to help their own: Jo-Jo Russo, Anthony Russo, and Joseph Monteleone (an accomplice on the pastry shop murder).

All the murder charges against Lin implicate Lin in murders carried out by Scarpa on his and Carmine Persico's enemies in Brooklyn. How do you go from proving Lin was involved in Scarpa's Brooklyn murders to the unrelated pastry shop murders in Nassau County on Long Island? Those are the murders for which Hollywood actor James Caan's "dear friend" Jo-Jo Russo is doing life. When Jo-Jo and company committed the pastry shop murders, Jo-Jo was also a "dear friend" of Greg Scarpa. They were on the same team, the Persico side of the war. Jo-Jo is Carmine Persico's cousin, and Scarpa was Persico's right-hand man. And if Lin were found guilty in Brooklyn, he merely would be put on that same team.

If you prove that Lin teamed with Scarpa to kill Persico's enemies in Brooklyn, what does that have to do with the unrelated pastry shop killing of some more Persico enemies on Long Island by other members of the same team? As I mentioned in discussing the Scarpa Defense, Jo-Jo had gotten his conviction reversed, strangely, because the prosecutor had not informed the defense that Scarpa was a government informant working for Lin. That reversal was reversed on appeal as being an unrelated fact that was beside the point, and Jo-Jo remained in the can. Now if Scarpa and Lin could be proven to have been a two-man Murder Incorporated, you can't blame the Persico team for hoping that maybe that could spill over and help Jo-Jo on appeal. But legally and geographically, it's a huge stretch.

An appellate lawyer would need to have something meatier.

• • •

A week after the setting of bail for Lin, the *New York Daily News* reported that Angela Clemente was engaged in another investigation.

Guess what? Bingo. A pastry shop in Nassau County. According to the News, Clemente "spotlighted the testimony of another federal informant who claimed others admitted to the" pastry shop murders. Now, these jailhouse ruses of someone else confessing to a crime for which someone was convicted, are a dime a dozen. You can "spotlight" them all you want. You still need more.

But you've got to admit, this Angela gets around.

The next plot twist occurred on June 17, 2006. On that day, Angela Clemente—after first warning the DA's office that the lives of those involved in investigating Lin's case were in danger—got herself discovered beaten and bruised at 6 a.m. in the parking lot of Caesar's Bay Shopping Center in Bensonhurst, Brooklyn.

Angela said that on the morning of the day before her beating, her assailant had put a note on her car. The note writer claimed to have information that would help with her investigation into clearing Jo-Jo Russo and company of the pastry shop murders. She believed this would lead her to an eyewitness who saw that the murders were not committed by Jo-Jo and company but were linked to Scarpa and Lin. The anonymous note writer said for her to meet him at midnight at 82nd St. and 3rd Ave. in Brooklyn—Scarpa territory. Angela told a law enforcement official about the note and he advised her not to go. She went anyway, but the note writer did not show up.

The next day Angela got another note on her car. This time she called a crime reporter at the *New York Daily News*, Angela Mosconi.

"What do you think I should do?" Angela asked the reporter.

"Don't go—it's the heart of Colombo territory, and it's dangerous. But if you do go, bring backup."

Angela had a better idea. Do go and go alone without back up. But she gave the reporter the DA's phone number and said, "Just in case, if I don't call you by 6 a.m.—call them."

Angela had already written a three-page letter to the authorities claiming that ex-FBI agents were engaged in "witness tampering, harassment and intimidation" on Lin's behalf. That got some media coverage, and now she'd lined up a crime reporter, "Just in case. . . ."

For the second night in a row, the fearless unlicensed private eye drove to Scarpa territory to meet with the leaver of windshield notes. Again, the note writer didn't show up. So Angela, instead of going home, began "driving around" in the opposite direction and ended up in the isolated parking lot at Caesar's Bay. There a man approached her. He had obviously been following her. He asked her, "Are you going to keep investigating DeVecchio?" The brave Angela said, "Yes," and the man began punching, choking, and kicking the 5'4" woman.

Angela was taken to the Lutheran Medical Center where she was protected by cops at her bedside. Also at her bedside was Vecchione. "We consider this very serious," Vecchione said. "She was working on a case not unrelated" to his case against Lin.

"Not unrelated" means related. Well now, that pastry shop in Long Island was getting closer to Brooklyn by the day. It was now officially "not unrelated."

Against the hospital's advice, mission accomplished, Angela walked out of the hospital.

For the next scene, cut to the next day. Angela and her children went into hiding. Angela told the press that she had received a post-beating threat that had now finally scared her off the case. "I'm in danger," Angela said. "What happened to me today is far worse than the attack."

The *New York Daily News* reported Angela telling a source, "The threat that came after the attack was far more alarming than the attack itself. I'm in hiding. I'm very nervous. I'm scared. I'm not going to do any further investigation."

About the physical attack, Angela said, "I never thought I was going to die. They were just trying to scare me." Think about that for a second. You're a woman alone in Mafia land in a remote area with no witnesses at 2:30 in the morning; a stranger has set you up; he begins beating you; and somehow you can read his mind that he will know when to stop. Oh, I just got it. The reason she "never thought" she was going to die is that it was the retired FBI agents out of control again—not the Mafia. Presumably, my colleagues would have sense enough not to kill her.

I know it will take a long time, but if my ex-agent pals apply themselves they can do the same thing to scare off the DA's professional investigators, one at a time.

As to the unnamed threat, Angela said, "I'm withdrawing from this entire thing due to financial reasons. I don't make any money on this." (Yet.)

"It's been a lot of headaches," she continued. "Why should I continue? I'm getting mobsters pissed off at me and law enforcement angry with me. Why continue on a path that's harming me. . . . I don't know if justice will be done. There's so much corruption in this case."

Vecchione assured the voters of Brooklyn, "We're vigorously pursuing the assailant."

A week later it surfaced that Vecchione had a new, as yet unidentified witness—a "middleman" who helped intimidate Linda Schiro into perjury in her 1994 interview by the FBI. "He had the middleman to pass along to Ms. Schiro what to say to the FBI when they came to her," Vecchione said. So Linda was good and intimidated. FBI agents and this middleman were double-teaming her. That's why she didn't tell the FBI in 1994 what she told the Brooklyn DA's office in 2006, namely, that she saw and heard everything. She saw Scarpa every week give Lin a roll of bills totaling thousands of dollars wrapped in a rubber band. Forget for a minute that no bribe would ever be given in front of a wife or a *cumare*. Nothing for nothing, but all bribes, all passing of money between Mafia men, is done in envelopes. That's just the way it is always done. Not in a rolled up wad that bulges in your pocket. The fact that Linda said it was a wad only shows that she never saw it done except in the movies.

Later that week Lin got court approval to be out late on the Fourth of July so he could watch the fireworks display and celebrate the independence of the nation he dedicated his career to. I understand a very tiny bit of how Lin must have felt, from the time Tony Mirra accused me of stealing drug money.

In the next scene, Angela failed to appear at the NYPD stationhouse to help "vigorously" pursue the assailant. Angela had two appointments with a sketch artist and blew them. She claimed to have kept the assailant's notes in the back seat of her car, but they never turned up. Maybe the intimidator saw the envelope and took it. Angela Mosconi, the crime reporter that Angela had called "Just in case" wrote in the *New York Daily News* that Angela "also gave police varying accounts of what her assailant looked like."

Angela responded immediately by claiming she had been in another state helping her ailing mother who had suffered a stroke. She said, "Never once did I fail to cooperate."   She blamed the cops and the stroke, but not the FBI. That's progress.

. . .

Unfortunately, frames are very hard to expose and the judge may keep all of Angela's hi-jinks out of the case as irrelevant to the charges. Because it is not that hard to frame an innocent man, it is vital that prosecutors exercise sound and sober judgment in evaluating witnesses. This case of changed testimony and incredible charges of corruption should have been squashed within the four walls of Vecchione's office. That is, unless Vecchione had something else on his mind and in his heart when he first heard the details of Angela's package.

In the middle of all this melodrama, I was reminded of the real world and the job Lin DeVecchio did supervising the Mafia Commission Case. In the early summer of 2006 Good-looking Sal Vitale and Frank Lino testified against my old friend, the zip Baldo Amato, for murdering a supervisor at the *New York Post* fifteen years ago. Good-looking Sal was concerned that the victim would cooperate and expose the Bonanno family's stranglehold on the *Post's* delivery operation—the no-show jobs and the like, one of which Sal's son had. The Bonanno family underboss and the very man who ordered the hit, Good-looking Sal, testified for the prosecution. "Baldo turned around and says to me, 'Mr. Sal, I'll take care of it, don't worry about it. You bring the guy and don't worry about it. I'll take care of it. I'll kill him.'"

Capo Frank Lino testified that he griped because Baldo did not take care of it. The victim was still alive when Frank got the body to bury. They had to finish the victim off with an ice pick through his ear. Frank complained to Good-looking Sal, "Next time you send somebody to get killed, make sure the guy is dead—when we walked up there, the guy was alive, he could have shot us."

One of Baldo's co-defendants took the stand and testified that he had never become a made man in the Bonanno family; therefore, he was not part of the corrupt organization under RICO. This kind of testimony, with its admission that there was such a thing as a made man and a Bonanno family had always been forbidden testimony. Jerry Capeci was quoted on the testimony the next day in the *New York Times*. "If the Bonanno crime family still exists, he would need permission."

Baldo Amato had been Carmine Galante's bodyguard when Galante got whacked at Joe and Mary's in July 1979. Everybody with any sense knew he had to have been part of the conspiracy, but it was never proven. We got Baldo in the Pizza Connection Case, and now we got him again for murder.

Baldo got convicted, and Lin was out on bail. And Lin deserved some of the credit for Baldo's conviction based on the job he did on the Mafia Commission Case twenty years before.

That early summer I got another reminder about the real world while watching the NBA All Star game. Bobby Delaney was a referee in the game. While a young New Jersey State trooper many years ago, Bobby infiltrated the Mafia. At halftime, they did a segment on Bobby about how dangerous his undercover assignment had been, and how dealing with the tempers of NBA players was child's play compared to what he had been through. For Bobby's segment they interviewed me, not as a high school basketball star, but as an undercover who knew the dangers first hand. Watching myself on TV always reminds me of those dangers.

I recalled the time, before Galante got killed, when Lefty and I were under Mike Sabella and I had been called in by Lefty for a meeting about Milwaukee boss Frank Balistrieri and undercover agent Tony Conte—a meeting I thought could be my last. I was in Chicago pretending to be waiting for Tony Conte to return to the hotel with his share of an art heist. Lefty knew Tony would not come back. Lefty wondered out loud if Tony was an agent. Lefty called me in to a remote bar on the Upper East Side of New York. In pursuit of the day that there would be a Mafia Commission Case, I attended the meeting anyway. I just didn't tell Jules about it.

I recalled something I'd forgotten. Funny how there was so much danger that not all of it springs to mind. But there was an additional real-world danger during that whole last two years when I was working to gather evidence on the Mafia hierarchy and structure—harvesting the crop from the seeds I had planted. At first, Lefty and Mike Sabella and I had no known reason for Milwaukee boss Frank Balistrieri not returning their calls. But three months after Galante got whacked, an FBI handler got word from his high-level informant that Frank Balistrieri in Milwaukee had discovered that Tony Conte was an agent and that Balistrieri was "spooked" by it. Balistrieri had cut off contact with us, not because Conte had flirted with his girlfriend as we had guessed, but because of this discovery. These high-level informants, like Scarpa had been for Lin, were worth whatever you paid them.

Headquarters wanted to pull me out at once. If Balistrieri knew Conte was an agent, he also knew I was the one who had vouched for Conte. That made me a dead man. This was close to two years before I surfaced. I was now with Sonny Black and cementing my relationship with him. It was way too early for me to come out if we ever expected to topple the Mafia from the top down.

"Believe me," I said. "Balistrieri is embarrassed. He won't want anybody in New York or Chicago to know that he was careless and was taken in by Conte. He could get whacked for that. With his ego, the way he bosses his own sons and his brother, he wants this covered up."

I persuaded Headquarters to let me continue to risk my life. Every time I was called in for a meeting with anybody in the family, I wondered whether it might be because Balistrieri had finally passed on the information and my number had come up.

This was the real world that Lin was an important part of, and he was on our side with every step we took.

. . .

Meanwhile, back in Brooklyn the Mafia Cops appeared to be getting what they deserved.

On June 5, 2006 Lou Eppolito and Steven Caracappa got life without parole. "This is probably the most heinous series of crimes ever prosecuted in this courthouse," Judge Jack Weinstein said.

Before sentencing, they had fired their trial lawyers and had gotten new lawyers who turned on those trial lawyers, claiming incompetency of counsel as grounds for a reversal.

Caracappa's fired lawyer, Eddie Hayes, was accused of getting a $200,000 fee while he made "no serious effort to prepare for trial and remained unfocused throughout the trial. . . . The only effort by Mr. Hayes to present a theory of defense before the jury was the totally confusing and disjointed effort to blame the prosecution on an undefined conspiracy emanating from Washington, D.C."

Eppolito's fired lawyer, Bruce Cutler, was accused of getting a $250,000 fee, and for that money Cutler "spent the majority of Mr. Eppolito's closing argument speaking about himself."

Later that month, the fired trial lawyers and the Mafia Cops were brought in for hearings. Eppolito admitted on cross-examination that he would have no problem telling a lie "if it will help me get a movie done." Judge Weinstein ruled that the trial lawyers were both "highly professional" and had done an "excellent" job. The judge accused Eppolito of "immorality and a lack of credibility."

To the relief of the victims' family members who had waited so long and grieved so hard, it appeared to be finally over. After the hearing on all the motions, the family members had the privilege of reading in the paper that Caracappa's new lawyer had advised his client that there wasn't "a snowball's chance in hell" of getting the case overturned by Judge Weinstein.

Meanwhile, another hopeful book deal surfaced. Lou Eppolito, Jr., the son from Eppolito's first marriage, was going to write a book on being the gay son of the Mafia Cop and the gay grandson of a Gambino family made man.

Then the judge, who a month before had thrown the book at the Mafia Cops, now overruled his pre-trial decision and the trial jury's specific verdict on the statute of limitations issue and, on July 1, 2006, entirely reversed all 70 convictions.

This was a RICO conspiracy case with a five-year statute of limitations, requiring the last act of the conspiracy to have been committed within the last five years—not a murder case with no statute of limitations. Although the government indictment claimed and the jury found that the corrupt organization was the partnership between Eppolito and Caracappa to commit crimes—some of which were committed with the Lucchese family and some were committed years later on their own in Las Vegas after their retirement from the NYPD—the judge decided it was a Lucchese family enterprise, period.

In a 77-page opinion Judge Weinstein wrote, "It will undoubtedly appear peculiar to many people that heinous criminals such as the defendants, having been found guilty on overwhelming evidence of the most despicable crimes of violence, should go unwhipped of justice.

"The evidence presented at trial overwhelmingly established the defendants' participation in a large number of heinous and violent crimes, including eight murders. While serving as New York City police detectives, the defendants used their badges not in the service of the public, but in aid of organized crime. They kidnapped, murdered and assisted kidnappers and murderers, all the while sworn to protect the public against such crimes. . . . It is unclear precisely when this conspiracy came to an end. . . . Once the defendants had both retired from the police force and re-established themselves on the opposite side of the country, the conspiracy that began in New York in the 1980s had come to a definite close. . . . The defendants were no longer in contact with their old associates in the Lucchese crime family."

The judge called the 2004 drug deal and laundering of Mafia drug money to be "sporadic acts of criminality."

We finally had a film editor. Judge Weinstein preferred *The Godfather* storyline that dealt with the Mafia family as the corrupt organization of RICO and not the *Butch and Sundance* theme of a partnership that began in the hills of Wyoming, had a lull while they lay low doing tricks on a bicycle with Katherine Ross, and resumed in Bolivia. The media calling them the Mafia Cops may have backfired. If they had been called the Two-Man Crime Wave it would have been a different story line. The criminal partnership that began with the Gambino family—even before the Lucchese association began—would have been understood by the film-editor judge to have had a lull due to adverse publicity from Gaspipe Casso and to have resumed in 2004 in Las Vegas with the drug deal and the laundering of Mafia drug money. Last I knew, even a two-man partnership was a business organization. But as an experienced film producer I can see how the storyline is neater, cutting it off around 1990 with the hit on Eddie Lino on the Belt Parkway.

It shocked one and all, including yours truly, and including the jury. The jury was asked to decide and did decide, "precisely when this conspiracy came to an end," and precisely whether the two-man partnership was a corrupt organization. The Draft Board was done away with, except for jurors, so to speak. These poor jurors lost time from their lives, got a pittance for the privilege of serving, and then got what one juror called a "slap in the face. I don't think twelve people could not understand the letter of the law. . . . I know we didn't misunderstand it. The conspiracy went on. . . . There was a conspiracy here. There was a conspiracy even when these guys left the force. That was the first thing we hit head-on."

Another juror who was interviewed raised an obvious point. "We should have probably known upfront that this was going to happen if this was a problem."

Why didn't the judge decide against the prosecution in the first place when the defense first made their statute of limitations motion before trial? Why didn't the judge avoid putting the families and the jury through all this aggravation?

"It's taken the breath out of everybody. It's just shocking. I'm still in shock, honestly," said victim Israel Greenwald's daughter.

"I never heard of anything so stupid," said Betty Hydell, the woman who brought the first lead in the case to a top-notch investigator and good man, Tommy Dades, who was later barred from the case because he had the conflict-of-interest of a book deal on it. Betty's daughter Linda said, "There's no closure on this for my family. It just keeps getting worse and worse and worse."

From his 6x6 jail cell Eppolito admitted he was "completely stunned," and praised the judge because he "stood up like a man." Eppolito said, "The judge's statement is that he believes I'm guilty." But Eppolito cleared that up by explaining that there is a conspiracy here involving the FBI and the NYPD, and "... when I get out your head's going to spin around. There was always somebody behind this case pulling the strings of the marionettes." I hope he didn't mean retired FBI agents. That conspiracy has already been taken.

When told of the decision, Eddie Hayes was reported to be speechless. When he composed himself, he went back to the Washington D.C. conspiracy. "But this is a Justice Department that more than any in my lifetime has shown a mad-dog desire to control everything."

Or maybe the star witness, Burton Kaplan, was a sentenced federal prisoner who needed considerations that the federal authorities could best provide, and maybe that's one reason that Bill Oldham of the "mad-dog" Justice Department was brought into the team early on by the Brooklyn DA's investigations division. Not to mention the need for federal "mad-dog" activity in Las Vegas to run a Hollywood drug and drug money sting on tape to deprive Butch and Sundance of any reasonable defense at trial.

Caracappa's new lawyer said, "Mr. Caracappa is a realistic man. Obviously, he's pleased with the decision, but this is just one stage along the way."

In an editorial the next day in the July 2, 2006 edition, the *New York Daily News* explained why the realistic Mr. Caracappa was not jumping for joy in his jail cell. "For the time being government prosecutors will appeal. . . . And once those federal judicial processes are concluded, and if Weinstein's ruling is ultimately upheld, then the Brooklyn District Attorney will be free to slam Eppolito and Caracappa with state murder charges, no statute of limitations attached."

On July 4th Lin DeVecchio took advantage of the judge's order and stayed out past his 9 p.m. curfew to watch the fireworks.

And now it is likely that, after a judge appointed by LBJ allowed taxpayer money, victims' emotions, and jurors' sweat to be spent on a trial that he could have nipped in the bud before it began, the Two-Man Crime Wave, the Butch and Sundance of Brooklyn and Las Vegas—the Mafia Cops—will be tried in the same courtroom by the same prosecutor as Lin DeVecchio.

Or not.

A mere ten days after the judge decided that the Mafia Cops would go "unwhipped of justice" it was revealed that the Brooklyn DA's office had a little stumbling block to doing any future whipping.

It turned out there was yet another book deal out there that the public didn't know about. Unlike Louis, Jr.'s book on the gay son and the Mafia, this book already had a prominent publisher. It was due out in January. It was Michael Vecchione's book deal. It promised to be "the full inside story of the investigation" into the Mafia Cops case. It would be called "Mafia Detectives" and it would contain "never-before-released documents and information." That insider trading and personal use of information that belongs to the people of Brooklyn would give this book a huge advantage over the others by Bill Oldham, Nick Pileggi, Jimmy Breslin, whomever. "Mafia Detectives" would have the added advantage of being written with Tommy Dades, who, although tossed off the case because of a conflict-of-interest, still works for the Brooklyn DA's office.

Jerry Schmetterer, the flak for the DA's office, said that the DA Charles Hynes had "absolutely" approved Vecchione's book deal.

The American Bar Association's model code of professional responsibility forbids a prosecutor from entering into any media deal until all appeals are exhausted and a case he worked on is truly and finally over.

Schmetterer said that the detail of when the deal was entered into was "a personal matter." At least until the defense lawyers tear into this issue.

When asked his opinion, legal-ethics expert Professor Monroe Freedman was quoted as saying, "It's really egregious judgment, because it's the kind of thing every prosecutor should know. It clearly puts the prosecutor's personal interest in self-promotion and making money ahead of his obligations as a public official."

And Professor Eugene O'Donnell of the John Jay College of Criminal Justice offered that, "It would be absolutely inappropriate for a prosecutor involved in a case to be speaking in terms of furthering personal interests. No district attorney should tolerate a member of his staff discussing the business of the office in connection with any commercial benefit."

Nothing for nothing, but what are the odds that before the ink was dry on his "Mafia Detectives" book deal, Vecchione harbored a dream in his heart of a second book deal on a "not unrelated" case of a murdering FBI agent—let's call it, "Mafia Agent"? What are the odds that his publisher reads the newspaper and knows that Vecchione is prosecuting Lin's case and has discussed it with

Vecchione?

Even if Vecchione doesn't have a wink and a nod of an informal deal on "Mafia Agent," prosecuting Lin vigorously would still help Vecchione's first book sales. By prosecuting the Mafia Agent—win or lose—he'd get plenty of headlines that would help him promote "Mafia Detectives."   Next stop, Hollywood. Vecchione wouldn't even need James Caan to show up and throw him thumbs-up in front of the jury. Although, endorsement from a star is always a welcomed touch.

Could any of this "personal interest in self-promotion and making money" stuff have been on Vecchione's mind when he first opened Angela's package? When he opposed Lin's bail? When he accused retired dedicated FBI agents of conspiring to intimidate witnesses? When he publicly accused these decent heroic lawmen of planning to help Lin flee the country?

You swim right into a fish net when you cross over the line into your own self-interest. In the first *Donnie Brasco*, we stayed on the ethical side of the line and I'm not even a lawyer. Consider that Vecchione would actually be freer to write his book—as Marcia Clark was—if he lost Lin's case in front of a jury. He wouldn't have to wait for Lin's appeals to be exhausted.

As the songwriter Johnny Mercer put it, "Hooray for Hollywood, where you're terrific if you're even good."

CHAPTER 23
THE LAST DON

JUST BECAUSE YOU WORK for the government does not mean that you lack passion for your work, that you're in it for the security, the benefits, and the pension. Whether you're a postal worker or the president, you can still have a passion for getting your job done as well as you can get it done. Government workers, I found, are no different from a movie's cast and crew.

I knew only a handful of people in the FBI who somehow lost their passion along the way. And nearly every one of us agents retires with one case that still rankles because of the way it ended up—either in defeat, or unsolved, or in an incomplete victory.

You'd have no trouble guessing that the Bonanno family and I had a special relationship that lasted long after I left the Bureau both times. The Galante hit and the three capos' hit were crimes that went largely unsolved. Nothing for nothing, and I'll keep it short, but had I stayed under a couple more months I am certain I'd have brought home the goods on Galante and the three capos.

The hit that I would not have been able to get any evidence on was obviously Sonny Black's hit, because he went as a result of my coming out and he'd have gotten it just as surely no matter when I came out. And that's the hit that I still asked about from time to time over the years when I spoke to the agents working the Bonanno family.

The hit could not have been done without Big Joey Massino. Rusty was in jail when I came out and Sonny needed to go. Rusty used Joey on the outside to take care of business for him.

Joey, meanwhile, prospered from the hit on Sonny. Joey no longer had Sonny as a rival to take over the top spot when Rusty died. Everybody inside and outside the Bonanno family knew Joey was the top power now that Sonny was gone.

The first thing Joey did after Rusty died was to shut down the social clubs. Joey, who was an electronics whiz himself and very clever at finding bugs, learned from Gotti's mistakes at the Ravenite and the Bergin Hunt and Fish Club, as well as the bugs in the rest of the cases. Joey figured that the social clubs were no longer safe havens from the prying government. Joey knew he couldn't find all the bugs all the time, and the bugging devices were getting harder and harder to detect.

If I had been consigliere, however, I would have recommended against closing the social clubs because they gave a cohesiveness and unity to a crew that bred loyalty. It was a lot harder to turn on people you spent every day with at a club than people you saw only when your work required it. And any business you needed to discuss in a social club you could write down on paper and immediately burn the paper. If someone couldn't read or write you could always turn the TV up and whisper to him.

Big Joey was a dropout from Grover Cleveland High School, but what I'm talking about here isn't rocket science. It never occurred to Joey because he too, like the other bosses, was hearing our footsteps every time he made a decision.

The next thing Joey did was to isolate himself further from his men by requiring that they never utter his name. Like the Chin's men touching their chins, Joey's men would have to touch their ear. Some of the agents began to call him Joey the Ear.

Joey would conduct some minor business at his restaurant, the CasaBlanca. It was decorated in the motif of the classic Humphrey Bogart and Ingrid Bergman film. "Here's looking at you, kid" was Bogart's classic line. And business could be conducted there simply with looks.

But most of Joey's business was conducted on location in places like Monte Carlo, Paris, or Mexico. He was taking no chances on being bugged or having his activity filmed in the U.S.A.

By 2002, ten years after he got out, Joey had earned the nickname of the Last Don. His was the only family not to fall apart; the only family to prosper; the only family not to have a single made man ever turn for the 71 years of its life. Joey was also the only clearly identifiable boss of a family. Thanks to the Mafia Commission Case and the individual family cases, the other bosses were here today and gone tomorrow. All the major bosses were in jail except Joey. And Joey, for reasons known only to him, changed the ceremony for made men. They were no longer to be inducted into the Bonanno family. They were to be inducted into the Massino family.

For Christmas 2002 I got a present I could never have expected. A little birdie told me that the Sonny Black murder was solved and there would be an indictment on it. There sure was.

On January 9, 2003, Big Joey Massino was arrested under RICO for a single murder, the murder of Sonny Black Napolitano. Good-looking Sal Vitale, Joey's underboss and brother-in-law, was named in the same indictment, but for another murder.

A lot had changed since Big Joey orchestrated Sonny's murder and waited outside in a van with a gun in case Sonny ran out still breathing. The Bureau now used something called forensic accounting. They had agents who specialized in tracking down a criminal's assets and linking them to his profits from crime. Congress had passed civil forfeiture laws designed to strip these ill-gotten assets from Mafia members and others such as drug lords. Forensic accounting agents Kimberly McCaffrey and Jeffrey Sallet had been able to identify over ten million dollars worth of illicit assets belonging to Joey and his wife Josephine, who was Good-looking Sal's sister.

Another thing that had changed was the sentencing guidelines in federal cases. Congress had eliminated federal parole. A convicted criminal was required to serve 85 percent of the time he got.

Joey would have been better off getting arrested in 1981 for the Sonny Black murder.

Can you imagine how I felt to hear the news that Sonny Black's 22-year-old murder, which had been caused by the Donnie Brasco operation, was now about to bring down Big Joey Massino?

As the weeks went by the news got even better and better. Made men who had been indicted with Joey were jumping ship, going into Witness Protection, and being debriefed. Charges were being added. When all the debriefing was done there were six more murders added to the murder of Sonny Black. For example, Joey the Mook D'Amico, whose mother paid to have him made, admitted that he killed his uncle Tony Mirra on orders of Big Joey Massino on account of me. Another made man turned and admitted that Joey had ordered the hit on my old crewmember, Boots Tomasulo's son. This hit was done because when Boots died his son wouldn't share his father's gambling machines that he felt he inherited.

One of Sonny's shooters was Frank Lino, a Bonanno capo and the cousin and former roommate of Gambino capo and shooter of Big Paul Castellano, Eddie Lino, who the Mafia Cops whacked on the Belt Parkway. After 27 years as a Bonanno, Frank Lino turned. Lino described how he and Stevie Beef Cannone lured Sonny to a house in Staten Island. There was a meeting in the basement that was supposed to be held to discuss me. Sonny headed downstairs, but he turned when he heard the door slam. Lino shoved Sonny down and Sonny ended up on all fours. Another man fired into Sonny, but his gun jammed. Not wanting to prolong his agony the tough Sonny Black said, "Hit me once more. Make it good." And they finished him off.

Turncoats described how Big Joey and Sonny Black had orchestrated the May 5, 1981 massacre of the three capos and the accidental paralyzing of another made man. Good-looking Sal and three Zips from Canada were hiding in a cloakroom when the three capos walked into a social club with George from Canada. When George gave the signal, the four shooters burst out and opened fire on the capos. In 1987, Joey had beaten the charge of conspiracy to murder the three capos in our Bonanno family trial when he got back from the Poconos. But under the genius of RICO, he had been charged here with directly participating in the May 5 hit on the three capos. It was technically a different charge and therefore not barred by double jeopardy.

Goldie Leisenheimer, who hid Joey at his parents' home in the Pocono Mountains, was a lookout on the May 5 hit. Joey had to smart more than a little bit when he learned that his disciple, young Goldie, had turned.

But the unkindest cut of all came when Good-looking Sal flipped in front of his own sister. No doubt Sal flipped because of the deck that was stacked against him and because of all those who had already flipped. But Sal claimed that Big

Joey had frozen him out long before he flipped. From having been there, I can see how all that isolation that Big Joey had instituted for the Massino family influenced Sal against Joey long before Sal turned. Things such as closing the social clubs—including the club the two boyhood friends had together, J& S Cake—could not have endeared Big Joey to Sal. I'm sure that club meant the world to Good-looking Sal.

Another thing that had changed over the years was the 1994 federal murder-in-aid-of-racketeering law that provided for the death penalty. It was a federal penalty and could be enforced in New York City for any RICO murder that qualified after 1994 regardless of whether the State of New York had a death penalty that was useable in the same circumstances. Nothing for nothing, but Governor Mario Cuomo had vetoed the state death penalty time after time when he was governor, regardless of the will of the people—and here it was, about to be used against the old "ugly stereotype."

Thanks to Good-looking Sal, a separate indictment was brought against Big Joey for an eighth murder that subjected Joey to death. It was the March 18, 1999 hit on capo George from Canada. George had made the mistake of complaining to Joey about the excessive cocaine use of another capo. Big Joey thought the otherwise very loyal George from Canada was questioning his authority. Big Joey told Good-looking Sal, "George has got to go." Big Joey had planned to take Josephine to Cancun, Mexico, no doubt for a meeting down there with some capo or other. Joey said to Sal, "Get it done before I get home." Sal got it done as instructed, and now Joey was going to get a hot load from a needle if he got convicted for ordering it.

Every bit of this stemmed from the murder of Sonny Black. It was too good to be true, but it was as true as it gets. It was the domino theory in spades. The Donnie Brasco operation was finally finishing its unfinished business.

Jury selection began in April 2004 in what I'll take the privilege of calling the Sonny Black Plus Six RICO murder case. By the time it went to trial there was almost no one left in the Bonanno family to take to trial. Among the 422 people assembled for jury selection was the daughter of Bobby Boriello, one of the shooters of Big Paul Castellano and whose own murder was one of two dropped from the Mafia Cops case to satisfy the judge. The juror was excused.

It turned out they didn't need me in this case. In his opening statement to the jury, Joey's lawyer admitted that Joey was the boss of the Bonanno family. Hello. I heard that, loud and clear. The question of whether there was a Mafia or whether it was just "a lot of baloney" was now like the ancient question of whether the earth was round or flat.

Joey's lawyer, a Mafia defense attorney named David Breitbart, claimed in his opening statement that the turncoat witnesses against Joey had been subjected to "the same methods that were used in Iraq" against prisoners. The turncoats "were sleep-deprived and weakened. And then . . . offered a deal." The government got their witnesses to turn against Joey because the government endeavored to "bribe them . . . to torture them."

Once the witnesses took the stand and the jurors got a chance to see them, no juror in his right mind would think these tough men had been tortured—or if they had been tortured, that they wouldn't have stood the torture like men. These witnesses proved they weren't pansies when they stood up to Brietbart's desperate cross-examinations.

An old pal o' mine, retired agent Doug Fencl—the agent who had informed Sonny of my status as an agent—was subpoenaed as a prosecution witness. The prosecutor first wanted Doug to look at some photos in preparation. From behind him Doug heard a familiar voice call out, "Hey Dougie."

Doug turned around to face Big Joey Massino sitting with his lawyer.

"Joey, how're you doing?" Doug said, heading over to Joey to shake hands.

"Doug," Joey asked. "What kind of bullshit is this case?"

"I don't have a clue," Doug said. "I'm just here to testify on a minor point."

The two old adversaries had a pleasant visit with each other, talking about their health and the health of their families.

The trial, however, was an unpleasant slaughter for Big Joey.

After the anonymous jury found Joey guilty of all eleven counts, the United States Attorney for Brooklyn, Roslynn Mauskopf, said, "Joseph Massino reigned over the Bonanno crime family's bloody history for more than two decades. He was the last boss walking the streets of New York."

Joey's next scheduled trial was the death penalty case for the whack on George from Canada.

Immediately following the July 30, 2004 verdict in the Sonny Black Plus Six RICO murder case, and without leaving the courtroom, Joey told a court officer, "I need to talk to the judge."

Before the trial had begun in May 2004, nearly three months earlier, Joey had appointed an acting boss, Vinnie Gorgeous Basciano. Vinnie Gorgeous got indicted for RICO and murder after Joey's conviction and the two of them were able to chat one afternoon in jail. During the chat Vinnie Gorgeous proposed a hit on Greg Andres, one of the prosecutors in Joey's trial. Unknown to Vinnie, the acting boss, his own real boss, was recording the conversation.

When Joey had met with the judge immediately following the guilty verdicts, his first words were, "I'm ready to talk."

In exchange for saving himself from a death sentence, and while accepting life without parole, and in consideration of saving about ten percent for his wife and family of the over $10 million asset forfeiture, Big Joey Massino became the first real boss in history to flip and the first real boss in history to wear a wire against his own family—in this case against his own family's acting boss, whom he had just appointed.

Joey directed the Bureau to the buried bodies of the two capos whose bodies had not been found following the May 5 massacre of the three capos. They were buried right near where Sonny Red's body had been found wearing his Cartier watch. But for some reason no one had looked much further when Sonny Red's body was discovered.

Joey's jailhouse wire of Vinnie Gorgeous led to the arrest of one of his lawyers, a defense attorney gofer named Thomas Lee. The 39-year-old married father of three had passed along a message to have another Bonanno soldier whacked when he got out of jail. The hit would have been done to the actual shooter of George from Canada, no doubt to silence him just in case he thought about becoming a cooperator in the death penalty case.

. . .

In early 2006 Vinnie Gorgeous Basciano went to trial on his RICO murder indictment. The trial was overshadowed in the press by the Mafia Cops case going on at the same time, and the Lin DeVecchio indictment. Good-looking Sal was one of the turncoats to testify against Vinnie Gorgeous. You can't make these names up.

Big Joey was not used in the trial because the prosecutors felt he had too much baggage and the jury might think that, as boss, he had orchestrated all these other witnesses to turn and frame Vinnie as a sacrificial lamb to save their own hides. As it is, the turncoats turned the jury off anyway. Vinnie Gorgeous skated on the murder counts, but he was convicted on the rest of the RICO crimes. Vinnie is awaiting sentencing and could get 20 years. Thanks to the tough changes in the federal sentencing guidelines, he'd serve most of it and either die in the can or get out as an old man.

Meanwhile, the acting boss of the Bonannos is facing more murder charges and the conspiracy to kill the prosecutor Greg Andres. From what I hear, Big Joey will testify in those cases against Vinnie. On one of the tapes, Joey asked Vinnie why he had had a Bonanno member whacked a couple of weeks prior. Vinnie Gorgeous replied, "I thought this kid would be a good wake-up call for everybody."

Like Tony Ducks Corallo had said, "You pick them and you kill them."

. . .

Win or lose the single battle to defeat Vinnie Gorgeous, the destruction of the Last Don by turning him into an informer was a huge victory in the war against the Mafia.

In the end Big Joey Massino became what Sonny Black never would have become: a rat. Joey killed Sonny Black for being fooled by me, which was an honest mistake. But that murder caught up to Joey, and when it did it revealed his deep character to be weaker than anyone whose death he had ordered along the way.

In his summation in the Mafia Commission Case, prosecutor Mike Chertoff had said about the Commission bosses: "They joined an organization which was disciplined, which had rules that were enforceable by punishment, including the punishment of death."

Who out there could believe today—twenty years later—that the Mafia is a "disciplined" organization with "rules" that are "enforceable." If anybody said to me today what Mike Chertoff said to the Mafia Commission Case jury, I'm afraid I'd have to borrow the words of Governor Mario Cuomo and call that kind of talk "a lot of baloney."

I can still hear Rudy Giuliani's words when he announced the Mafia Commission indictment: "The case should be seen as the apex of the family cases. . . . It is an attempt, if we can prove our charges, to dismantle the structure that has been used since the beginning of organized crime in America."

And all it took was a little song, a little dance, and a little seltzer down their pants.

. . .

In 2005, thirty years after I had gone under, I had the privilege of being interviewed for a documentary on the Mafia in Little Italy. We were in front of CaSa Bella's restaurant, the place Kid Blast owns and Mike Sabella had owned. It was the place that Lefty and I had guarded the night Carmine Galante came down for a meeting with our capo at the time, Mike Sabella. That night Lefty told me a lot about the Zips and how Mike Sabella had taken the opportunity to smuggle heroin in with the marble he used in his restaurant's construction.

While I was being prepped for my interview, wearing dark glasses for a little disguise, a wiseguy came out of CaSa Bella's.

"Donnie," he said, "What the fuck are you doing here?"

"What does it look like I'm doing," I said. "We're shooting a documentary."

"Haven't you caused enough damage," he said. "Haven't you done enough to us?"

"Obviously, I didn't do enough," I said, "or you'd be in jail."

REST IN PEACE

The following is a list of Mafia men I associated with and hung out with who got whacked, whose business was finished, not necessarily on account of Donnie Brasco. This is a list I've managed to stay off:

Dominick "Sonny Black" Napolitano
Tony Mirra
Jilly Greca
Anthony Tomasulo
Carmine Galante
Alphonse "Sonny Red" Indelicato
Phillip "Phil Lucky" Giaccone
Dominick "Big Trin" Trinchera
Cesare Bonventre
Frank DeCicco
Robert Capasio
Gabe Infanti
Russell Mauro
Collie DiPietro
Johnny "Irish" Matera

Photography Credits

INDEX